EASTERN Siena

Don Villa Hotel
Lone Pine, CA

[Alabama Hills]
Margin's merry-go-round

COVER PICTURES

Milt & Maxine McAuley

Front: Zuma Canyon below the falls

Back: West Fork Santa Ynez Canyon

August, 1980

Hiking Trails
of the
Santa Monica
Mountains

by

Milt McAuley

Illustrated by

JANET WILSON SOLUM

Canyon Publishing Co.

TABLE OF CONTENTS

Where the Mountains meet the Sea

ACKNOWLEDGEMENTS

Many people contributed to the writing of this book; so many that I cannot hope to acknowledge each one. But I owe a debt of gratitude to:

* Maxine who endured the disruption of our home during the preparation of this guide, typed the original manuscript, and did the final typesetting.

* Scott McAuley who programmed our computer, and under "Help" listed his phone number. His contribution has been significant in making this a better book.

* Ron Webster, who marches to his own drummer, receives my admiration for leading hikes with a flair for innovation and with great inspiration. He also builds trails.

* Milly St. Charles for making detailed comments on the manuscript. She wants to hear "owls hoot," "crickets chirp" and "frogs croak," and has offered many helpful suggestions.

* Franklin Beylik has given help and guidance in the area of natural history.

* Jane Lewis has helped in the research of historical information, and has contributed much to trail details.

* Janet Wilson Solum illustrated this book, as well as being invaluable in advising on publishing details.

* Mary Ellen Dunlap edited the book, helping prepare the manuscript for final publication.

* Bill Crane and Ron Webster provided pictures, some of which were used as a basis for illustrations.

* Mary Gibson Park has provided details of the Backbone Trail. Her knowledge of the Santa Monica Mountains trails has been of great value.

* Joan Rummelsburg has supplied detailed information about the Stunt High Trail.

* Dave Brown for his active participation in environmental protection and for furnishing updated information on the preservation of recreational land in the Santa Monicas.

* Linda Palmer has furnished updated trail information. She plans trails, builds, and uses them.

* Jim Kenney for organizing and preparing the information on the plant life in the mountains. I especially appreciate his practical listing of plants in the appendix.

* Tim Thomas lives in the Santa Monicas, has built some of the trails we use, and has made all types of information available to me.

* Eileen Salenik furnished up-to-date information on the Backbone Trail and the trails over National Park Service Lands. Eileen plans trails and actively takes part in the construction.

* Everyone with whom I have hiked these mountains, all of the good friends that have given me information in casual conversation.

I thank you all.

INTRODUCTION

Welcome to this mountain range — bound on the north by valleys, on the south and west by the Pacific Ocean, and on the east and southeast by the Los Angeles Basin. A rugged bastion holding out against the population expansion, the Santa Monica Mountains offer lofty crags, cascading waterfalls, rugged boulder-filled canyons, beaches, and more.

Ancient home of Indians, landing site of Juan Rodriguez Cabrillo, site of surrender ending California's part in the U.S.-Mexican War, location of Mexican land grants, destination of early settlers, and now the Santa Monica Mountains National Recreation Area, here are the Santa Monica Mountains. (Cabrillo landed on the coast, 10 October 1542. After a brief, friendly meeting with Chumash Indians he sailed on. Several months later Cabrillo died as a result of an accident on San Miguel Island. He is buried there.)

Conceived as ocean deposits and born of compressive land forces, the Santa Monicas have grown through volcanic action, fire, flood and earthquake. For centuries, Chumash, Fernandiño, and Gabrieleno families hunted and gathered seeds in the mountains, fished along the ocean shore, and built their villages near the major watercourses.

Wild animals still haunt the rugged back country. Deer can be expected any time at any place; a coyote yip just after sundown will trigger a response from a dozen more; bobcats usually keep to themselves, but will occasionally surprise you by nonchalantly walking across a trail or across a road. Red-tailed hawks soar overhead; mountain lions exist but are seldom seen; at night owls hoot, crickets chirp and frogs croak. This is a rugged pristine panorama of mountain, animal, and plant life into which humankind has been invited.

The Santa Monica Mountains offer a unique opportunity for recreation, exercise, and the pure enjoyment of the out of doors. It is my desire that this guide book will open up new vistas, that you might savor and enjoy this unique range of mountains. So come on an adventure, walk the trails, absorb the history, and experience the beauty and friendship that is waiting for you.

THE SANTA MONICA MOUNTAINS

TOPOGRAPHY

The Santa Monica Mountains are an east-west trending range located in Los Angeles and Ventura Counties of Southern California. Including Griffith Park on the east and Point Mugu State Park on the west, the range is 46 miles in length. Bounded on the north by the San Fernando Valley, the Conejo Valley and the Oxnard Plain, and on the south by the Pacific Ocean, the range averages nearly 10 miles in width. There are 36 miles of Pacific Ocean shoreline, 29 intermittent streams entering the ocean, and a lesser number to the north. Sandstone Peak at 3111' is the highest point in the mountain range, Malibu Creek has its origin in the Simi Hills north of the central part of the Santa Monica Mountains, and is the only stream that cuts through the range. All other streams drain the same side of the mountains on which they originate.

Access to the trailheads in the mountain range is provided by a series of roads that parallel and traverse the mountains. Fireroads, firebreaks, and trails, provide further access to the hiker or equestrian.

PLANT LIFE

Vegetation is a vital natural resource to the area. It stabilizes the soil from erosion by providing a screen from rain. Root systems hold the soil in place, aiding in the prevention of slides, and by retaining much of the water from storms, reduces the chance of floods. Vegetation also forms the basis for the food chain for the animal community. And of course, I can't resist pointing out the beauty of Ferns, Oaks and Sycamores along the streams, the riot of flowers found in the secluded glens as well as open fields. There is nothing to compare with the chaparral in spring when thousands of acres of California Lilac overpower us with their beauty of sight and scent.

The plant references in this guide will usually be in a common name. These names are listed alphabetically in the appendix and are further classified as to genus and species. For further information either the botanical name or common name may then be referenced to "Wildflowers of the Santa Monica Mountains" by Milt McAuley, where each plant that grows locally is described, and most are pictured. "Flora of the Santa Monica Mountains, California" by Raven, Thompson, & Prigge is a technically oriented and authoritative work of the area.

PLANT COMMUNITIES

The plant life of the Santa Monica Mountains can be placed into a number of different Plant Communities, each having characteristics setting them apart from one another. All naturalists do not agree on the nomenclature and specific communities so I will try to describe plant life from the eyes of a hiker, as I see it. To read of other points of view, see any of the wildflower books dealing with California or the Santa Monica Mountains. At the outset I will omit plants growing in the ocean (Kelp, Surfweed, etc) and in quiet salt water (Eelgrass). I will list eleven communities: (1) Coastal Strand (Littoral zone), (2) Coastal Salt Marsh (and Brackish Marsh), (3) Freshwater Marsh, (4) Coastal Sage Scrub, (5) Southern Oak Woodland, (6) Chaparral, (7) Riparian Woodland, (8) Valley Grassland, (9) Vernal Moist Habitat (includes ponds that dry up in summer and intermittent streams), (10) Cactus Scrub, (11) Cliffside.

COASTAL STRAND

Coastal strand includes a narrow interrupted sand dune and green belt along the ocean from Santa Monica to Point Mugu. Much of this area has been altered or removed from the environment by construction. Pacific Coast Highway travels through the area. Some characteristic plants are: Sand Verbena, Silver Beachweed, Yerba Mansa, Sea Rocket, Beach Primrose, Beach Morning Glory, Dudleya and Ice Plant.

COASTAL SALT MARSH

A saltwater marsh is in the tidewater zone of the ocean. We have two of them — Mugu Lagoon and Malibu Lagoon. All plants of this habitat have adapted to survival in saltwater, at least part of the time. Hollow spaces in stems and leaves let air go to the roots. Salt concentration in roots reverses osmotic flow so that moisture is absorbed by the plant. Glands on the leaves and stems excrete salt. Some characteristic plants are: Salt Bush, Saltwort, Pickleweed, Jaumea, and Dodder.

Fresh water flowing into saltwater marshes places an extra demand on plants in that they must adapt to both salt and fresh water. Some characteristic plants are: Brass Buttons, Juncus, and Ditch Grass.

FRESHWATER MARSH

A freshwater marsh contains either standing or slowly moving water. Plants adapt to water living by having air tubes from leaves to roots, air pockets for bouyancy, and a concentration of photosynthesizing bodies in the upper leaves of floating plants. The edges of ponds, pools of slow-moving streams, and seepages are examples. Some characteristic plants are: Pond Lily, Cat-tail, Rush, Swamp Knotweed, Water-cress, and Common Knotweed.

COASTAL SAGE SCRUB

Coastal Sage Scrub is found on lower elevations in the mountains, both coastal and inland. It occupies drier locations than does Chaparral. Coastal Sage Scrub plants have shallow root systems, are spaced rather far apart and are much smaller plants than Chaparral. Some characteristic plants are: California Sagebrush, Bush Sunflower, California Buckwheat, Sawtooth Goldenbush, White, Purple, and Black Sage, and Laurel Sumac.

SOUTHERN OAK WOODLAND

Southern Oak Woodland is dominated by trees usually on north-facing slopes in heavy soil. Broad valleys having more than average ground moisture will often be covered with Southern Oak Woodlands. Some characteristic plants are: Coast Live Oak, Bay, Walnut, Poison Oak, and Woodfern.

CHAPARRAL.

Chaparral is composed mainly of evergreen shrubs that are adapted to fire and summer drought. The name comes from "chaparro" which describes oak thickets of Spain. The growing environment is characterized by poor, rocky soil, hot dry summers, and limited rainfall (12-14 inches) all falling in the winter. Only five places in the world meet this criteria: (1) coastal southern California and Baja, (2) the Mediterranean, (3) central Chile, (4) south Africa, and southwest Australia. Most growth occurs during winter.

Chaparral is typically found on the higher ridges and slopes, sometimes in almost pure stands of Chamise or Ceanothus but usually as a mixture of shrubs and understory. Nearly all Chaparral plants have the ability to crown-sprout after a fire or physical removal. Some plants protect their immediate environment from competitive germination by putting chemical toxins in the soil as an inhibitor. Characteristic plants are: Chamise, Ceanothus (6 species), Manzanita, Red Shanks, Mountain Mahogany, Scrub Oak, Laurel Sumac, and Sugarbush.

RIPARIAN WOODLAND

Riparian Woodland occurs in canyons and streambeds. Shores of man-made lakes (Century Lake in Malibu Creek State Park) support Riparian Woodlands. A perennial source of water or subterranean moisture is required. Characteristic plants are: White Alder, Sycamore, Cottonwood, Willow, Bay, Blackberry, Poison Oak, Horsetail, and Stream Orchid.

VALLEY GRASSLAND

Valley Grassland is located throughout in well-drained areas at all elevations. Most communities are small but a 600 acre grassland is found in upper La Jolla Valley. Introduced species of grasses and herbs have permanently altered the composition of the original grasslands and overgrazing has also had an effect. A lessened frequency of fires probably has changed the composition to some extent; cultivation most certainly has. Characteristic plants are

Needlegrass, Wild Oat, Foxtail Brome-grass, Rye-grass, Mariposa Lily, Tarweed, Blue-eyed Grass, Black Mustard, and Filaree.

VERNAL MOIST HABITAT

Vernal Moist Habitats are sinks or annual ponds that fill with water during winter then dry up in summer. Areas along intermittent streams can often fall into this habitat.

Some plants tolerate fluctuations of water level, in fact, may require it. Under these conditions plants that need submersion for germination and a lowering of the water level to flower and set seed have a competitive advantage over others. Trees, shrubs, and stem succulants do not prosper in this habitat. Some characteristic plants are: Long-leaved Ammania, Waterwort, Lowland Cudweed, Loosestrife, Woolly Heads, Alkali Mallow, Bull Clover, and White-tipped Clover.

CACTUS SCRUB

Cactus Scrub is a small community of one species of cactus (Opuntia littoralis or Opuntia oricola) of up to 200 feet in diameter. Normally on a south or west facing slope in an otherwise Coastal Sage Scrub community, Cactus Scrub is readily identified as a distinct habitat. Usually inhabited by ground squirrels and rabbits and possibly snakes, the community is structured so that coyotes and similar predators cannot enter. The rabbits and squirrels forage on grasses and herbs in the community and around the perimeter, probably aiding the expansion of the cactus patch by reducing other plant competition.

Individual plants are also found scattered in some Coastal Sage Scrub communities and on cliffsides.

CLIFFSIDES

Cliffs and the rock debris at their base provide a harsh environment for most plants, but some plants seem to thrive on rocks. Rock outcroppings are found throughout the mountains and "Rupicolous plants" (by definition, "live or grow on rocks") are usually found in the habitat. These same plants are also found in other areas. Some characteristic plants are: Dudloya, Golden Yarrow, Shrubby Bedstraw, Tejon Milk-aster, Spike Moss, Santa Susana Tarweed, Brickellbush, and Fuchsia.

ANIMAL LIFE

The wildlife of the Santa Monica Mountains makes every effort to remain hidden — and with just cause. People, dogs, and cats have encroached upon the terrain of the native animals and caused severe losses. It has been more than forty-five years since a giant California condor soared overhead or made a dive down into a canyon; bears no longer range their 100 square mile territory (thank goodness); and even the California mule deer is hard to find in some areas. The urban dream continues to take its toll; but if you walk into the mountains often enough, you are bound to find wildlife.

California quail are found in the fringe area between chaparral and riparian woodland as well as in coastal sage. Sometimes they are found near homes, especially when water is available. Deer are full of surprises. I've seen them crossing Mulholland Drive during mid-day, as a silhouette at night on a ridge, and as a flash up from a stream that I was walking along. Seldom seen, but often heard, is the kr-r-r-eck-ck of the Pacific tree frog. Most intermittent streams and even small temporary ponds are places to look and listen.

The coast horned lizard is often seen in the fringe area of the chaparral. This 3 to 4 inch long, flat, wide lizard is active during the daytime and will be seen in rocky, sandy, or gravelly places. It can change color from a dark to a light phase in only a few minutes and often closely matches the color of the background. This refugee from prehistoric times looks ferocious, but is really tame. This lizard feeds on insects, including bees. Beekeepers who place hives near the chaparral have reported that occasionally a horned lizard will take up a station near a hive entrance and grab a bee now and then.

Four kinds of salamanders live in the Santa Monicas: the arboreal salamander, the California slender salamander, Eschscholtz's salamander, and the California newt.

The California newt lives on land most of its life but returns to water to breed. The migration to water usually occurs in winter and spring during or after a rain. The eggs are attached to rocks, sticks, or other objects in the water, and hatch 5-10 weeks later.

15

The California newt spends its larval state in the water, usually a coastal stream. Transformation takes place late in the summer and the young newt leaves the water and hides in damp areas nearby.

The other three salamanders are terrestrial through all phases of life. During the dry part of the year they stay under rocks, in burrows in the ground, or other subterranean retreats that afford some protection from becoming dry. When the ground becomes wet from the winter and spring rains these salamanders emerge and may be found under leaf litter and other surface material. Courtship and breeding may occur anytime that they are out on the surface. The California slender salamander lays eggs in late fall and winter, with hatching in the spring. The eggs are deposited under rocks and other underground places. The arboreal salamander deposits eggs in rotten logs or hollows in trees in late spring or early summer. Hatching takes place in fall and early winter. The eggs of the Eschscholtz's salamander are usually deposited underground. The young of all three terrestrial salamanders hatch as miniature adults, the transformation from larvae having taken place in the egg.

You will seldom see, but often note, the presence of coyotes in the mountains. If you are high on a ridge at evening you may hear the staccato yipping and then howling down in a valley; if you are in the valley they will likely be on the ridge. Also watch underfoot. Coyote "scat," characteristically containing the big Islay seeds will often be deposited right on the trail. There is no modesty about coyotes; they find an open spot away from trees and bushes, usually in the middle of the trail, and make their deposit. Unknowingly, this insures the optimum condition for the Islay seed to sprout, processed whole through the intestinal tract, placed in an open, sunny spot and provided with its own fertilizer! October ends the Holly-leaf Cherry season and the Toyon season begins for the coyote. Walnuts, Acorns, and Laurel seeds are not on the coyote diet.

The Southern Pacific rattlesnake is an important resident of the Santa Monicas. They are seen often enough that it is prudent to be aware of their characteristics. Because they are unable to control body temperature as mammals do, they seek an area in their temperature range between 64° and 89° F., with a preference for the mid 80's. This means that during the heat of the day in summer the rattlesnake will find shade and wait for late afternoon or evening to move around. They hibernate in the winter, coming out in early spring, and are then likely to be seen during the day.

Most snakes stay in an area for their lifetime rather than travelling great distances. Over a period of months it is not likely that a snake will travel more than 100 feet or so from home, with some exceptions.

Breeding usually takes place during March or April with the young being born alive 6 months later. A brood of 11 is average. The recognition of a sexually receptive female by an active male appears to be by sight and smell. Some snakes have a 2-year reproductive cycle, the ripe female copulating in the fall and ovulating the following spring.

The mating act as witnessed by me on one occasion, involved an entwining in slow but constant twisting and swaying motion. The heads and about 1/3 of the bodies were off the ground. A hiking group out on Sullivan Ridge came upon two mating rattlers about 9:30 p.m. on 16 August. Both snakes were rattling rather gently and did not appear to change their activity, nor seem to be threatened by the presence of a group of people shining flashlights.

Rattlesnakes sense the presence of warm animals by heat sensitive pits that are located below and forward of each eye. Good depth perception in locating prey is important because most foraging is done when visibility is poor at dusk or after dark.

Rattlesnakes do not hear in the normal sense. They probably detect ground-borne vibrations through their body or head if in contact with the ground, but do not hear air-borne vibrations. Rather unique, but they don't "hear" their own rattle.

Smelling is done in a pair of spherical chambers in the roof of the mouth. The forked tongue flicks out, picks up odorous particles from the air and transfers these samples to the chambers where sensory cells transmit the information to the brain.

To conclude this segment on the rattlesnake, it can be noted that the pupil of the eye is vertically elliptical and that the pupil of all other Santa Monica Mountain snakes is round. If you are close enough to note this difference, you are TOO CLOSE.

GEOLOGY

The Pacific Plate — the part of the earth's crust under the Pacific Ocean and as far inland as the San Andreas Fault — has been slowly moving against the North American Plate. This action is a major cause of mountain building in California. The land was forced up to become the Santa Monica Mountains less than 10 million years ago. Most of the geologic history prior to then happened as sedimentary deposits on the ocean floor. Land rose above the ocean on several previous occasions and later subsided. Volcanic activity resulted in massive igneous intrusions about 16-12 million years ago (mya), but for the most part the land was at the bottom of the ocean.

Although nowhere exposed, the 200 million year old ocean floor — the crustal section of the Pacific Plate — is the oldest formation in the Santa Monica Mountains. Santa Monica Slate, the first sedimentary deposit, was laid down in a shallow sea during the Jurassic Period, 190-135 mya. Santa Monica Slate is found in roadcuts in Sepulveda Pass and as far west as Sullivan and Rustic Canyons where outstanding examples may be seen. During late Jurassic and early Cretaceous Periods (about 135 mya) granite intruded into the slate.

The Tuna Canyon Formation, an Upper Cretaceous, 135-70 mya, marine sediment of sandstone, siltstone, and conglomerate, overlies the Santa Monica Slate. The land rose above the ocean during several significant periods of time, only to subside again. One such time occurred in the Early Paleocene Epoch, 70 mya, when the Simi Formation nonmarine conglomerate was deposited. This layer, characterized by rounded cobbles and boulders of quartzite, granitic, rhyolitic and gneissic rocks, is limited in its occurrence — the best known exposure is in Upper Solstice Canyon on private property.

Later, during Lower Paleocene and Eocene times, 60-50 mya, a fossil bearing marine sequence of pebbly conglomerate, sandstone, and siltstone was deposited on the Tuna Canyon Formation. Examples of this Coal Canyon Formation are found in Carbon (formerly Coal) Canyon.

The Llajas Formation is a marine sequence of sandstone, siltstone, and pebbly conglomerate that overlies the Coal Canyon Formation in a few places in the Santa Monica Mountains. A well exposed 1300' thick section of this Eocene, 50-40 mya, formation is seen in upper Solstice Canyon along part of the trail that goes west from the parking lot at the end of Corral Canyon Road.

During the late Eocene, Oligocene, and early Miocene times, 40-25 mya, the land again rose above the ocean and the nonmarine Sespe Formation of pebbly sandstone, mudstone, and coarse grained sandstone was laid down in flood plains. Examples may be found on Corral Ridge and Upper Solstice Canyon above the Llajas Formation. A prominent ridge is seen along East Topanga Fireroad.

The marine Vaqueros Formation containing shellfish fossils, characteristically TURRITELLA INEZANA, overlays the Sespe. This fine-grained sandy siltstone, mudstone, medium-to coarse-grained well-sorted formation was deposited during the Lower Miocene Epoch, 25-20 mya. Upper Trancas Canyon is one of many places to find this rock.

The Topanga Group is a Middle Miocene, 20-12 mya, sequence of sedimentary and volcanic rocks totalling about 18,000 feet in thickness. It is divided into three formations: a lower formation of sedimentary rock (Topanga Canyon Formation), a middle formation of volcanic rock (Conejo Volcanics) and an upper formation of sedimentary rook (Calabasas Formation) that intertongues with and overlies the volcanic. Examples of Topanga Group formations are widespread and common. A well-known collecting area for a variety of molluscan fauna is from the Topanga Canyon Formation along Old Topanga Canyon Road. The Conejo Volcanics are widespread in the central and western part of the mountains. Good examples are Goat Buttes in Malibu Creek State Park, but many other volcanic rocks are found throughout. The Calabasas Formation is a thick wide-spread sequence of sandstone, siltstone, and breccia. It receives its name from an exposure in Stokes Canyon about 2 miles west of Calabasas Peak. (The rock on Calabasas Peak is the Topanga Canyon Formation.)

The Modelo Formation was laid down during the late Miocene and early Pliocene Epochs, 12-8 mya, when the land was under a deep sea. Diatomaceous shale, siltstone, shale, and sandstone overlies the Topanga Group. The north slope of the central part of the mountains is made up of Modelo shale. Good examples can be seen in the roadcuts along Topanga Canyon Blvd. south of Mulholland Drive to the summit and 1/3 mile beyond.

The Malibu Coast Fault runs east-west from the mouth of Carbon Canyon to Leo Carrillo Beach. South of the fault the sequence of rock differs from that found in the rest of the Santa Monica Mountains. A 4000' exploratory well drilled near Point Dume determined the sequence, starting with the oldest rock: Catalina Schist, Trancas Formation, Zuma Volcanics, and Monterey Shale.

Catalina Schist of late Mesozoic Era is the underlying formation, and is not found anywhere on the surface.

The Trancas Formation is sandstone, mudstone, shale, claystone, and breccia of the early and middle Miocene epoch, 25-15 mya. Zuma Volcanic is of about the same age and interbedded with the sedimentary Trancas Formation. Neither formation is exposed at their base, and most of the information regarding thickness comes from core samples from oil well drilling.

Monterey Shale is of middle and late Miocene ages, 18-11 mya, of marine clay shale that is variably diatomaceous, bituminous, siliceous, and sandy. Dolomite and chert are common. The formation is about 3000 feet thick at Point Dume. Much of the area is overlain by marine terrace deposits of upper Pleistocene age, 3 mya and less.

GEOLOGIC COLUMN - SOUTH OF MALIBU COAST FAULT

Era	Periods / Epochs	Time in million years	Formation	Where to find examples
	Quarternary		Terrace deposits	On the Point Dume plateau
	Pleistocene			N. of PCH in the Zuma Beach Area
		3		
Tertiary				
	Pliocene			
		11		
			Monterey Shale	Point Dume Cliffs on inland side of PCH along Zuma Beach
		18		
	Miocene		Zuma Volcanics	Point Dume
			Trancas	N of PCH in Trancas Cyn Area
		25		
				Missing
		70		
				Missing
		100		
			Catalina Schist	Not exposed

GEOLOGIC COLUMN - SANTA MONICA MOUNTAINS

Eras	Periods / Epochs	Time in million years	Event or formation	Where to find examples
	Quarternary		Continued mountain building	
	Holocene	0.01		
	Pleistocene		Faulting Erosion	Everywhere
		3		
	Tertiary		Mountain Building	
	Pliocene			
		11		
			Modelo	North slope of Mts
	Miocene		Topanga SS Conejo Volc.	Calabasas Pk Mulholland HWY NW of Calab. Pk
			Vaqueros	Upper Trancas Cyn East Topanga F.R.
		25		
	Oligocene		Sespe	Upper Solstice Cyn
		40		
			Llajas	Upper Solstice Cyn Carbon Cyn
	Eocene			
		60	Coal Cyn	Los Flores Cyn
	Paleocene		Simi Congl.	Upper Solstice Cyn
		70		
				Garapito Cyn
	Cretaceous		Tuna Cyn	Pena/Tuna Cyn
		135	Granite	Griffith Park
	Jurassic		Santa Monica	Rustic Cyn Sullivan Cyn
		180	Slate	Sepulveda Cyn
	Triassic	200	Floor of the ocean	

UPWARD FOLD OF STRATIFIED ROCK
caused during uplift of Santa Monica Mountains
(located in roadcut on south side of Mulholland
Highway near Malibu Creek State Park)

THE PEOPLE THAT CAME TO
THE SANTA MONICA MOUNTAINS

THE INDIANS

Southern California experienced a decisive climatic change at the end of the Pleistocene Age about 11,500 years ago. The period of lessening moisture caused competition for water and plant food sources among the large land mammals that man used as a source of food. Over a period of several thousand years many of the large mammals became extinct causing man to experiment with new food sources and population movement. The selective processes resulted in man being forced to move out of a less productive desert environment into a new area.

The archaeological evidence shows that the Santa Monica Mountains were not extensively used prior to 7500 years ago. The earliest inhabitants were probably hunters that followed game through the valleys. This period coincides with the shortage of water that was evident in the desert region and coastal rivers of Southern California. The Santa Monica Mountain coastal area provided a highly productive environment for plant food as well as fish, and made for an attractive settlement area.

Most of the village sites of this time period are found on the coast rather than inland, usually located at low elevation near the mouth of a major stream in grassland and sagebrush plant communities. four main areas along the coast show permanent occupation beginning about 7000 years ago: Malibu Canyon, Point Dume, Little Sycamore Canyon, and La Jolla Valley. The plant food sources were mainly the hard seed variety (grass and sage) which were available through much of the year. Walnut, Toyon, and Holly-leaf Cherry were available during fall and winter. It was later that acorns, with the need for processing, became a major part of the diet.

The year–round subsistence system of living in a permanent site and foraging for plant foods continued without any major change of strategy until about 3500 years ago. During this period of time many minor changes occurred. About 5000 years ago the processing of acorns for food became known and with this plentiful food source, there was an increase in population. Village sites expanded in size and number with some developing inland. This period of permanent settlement and vegetal subsistence system was given the name Millingstone Horizon, and is quite descriptive of the processing of the basic food which consisted of hard seeds.

The gradual transition from dependence on seed gathering from a permanent site to a subsistence system that included divergence in settlement pattern may have taken 1000 years. An increase in hunting, particularly resources from the ocean, and a decrease in the proportion of seed use, is characteristic. Fish became an important source of food. During this period, some significant improvements in fishing technique were made. A circular shell fishhook was developed. This allowed fishing from shore by hook and line. New coastal villages evolved and around 2300 years ago, the pattern of village distribution was established that remained constant until the time of the Spanish invasion. Many inland sites were also settled.

This middle period of history lasted until about 1500 years ago and is called the Intermediate Horizon. This 2000 year period of cultural evolution is characterized by a shift from almost total dependency on vegetal foods to one that included hunting, the increase in the use of seafood in the diet, the development of large spear points, (the bow and arrow came late in the period) and shell ornaments.

At this time (Late Horizon) the Chumash culture emerged. The heritage of the people did not change but a definite change occurred in the social structure. Nucleated villages developed, each supporting several smaller living sites away from the main village. These smaller sub-villages in turn temporarily allocated foraging areas to sub-groups. This concept intensified the exploitation of the natural food that was available, and was not abandoned until after the Spanish invasion. Land ownership became recognized, first as village-owned and in some cases family-owned.

Task specialization developed actively and the Chumash traded goods with their neighbors; technological changes occurred in such basic improvements as the evolution of pestle shape from heavy and short, to slender with increased efficiency; fused shale was discovered in Grimes Canyon and elsewhere, resulting in its use in projectile point making.

The Chumash had a well established political organization that stood the test of centuries. The technical accomplishments of the Chumash were noted by the Spanish and the records show that they were amazed at the finely made tools and equipment. They had a serviceable economic system.

A discussion of the Chumash society would not be complete without noting that their advancement in the fields of astronomy and cosmology can be considered highly developed.

The Chumash language is related to other languages of central and northern California yet is uniquely distinctive, showing a separation from other languages for thousands of years. Although not known, it is likely that the people that occupied the area 7000 years ago and more are the ancestors of the Chumash people.

There is some evidence to show that about 3000 years ago Shoshonean speaking people moved into the Los Angeles basin area, displacing the people there.

At the time of the Spanish invasion, the Santa Monica Mountains and adjacent area were home for two different Indian language groups, the Chumash speaking people in the west, and the Shoshonean speaking people in the east. The division line was between the Malibu Creek watershed and the Topanga Creek watershed. The Chumash were represented by the Ventureños whose territory included the west end of the Santa Monicas and basically Ventura County. The Shoshonean family in the mountains was represented by the Fernandeños east of the Ventureño territory except for the Griffith Park area occupied by the Gabrielinos.

THE SPANISH

Upon the overthrow of the Aztec empire by a Spanish force under Hernando Cortez between 1519 and 1521, there was a rapid expansion of the exploration and occupation of Mexico. Immediately a succession of explorers fanned out from Mexico City, one of whom was Juan Rodriguez Cabrillo who arrived off the coast of the Santa Monica Mountains in 1542.

This expedition marks the first known view of the Santa Monica Mountains by Westerners.

On the return trip from sailing north along the California Coast, Cabrillo anchored at San Miguel Island and spent the winter. In 1543 Cabrillo died as a result of an injury sustained when on the island before. It is supposed that he lies somewhere under the drifting sand of San Miguel.

Periodically, ships on the trade route from the Philippines to Mexico sailed past the Santa Monica Mountains. Sebastion Vizcaino sailed the coast in 1602, then for 167 years the Spanish ignored the area. Then Gaspar de Portolá made his first historic trip north.

Upon reaching the Santa Monica Mountains, scouts were sent out to find a way around or thru the mountains. A high, steep cliff down to the ocean prevented passage along shore. On Saturday, 5 August 1769, the party went over the mountains thru a rough and difficult canyon. The route was over Sepulveda Pass. The mountains were named after Saint Monica.

After reaching the north side of the mountains they crossed the San Fernando Valley and went on to Castaic, then followed the Santa Clara River to the coast.

On the return trip from searching for Monterey Bay, Portolá came inland from the Oxnard Plain staying close to the north edge of the Santa Monicas, crossing the mountains thru Cahuenga Pass along the route of an Indian trail — now the Hollywood Freeway.

This expedition introduced the missionization of the coast of southern California. No missions were built in the Santa Monica Mountains but all of the Indians were within mission influence.

The contact of Indian culture with Westerners can be conveniently divided into four chronological periods:

Spanish Exploration (1542-1769)
Mission   (1769-1834)
Rancho   (1834-1848)
American   (1848-)

During the exploration period the effect on the Indian culture was minimal.

The culture impact of the missions was significant. When the Spanish arrived in California they brought an inherent cultural concept very different from the Native Americans. The Spanish subjects belonged to an authoritarian state, had a history of religious intolerance and conformity, for centuries had been embroiled in almost constant war with other peoples, usually with conquest as a goal, and had a manic zeal to impose their culture upon others. The Native Americans of southern California were almost the opposite in that they functioned in small political groups whose leaders did not have strong authority, were not warlike, tolerated other people's religious beliefs, and had no desire to exploit others.

Coupling these basic differences with the duplicity exercised by the Spanish speaking invaders, and the mass deaths because of introduced diseases, the Indians lost their land, their culture, and their lives.

THE MEXICANS

After Mexico declared independence from Spain in 1821, a shift in authority took place with the missions losing their vast land holdings and political domination. The Mexican colonization law of 1824 and the Reglamento of 1828 were passed and land grants were made. by 1834 the transition from religious to civil control was complete; mission lands had been sold and large ranchos established. Most of the Santa Monica Mountain area was claimed — current 7½ minute series topographic maps show boundaries and names of these Mexican land grants.

The Rancho period was of short duration because the Mexican-American War of 1846-1848 ended with California passing into the hands of the United States.   The Ranchos remained but an era passed.

THE AMERICANS

The Mountain Men in search of beavers had entered Spanish territory as early as 1817, and then Mexican territory in the 1820's, affecting a degree of commercial annexation. Efforts were made to keep them out. Despite some jail sentences and forced ejections from the area, the intruders kept coming. Jedediah Smith arrived at the San Gabriel Mission in 1826; James Pattie made it to a mission in Baja in 1827; Ewing Young came to Los Angeles in 1832; Joseph Walker and many others explored the State: and in the early 1840's, immigrant parties were coming to California. Most of the settlers went to the San Joaquin and Sacramento Valleys.

John C. Fremont led an Army force into California in 1845 and was in position when the Mexican-American War began in 1846. Sporadic fighting for California lasted until 13 January 1847, when the peace treaty was signed at Campo de Cahuenga, at an adobe building at the foot of Cahuenga Pass in the Santa Monica Mountains.   Another year was to pass before California became United States Territory, but a new page in history had been turned.

27

On 2 February 1848, the United States and Mexico entered into an agreement that officially ended the war, with negotiations being conducted at Guadalupe Hidalgo on the outskirts of Mexico City. A part of the treaty included the securing of California by the United States.

The "Gold Rush" of 1849 brought thousands of people to California and made a significant change in the way of life that had existed in the Rancho period. Flourishing towns developed overnight; local law became the rule; most of the population consisted of men without families, and the pastoral scene that characterized life was temporarily stayed. California was admitted as the 31st State in 1850.

The concept of land ownership made a dramatic shift. During the Indian occupation the land belonged to the people as a group, and usage was for all. There were some use agreements between families, but land titles as we know them today were not the rule. Under Spanish rule the land belonged to the King of Spain with the Church administering much of it. Usage permits were issued to ex-military men, but title to the land was not transferred. Under Mexican rule large land grants were made giving ownership of ranchos to relatively few individuals with the majority of the people living and working on someone else's land. The title to lands held under Mexican rule was honored by the United States upon obtaining California. Additionally, there was a strong demand for private ownership by the incoming settlers. Limited access to ownership of public property was available from the time that the United States acquired California, but the Homestead Act of 1862 made it possible for any adult citizen or applicant for citizenship who was the head of a family, to apply for 160 acres of unappropriated public land. This act, coupled with the growth of stage lines and established emigration routes, brought a lot of people to California.

The growth of population in the area surrounding the Santa Monica Mountains has had its effect on the mountains. The building of roads and the pressure to build more; the building of homes and the constant subdivision of new areas; the use of canyons as garbage dumps; the need to crisscross the mountains with power lines, telephone lines, water pipe lines, and gas lines; the demand for parks, equestrian trails, hiking trails, camping areas, picnic grounds and other recreation uses; and the desire to preserve the hundreds of archaeological sites that have survived thousands of years — all place a great demand on the mountains and those of us who use them.

HOW TO ENJOY THE
HIKING EXPERIENCE

"Study nature, not books" is an old axiom that suggests that we emphasize the personal experience of observing nature rather than reading what others have written on the subject. The intent of this book is to help you to better enjoy what the Santa Monica Mountains has to offer you as a participant. Most of what is written here is done with the intent of your having a safe and interesting hiking experience. I have been known to get carried away and describe nature as I see it rather than as you do. My "thundering cascade" over a waterfall as witnessed during a heavy rain may seem rather extravagant to one who arrives late in summer and finds a mere trickle down the face of the rock. What I am trying to say is that to hike these trails is to enjoy nature at its fullest; read this book to get you out there!

SELECTING A TRIP

This book describes more than 70 hiking trips. Some are easy, some are very challenging. Choose a trip that you believe you would enjoy and is within your hiking ability. Unless the drive is especially appealing, you might want to select a trip near where you live. The heading of each trip includes information on the type of terrain, the distance, the elevation gain and the expected walking time. If hiking is a new experience for you, visit Topanga State Park and do the Eagle Spring Loop Hike. This is a safe hike in that you may turn back without doing the complete loop and still have an enjoyable experience. Any trip on good trail with not more than 1000' elevation gain and in the 5 or 6 mile distance range would be suitable. As you gain experience expand your horizons.

OBSERVE THE AREA

The beauty of the trip is not so much in the trail underfoot as it is in the landscape about you. The benefits of looking about and mentally noting the landmarks and features of the terrain are twofold at least. Not only will you see more of the physical sights that the mountains offer, but you will become familiarized with the area to the point that you will know the trails, points of interest, and be able to find your way.

DON'T GET LOST

Who can get lost? Anyone can — all ages, both sexes, people alone or in groups. There is one very important thing to do the moment you recognize that you are lost; stop and sit down and think. Then mark your location, try to signal, relax.
Or to state it poetically —

When lost or confused
and when in doubt
Don't run in circles
Just wave and shout.

FOOTGEAR

Many of these hikes can be taken wearing tennis shoes or jogging shoes; a friend of mine wears hush puppies. The evidence leads us to believe that the Indians were barefoot or at best had fiber sandals or leather moccasins. All of these facts notwithstanding, my recommendation for any but the short hikes on good trail is to wear a sturdy hiking boot. Wear wool socks winter and summer. Have someone knowledgeable fit your boots. You should break them in on the shorter trips. It may sound like I am overdoing foot protection; but a blister, stone bruise, or twisted ankle sure takes a lot of the fun out of a good hike.

CLOTHING

Choice of clothing will depend on the season, weather and hiking terrain. My choice for warm weather open trail day hiking is shorts, T-shirt and a hat that keeps some of the sun off my face. Cooler weather requires more protection so wear long pants and a long sleeved shirt. A lightweight windbreaker will give added protection and should always be carried in the pack. Bushwhacking through chaparral is another matter. Wear close-weave long pants and long sleeve shirt, gloves and goggles. Very few of the trips suggested in this book deliberately get off an established trail but once in awhile, like on the "Lemming Hike," chaparral is encountered; so if you plan to go through it, be prepared. Some rain will be encountered in the winter. This should not be an absolute deterrent to hiking because hiking in the rain adds a new dimension to the experience. Various types of rain gear are available, probably none of which work perfectly. I expect to get wet and have muddy feet.

EQUIPMENT

The tendency is to carry more than one needs, but some items could be termed essential. Needed are a day pack, water, a first aid kit, a map and a compass for some of the hikes. Cameras, binoculars, books on birds, plants, animals and geology and other items can add to the hiking experience. Take a little something to eat if you like.

FOOD

What can I say about food that has not been said many times before? Anything goes — just as long as fire is not needed to heat the food. I've seen some very exotic meals out on the trail and also some austere ones. For myself, I prefer to keep it simple and light. A large lunch discourages vigorous hiking. Sandwiches, carrot sticks and apple would do it. Or if you are not serious about hiking, some day take a loaf of sourdough french bread, a chunk of cheese and a bottle of Chablis.

WATER

Take some water. Generally avoid water from streams and ponds; it is difficult to know for sure what is happening upstream. Water is necessary during exercise, so be on the comfortable side and bring a canteen.

ROCK CLIMBING

Most of the hiking you are likely to do will be on a fireroad or trail. Occasionally some off trail travel will be required to reach an area like middle Zuma Canyon. When this type of terrain is encountered on the described hikes I will sometimes use a classification such as class 2 or class 3. The difficulty increases with the class:

CLASS 1: Walking upright usually on a trail but not necessarily so. Special footgear is not required.

CLASS 2: Use of hands is required for balance. Proper footgear is required.

CLASS 3: Climbing technique is required. Hands are also used for climbing. Rope belay should be available. Proper footgear is essential.

None of the hikes described call for climbing techniques more difficult than class 3.

A word of explanation is in order. The classification is made under the assumption that the weather is good and that the prescribed route is followed. Rain or darkness can increase the difficulty so it is best to plan for a margin of safety.

DOGS, HORSES, and BICYCLES

Dogs are not allowed in any of the State Parks except for the blind, and in a few designated areas. The National Park Service normally allows dogs on leash. Horses, bicycles, and people use trails differently and this mixed use presents problems to all concerned. The State Park system has designated some trails for foot travel only and has banned bicycles from trails — allowing use of fireroads only. As hikers we can lessen the danger by being alert and doing whatever we can to make encounters safe.

HIKING COMPANIONS

Last but not least is the people you hike with. Try to find a group that hikes your speed and ability. Most people that hike are there because they want to be, and are easy to get along with. Occasionally circumstances provide difficult conditions that might test a group's compatibility, such as becoming lost in chaparral while it is raining. It is better to be in the company of optimists than pessimists.

Some of us hike alone quite often. This reduces the safety factor some. Leaving word as to your proposed itinerary and time of return is sensible.

ENVIRONMENTAL HAZARDS

Because these mountains are close to civilization there could be a tendency to overlook the fact that it is wild country. A much different environment is out there — probably safer than downtown but still with some unique hazards of which to be aware.

FIRE

Much of the hiking in the Santa Monicas is in the chaparral area. Dry winds for an extended period in conjunction with several months without any rain causes a potential fire hazard. Under these conditions a rampaging fire can sweep up a slope faster than you can climb out. Fire closures are posted during periods of extreme fire danger, both to reduce the possibility of starting a fire as well as to prevent danger to people in the area. Nearly all fires in the Santa Monica Mountains are man caused; needless to say, we of the hiking community should make sure that we do not contribute.

SUN

We have often heard that chaparral is "too high to see over, too thick to go through, and too low to give shade." The next time that the sun beats down on your unprotected head, give some thought to protection. Summer calls for a hat. Depending on the state of your tan, the rest of your body also should be shaded from the direct rays of the sun.

Heat exhaustion and heat stroke are both brought about by overheating, not necessarily sunshine. There are differences between the two ailments: heat exhaustion occurs to someone that has perspired heavily during exertion or because it is very hot and the body loses both water and salts. Heat stroke can occur on a hot, humid, windless day that doesn't allow sweat evaporation to cool the body.

With heat exhaustion the person feels tired, faint, has a headache, could be nauseated, has moist skin, or may be pale. The body temperature is normal, fast and feeble pulse, possibility of cramps. The treatment is to find a cool place and lie down, loosen clothing, raise feet, drink fruit juices, or water with some electrolytes added. Drink 1/2 cup every 15 minutes. Recovery is probable but get medical advice.

Heat stroke is identified by restlessness and confusion and sometimes unconsciousness. The skin is hot and red, and becomes dry at the onset of trouble. Pulse is fast and strong, body temperature is high. Treat by getting the person to a cool place. Remove the clothing and sponge the body with lukewarm water to bring the temperature down a few degrees. The condition is very serious — get medical help.

WATER

Flash floods such as occur in the desert are rare in the mountains. A heavy downpour will swell the streams and increase the difficulty of travel and occasionally cause a mudslide, so some care is required. Travel along some streambeds becomes virtually impossible when the water is high and crossings become hazardous. Rocks rolling down into the canyons are a definite hazard.

Automobile travel along the Pacific Coast Highway and on nearly all of the mountain roads is hazardous because of falling rocks during a storm.

PLANT LIFE

Immediately what comes to mind but Poison Oak? The juices from the leaves, stems or any part of the plant can cause a persistent rash. There is some claim that washing with soap and cold water as soon as possible after contact will prevent the rash. Also, a native plant, Mugwort, is a favorite "rub-on" antidote.

The leaf print is
a pencil rubbing. You are
not likely to catch poison
oak from this page!

A similar plant called Squaw Bush, also belongs to the Sumac family, but is nonpoisonous. It resembles Poison Oak closely, and because it can grow in the same area, is frequently mistaken for Poison Oak.

Other plants such as Phacelia and nettles cause a temporary skin irritation.

There are some thorny shrubs to be wary of.

A number of plants should not be eaten, some are toxic.

ANIMAL LIFE

Most people never see a rattlesnake. I have talked with people that have hiked the Santa Monicas frequently over a long period of time — 20 years or so — and some have never seen a rattler. But as for myself, I have seen dozens of them. There should be a reason for this apparent disparity, and there is.

A lot of my hiking is late afternoon and night. During the hot summer, rattlesnakes keep in the shade during the day and begin to move around when the temperature drops. Having no temperature regulating device, as mammals do, they must seek a spot that keeps them in their preferred temperature range, somewhere between 64° and 89° F. — with a real preference for the mid 80's. This means that from late spring until late fall they are often nocturnal. Occasionally I have seen a rattler lying in the hot noonday sun during the middle of summer, but not for long. As soon as the heat is absorbed, he'll become active and head for shade.

So----look for snakes in late afternoon or evening from late spring to late fall, and during the day at other times, except in the winter when they stay underground.

Also, it is very important to look where you step and avoid probing around in clumps of grass or around rocks unless you can see clearly. If you spot a snake, avoid him and nothing will happen. If you come close the snake will move away or take a coiled defensive position, depending upon the threat. I have had only one snake move toward me, that was early April, and from a coiled rattling position.

One thing further — if I owned a dog I'd either leave him at home or keep very close track of him while hiking. A dog's curiosity can cause trouble very quickly — for the dog.

Several methods are recommended for treating snakebite. The following method appeals to me: Lay the person down; wipe venom away from the puncture area; wash with soap and water; pat dry, do not rub; apply a clean dressing; give pain pills; carry the person to a hospital as soon as possible, keeping the bitten area low. Do not apply a tourniquet; do not cut into the area; do not apply chemicals; do not suck the wound. Keep calm. Do not let the patient exercise.

Also, avoid the small animals: gophers, rabbits, mice, etc., alive or dead. Fleas that sometimes carry germs may be looking for a new host and even though the chance is remote, nobody needs the bubonic plague. (The State Dept. of Public Health recognizes this as Sylvatic [wild rodent] plague since the term "bubonic" refers to only one of the three clinical forms.) Also the pustules on a diseased animal are a source of infection.

The larger animals: deer, coyotes, bobcats, all will avoid people and do not constitute a hazard.

Insects live in the Santa Monica Mountains and can be a factor in your enjoyment. The usual flies, mosquitoes, and other bothersome insects are evident, although not to the degree they would be in a damper environment. The description of the trails will normally omit any discussion of insect life because the distribution of any species does not appear to be localized, and their presence doesn't appear to cause much of a problem. Well, there are those "bee trees" down in Santa Ynez and Rustic Canyons.

I have some general words of advice, however. Such as — don't become so engrossed in watching the behavior of a colony of Harvester ants that you allow one of these 1/4" long red ants to crawl up your leg and bite. It's quite interesting to watch one group of ants gather seeds from the Buckwheat plant and carry them down a hole in the ground while other ants from the colony bring up the chaff and deposit it. Even though each ant seems to have an assigned work role it appears any one can bite.

Mites (chiggers, "red bugs") are not a serious problem in the dry areas and people only occasionally become a target.

Ticks climb to the tips of blades of grass or brush and wave their eight legs when disturbed, thus attaching to an unsuspecting host. A recommended procedure for removing a tick that has become attached is to use a pair of tweezers or a piece of paper or leaf or just your finger and thumb to hold the tick as you exert a straight steady pull until the tick releases its hold. The time for this to occur varies; my experience has been that some ticks persevere longer than others, but eventually give. Then apply antiseptic. My Dad added a counterclockwise twist of one revolution while steadily pulling on the tick. It always worked. If all of the tick doesn't come out, then it will probably become infected and come out in a couple of days. Once a tick is firmly attached and beginning to swell up, a drop of alcohol every minute or so for 10 minutes will cause him/her to relax enough for easy removal. Another method is to cover the tick with oil — any kind — for half an hour, then gently remove the tick. See a physician if you become ill after a bite. Ticks are carriers of Lyme disease (named from Old Lyme, Connecticut) which has been reported in California, mostly in northern, wetter counties. Two cases have been reported in Los Angeles County. Dogs, deer, coyotes, and horses would seem to be main hosts for ticks.

The cone-nose bug can cause a serious allergic reaction in some people. Normally the cone-nose bug lives in a wood rat den so one can avoid the possible encounter by not poking around any large pile of sticks and twigs.

HOW TO USE THE GUIDE

"Pick up the book, turn to a trip that appeals to you, and follow the instructions." At least that is my intention in the preparation of this guide. This concept needs some modification however; every year the rains come and flood out some trails and cause some landslides; periodically bulldozers scrape large amounts of vegetation from ridges covering some trails and causing massive erosion; and with some regularity, areas are subdivided and open area converts to housing developments. So — a trail that exists today may not necessarily be the same a few years from now.

In addition, trails that hikers have used for years may suddenly become unavailable for use because of land ownership transfer, or the owner may just get tired of picking up beer cans and decide to post a "no trespassing" sign. One property owner told me that in 5 years 3 fires have been started on his property by hikers. I have seen people light up a cigarette while sitting on dry grass and the wind is blowing. Admittedly, these instances are rare, but for someone who loses a house, once is more than enough. A lot of the Santa Monica Mountains is privately owned and the owner of property has the right to use of the property. None of the hikes I have described deliberately trespass; but times and conditions change, so be alert to posted notices and abide by them.

Temporary closures also exist on both public and private land. Point Mugu State Park, Malibu Creek State Park and Topanga State Park are frequently closed for fire hazard during warm or windy weather. Flood conditions will also close a park. A daily updated recorded status of the State Parks may be obtained by dialing (213) 454-2372.

Most of the hikes are over land in the State Park system and are open to the public, sometimes for a fee. Rules and regulations are posted and available as handout information. Except in designated campgrounds, dogs and other pets are not allowed; smoking and other fires are not allowed in the back country; camping is permitted only in designated campgrounds; removal of flowers, rocks or other natural items is prohibited; littering or defacing the environment is not allowed; and all motorized vehicles are banned from the roads and trails.

Each trip writeup has information as to the maps used, the distance travelled, the elevation gain and loss, the terrain, and the walking time for an average person. I have included a brief explanation of getting to the trailhead — this can be further clarified in some cases by referring to the map and charts showing main driving roads and the charts showing distances. The trip writeup itself describes the general concept of the hike with specific attention to the detail of road forks, landmarks, and items of interest.

Other information is occasionally included in the trip writeup. Plant life, geologic information, historical, or archaeological facts may sometimes be a part of the hike and provide interesting background. My intent has been to place the emphasis on describing how to get into and out of the mountains.

The trips in this book are listed from west to east; that is, trip number one is in Point Mugu State Park at the western end of the Santa Monicas and the last trip is in Griffith Park at the eastern end. How to judge the time required to walk a given trail takes some experience. Some of us with a good steady pace on level ground slow down when going uphill. Some even slow down going downhill. Your own speed can be determined by timing yourself while walking a measured distance on level ground, then doing the walk with a hill added. If your level trail hiking speed is 3 mph and it takes an extra 30 minutes to gain 1000 feet, then the walking times listed in these trip writeups will match your speed close enough.

Another type of factor that enters in is the type of terrain. Boulder-hopping and bushwhacking throw this system out of balance. Some of us really slow down under these conditions. A good stand of chaparral will stop me completely.

One other factor is the size of the hiking group, If there are a dozen people on the hike, I automatically add 20 minutes to every hour estimated. If the hike walking time is listed at 3 hours, it will take a group of 12 about 4 hours. This takes into account waiting for people as they bunch up for bottlenecks such as crossing a stream or a log, or for someone who decides to stop and take off a sweater. All these things slow down the group.

The times shown on the individual hikes are the actual time that it took me to walk the trip, modified by time-outs I may have taken for picture-taking or investigating some local item of interest. Short rest stops are included in the hiking time. My hiking speed is just under 3 mph and I am slower going uphill. Since my hiking speed undoubtedly varies on different days, absolute accuracy is not possible.

MAPS

Don't get lost! This is not as impossible as you may think. The Santa Monica Mountain range is surrounded by civilization and there are some roads and also small communities, but the terrain in between is quite rugged. The possibility of losing your way is real, so a good map and the knowledge of how to use it will add to your enjoyment of hiking.

This guide book is written so that you may conveniently take a number of established trips, using the book as reference, but when the time comes that you want to explore on your own, you should carry a map.

Maps of this area are available from a number of sources. Many of the backpacking stores carry the topographic maps published by the U. S. Geological Survey. The 7.5 minute "topos" have a scale of I inch = 2000 feet, the contour interval of 25 feet makes it possible to estimate elevation gains and losses accurately. The maps do not have an explanation of the symbols used — a booklet describing topographic maps and symbols is available, free from the Geological Survey. In the event that local sources of maps cannot supply your needs, order directly from Distribution Section, Geological Survey, Federal Center, Denver, Colorado 80225.

Some of the State and National Parks give away maps of their own area, showing the trails and major points of interest.

Street maps of the local metropolitan area are helpful in locating the roadheads of the hikes described in this book. I have found the Street Atlas published by Thomas Bros. Maps to be convenient.

And of course this book is written so that by reading the trip descriptions and referring to the maps included, all will go well.

Road guides are also important in locating the roadhead. On occasion it will be helpful to understand some of the signs that are posted alongside highways. Following these signs can sometimes become a two person affair; one to pay attention to the driving, the other to read the map and the signs. You may have already developed superior route finding techniques but I shall list some traditional methods for those that have difficulty.

A logical and mathematically correct method is to note mileage at the passing of some checkpoint then project ahead to the mileage at the next checkpoint. As any of us who has used this method knows, it has limitations. Watching the odometer very closely can cause you to miss the scenery and even the landmarks. And for some unknown reason there is accuracy of 0.l mile. Also if somehow you lose track of either a checkpoint or mileage the system deteriorates quickly.

So instead of complete reliance on this mileage method I will attempt both on highway or trail, in auto or afoot, to augment mileage with prominent features that can be used to crosscheck position.

Many of the highways in California are lined by small metal markers, 8x24 inches, set on a three foot post. Usually white, often with reflectors mounted on the side facing traffic, but sometimes with lettering and numbers in black. This will identify the County, the highway number, and the distance in miles, from either the county line or the beginning of the highway or some other reference point. As an example: the accompanying figure reads 27 LA 7.01. This is interpreted as being Hwy #27 (Topanga Cyn Blvd.) in Los Angeles County and 7.01 miles from some reference point — in this case 7.01 miles from the Pacific Coast Hwy. Bridges and overpasses are marked the same, with the added benefit of naming the stream or roadway. Wherever it may be of help, I'll include this road marker information.

Thirteen topo maps in the 7.5 minute and one 5x10 minute series cover the Santa Monica Mountains. The map needed for each of the hikes is listed in the trip heading. The following chart shows the maps.

Camarillo	Newbury Park	Thousand Oaks	Calabasas	Canoga Park	VanNuys	Burbank
Point Mugu	Triunfo Pass	Point Dume	Malibu Beach	Topanga	Beverly Hills	Hollywood

Symbols and key usually used in the maps of the hikes in this book:

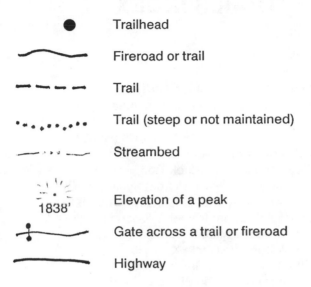

●	Trailhead
	Fireroad or trail
	Trail
	Trail (steep or not maintained)
	Streambed
1838'	Elevation of a peak
	Gate across a trail or fireroad
	Highway

(Backbone Trail Key is found on page 273.)

TRAILS INDEX

CHUMASH TRAIL into LA JOLLA VALLEY

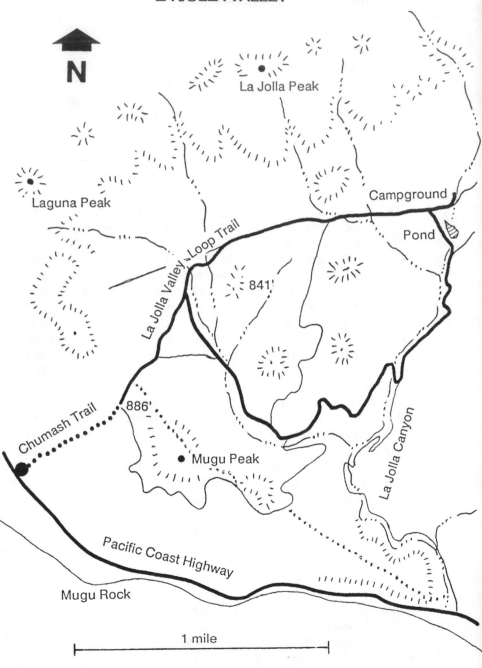

N

La Jolla Peak

Laguna Peak

Campground

Pond

La Jolla Valley Loop Trail

841'

Chumash Trail

886'

Mugu Peak

La Jolla Canyon

Pacific Coast Highway

Mugu Rock

1 mile

HIKE 1

LA JOLLA VALLEY LOOP
from the Pacific Coast Hwy
via The Chumash Trail

Maps:	Point Mugu, topo
	Point Mugu State Park
Distance:	6 miles roundtrip
Elevation:	1200' gain and loss
Terrain:	Trail; some steep,
	some easy
Time:	2-3/4 hours
Trailhead:	Pacific Coast Hwy

Indians lived in La Jolla Valley early in man's occupation at the Santa Monica Mountains, probably as long as 7000 years ago. A trail into the valley comes up from the east end of Mugu Lagoon, and was one of the routes used by the Indians.

To reach the beginning of the trail, go 24 miles west of Malibu on the Pacific Coast Highway. Park two miles beyond the La Jolla Canyon Road in a large parking area on the right. The road marker nearby reads 8[07]. Across the highway there is a military small arms firing range.

The trail goes straight up the hill to the east without any switchbacks. This is characteristic of the Indian trails — steep and direct — no frills. In a little over 1/2 mile the trail crests at a saddle just northwest of Mugu Peak at an altitude of 886'. Broken seashells litter the route, giving mute evidence of its previous use.

Take time to look back at the sprawling Pacific Ocean. On occasion it will storm, but usually you will see gentle rolls of waves softly caressing the shore below. Off to the right and out at sea are the Channel Islands. Indian tradition says that when a certain type of cloud forms over Anacapa that rain will follow in a few days.

La Jolla Valley extends northeast of the crest of the trail. It is a surprisingly large area of grassland cut by the two main forks of La Jolla Creek. Trees line the streambeds and in a few places there are oakgroves. At one time Chumash villages and camps dotted the valley. Springs and permanent running water made this an attractive living area for the Indians as well as the ranchers that followed.

Several trails in La Jolla Valley give you an opportunity to crisscross the valley as well as to see the canyon downstream. This hike will guide you on a loop trip around the upper part of the valley.

Continue on the trail as it heads northeast from the saddle. The gentle downhill grade takes you through a mountain rimmed savannah, rich in Indian history and valuable as a preserve for rare native grasses. Several trails come up the valley from the right and join the one you are on. A trail that comes from the direction of Laguna Peak enters on the left. (Laguna Peak supports a radar facility in a fenced-in area and cannot be reached.) About a mile after leaving the saddle, the trail goes through an area of head high mustard plants, crosses two tributaries of the west fork and turns east. As you continue east for another mile, several trails come up the valley from the south. These all come in from the main trail that starts at the La Jolla Canyon parking lot.

The La Jolla Valley Walk-in Camp is on the left. This camp is a primitive overnight camping spot with drinking water and restrooms. Permits for overnight stay may be obtained from any of the main entrance stations. The campground is in an oak grove with lots of shade and level grassy areas. It's a good place for a lunch stop.

Continue the loop of the valley by backtracking a short distance and branch off the trail to the south, along a pond. That black bird swimming among the tules is a coot. Just after passing the pond, the trail intersects the main La Jolla Canyon Trail as it gently follows downstream along the east bank. Walk this trail for about 3/4 mile until reaching another well marked and clearly visible trail on the right. (If you happen to miss it you will soon start dropping down into the splashing waters of La Jolla Canyon and arrive at the wrong roadhead.) Take this trail, initially heading northwest, until you cross the stream. The route then makes a southwest to westerly sweep, starting up the west fork of the stream. Eight-tenths of a mile after leaving the Canyon Trail, you are on a spot with some options: option #1, take a trail on the left which drops down, crosses the stream and climbs around the south and west shoulder of Mugu Peak intersecting the Indian trail that came up from the roadhead; or option #2, continue ahead, following the stream, taking care to notice that the trail forks again. Take the left fork, and in about one mile you intersect the Indian trail on which a left turn takes you back to the roadhead.

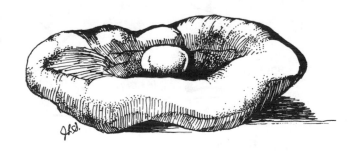

Millingstone and Muller

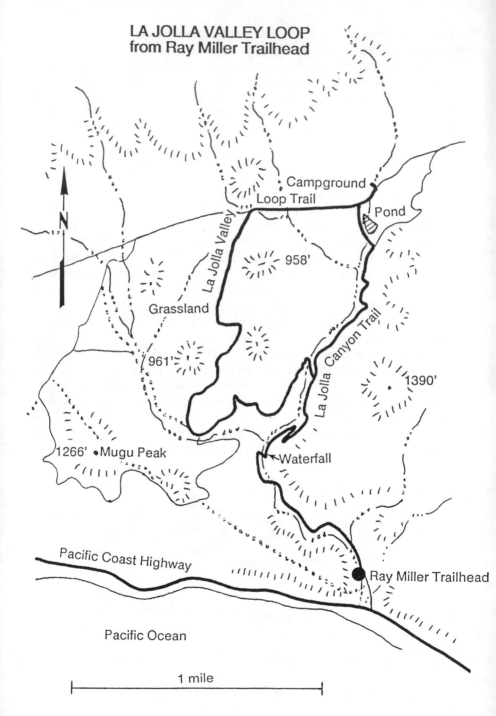

LA JOLLA VALLEY LOOP
from Ray Miller Trailhead

N

Campground
Loop Trail
Pond
La Jolla Valley
958'
Grassland
961'
La Jolla Canyon Trail
1390'
1266' •Mugu Peak
Waterfall
Pacific Coast Highway
Ray Miller Trailhead
Pacific Ocean
1 mile

HIKE 2

Maps:	Point Mugu, topo
	Point Mugu State Park
Distance:	6½ miles roundtrip
Elevation:	1000' gain and loss
Terrain:	Trail; some very steep,
	some level
Time:	3 hours
Trailhead:	Ray Miller Trailhead in
	La Jolla Canyon

Drive west on the Pacific Coast Highway, 22 miles from Malibu to the La Jolla Canyon parking lot. As you drive along, the lazy Pacific surf noses in on your left; and up ahead Mugu Peak is still shaking the morning mist from its crest. La Jolla Canyon is east of Mugu Peak.

Walk north from the parking lot at the Ray Miller Trailhead, going upstream on the La Jolla Canyon Trail. An old road, built in the '20s and used to haul rock for building the Pacific Coast Highway, goes about 3/4 mile into the canyon. We can see the quarry on the left as the trail starts up to the waterfall. Stop in the shade at the waterfall and notice the red roots of willow trees growing in the water. A rocky, steep, narrow segment of the trail lies ahead for a few hundred yards so we use an added amount of caution until the tread underfoot becomes wider. The waterfall is at an elevation of about 250'; the levelling off point after the two big switchbacks is at an elevation of 500' so we will have gained one quarter of the entire hike's elevation in just a few minutes.

At this temporary high point look at the sandstone along the trail — a layer of fossil shells is exposed. These shells were imbedded in sand when the land was ocean floor. Giant Coreopsis plants are in bloom during February through April. Come here then, if for no other reason. Continue along the trail for a few minutes and reach a side trail branching left. Take the left trail and it immediately drops down to the stream in the shade of oaks before making a left turn to climb along the shoulder of the mountain. A viewing spot lets us look down on the trail we came on earlier, and on a clear day an exceptional view of the ocean. On the uphill side of the trail look for a Cholla cactus — a rarity in the Santa Monica Mountains.

The trail heads west toward the approach to Mugu Peak, then turns north for an uphill climb to La Jolla Valley. Our first view of the upper valley is astonishing. The Valley Grassland plant community that we see is included in the <u>Inventory of California Natural Areas,</u> and is one of the best existing relict stands of native California grassland, anywhere. Chumash Indians lived here for thousands of years, then it became part of a provisional Mexican land grant to Isabel Maria Yorba in 1836. The official grant of 30,594 acres, called Rancho Guadalasca, was awarded in 1846. In 1871 Isabel Yorba sold 22,000 acres of the Rancho to a land company that resold to William R. Broome in 1873. Under the Broome family, Rancho Guadalasca has functioned as a ranch into the present. Part of the ranch, including La Jolla Valley, sold to the State of California in 1966 for recreational use. In February 1971 the State Park and Recreation Commission classified the land as Point Mugu State Park, and adopted a use plan that has kept La Jolla grassland in its pristine state.

One of our favorite lunch spots is on a knoll east of the trail, and if anyone out there leaves so much as an orange peel, I will regret telling this secret. Continue north on the trail and we are on the eastern edge of the grassland. Not all of the vegetation is native; we will recognize introduced grasses mixed with the natives, and in springtime might even taste the waist high Mustard flowers. For the first ten seconds or so they have a slightly sweet taste — then hot!

Our trail intersects a west to east trail that comes from the saddle north of Mugu Peak. Turn right and follow this trail — more a road — until reaching a walk-in campground on the left. Restrooms, water, and shade under the oaks are available. If the sun was too hot to have lunch back along the trail, this is a good spot for eating.

To return we walk about 150 yards back on the trail we came on, then turn left onto a narrow trail and stay left until we pass by the pond, then angle right and meet the main trail down into La Jolla Canyon. A brisk 45 minute walk takes us back to our cars.

La Jolla Canyon Waterfall

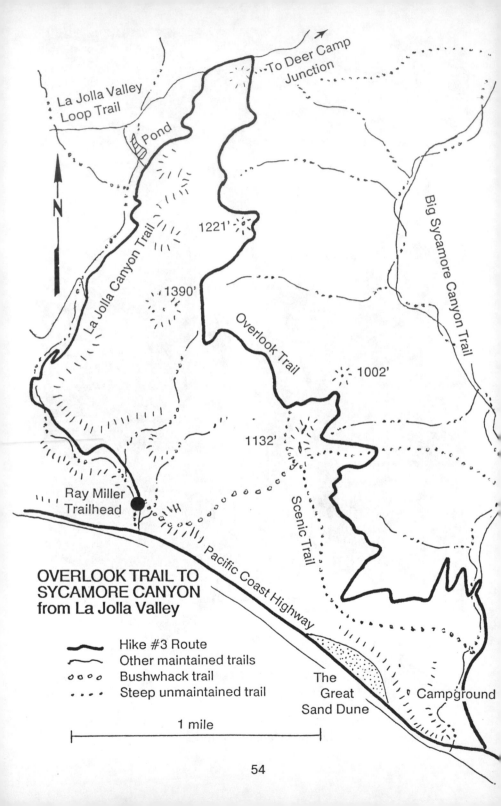

To Deer Camp
Junction

La Jolla Valley
Loop Trail

Pond

N

1221'

1390'

La Jolla Canyon Trail

Overlook Trail

1002'

1132'

Ray Miller
Trailhead

Scenic Trail

Big Sycamore Canyon Trail

**OVERLOOK TRAIL TO
SYCAMORE CANYON
from La Jolla Valley**

Pacific Coast Highway

The
Great
Sand Dune

Campground

— Hike #3 Route
— Other maintained trails
oooo Bushwhack trail
.... Steep unmaintained trail

1 mile

HIKE 3

SYCAMORE CANYON
from La Jolla Valley
via The Overlook Trail
(shuttle)

Maps:	Point Mugu, topo
	Point Mugu State Park
Distance:	9 miles roundtrip
Elevation:	1400' gain and loss
Terrain:	Trail
Time:	3-3/4 hours
Trailhead:	at Ray Miller trailhead
	La Jolla Canyon (beginning)
	Big Sycamore Cyn (ending)

This trip requires a short car shuttle, because the hike starts at La Jolla Canyon and ends at the Sycamore Canyon Campground.

To reach the beginning of the hike, drive west on the Pacific Coast Highway 20 miles from Malibu. Leave a car at Sycamore Canyon, then proceed past the Great Sand Dune and along the highway another 2 miles from Sycamore Canyon to the La Jolla Valley parking lot.

Walk north from the parking lot going upstream on the La Jolla Canyon Trail. The first 3/4 mile of the walk is gently uphill, then the trail winds through a rocky area under some trees as it crosses the stream near a waterfall. Immediately after the stream crossing, the trail climbs past the waterfall then gains altitude by going through two switchbacks. In a half mile a trail branches off to the left that would take you to the west end of the upper La Jolla Valley and to Mugu Peak. Today's trip will go into the eastern end of the valley so stay on the main trail.

In about 1/2 mile, another trail branches left and goes along the south shore of a pond. That trail would take you to the La Jolla Valley Walk-in Camp, where there is water and a restroom; and then you could continue on and meet the La Jolla Canyon Trail. However, stay on the La Jolla Canyon Trail and in another 1/2 mile you find a succession of trail junctions. At each decision point follow the trail on the right until you are on the Overlook Trail going south. Overlook Trail stays well up on the ridge between La

Jolla and Sycamore Canyons and true to its name looks into both canyons. Generally heading south, this trail twists and turns, climbs and dips for 4 miles before making a decisive turn toward Sycamore Canyon and a downhill drop to the trail along the stream. Cross the stream and follow the trail down to the campground and parking area where water and restroom facilities are available.

An alternate and slightly more daring route branches from the Overlook Trail near Peak 1132. See hike #6 for a description of the Scenic Trail.

Bulletin Board at Ray Miller Trailhead

HIKE 4

Maps:	Point Mugu, topo
	Camarillo, topo
	Newbury Park, topo
	Triunfo Pass, topo
	Point Mugu State Park
Distance:	26 miles roundtrip
Elevation:	4700' gain and loss
Terrain:	Road and some very steep
	trail; some stream crossings
Time:	Sunup to sundown
Trailhead:	La Jolla Cyn (beginning)
	Sycamore Cyn (ending)

This is a strenuous hike, some of it on very steep trails. "Walkabout" is a mild term that is deceiving; this is a real hike.

The car shuttle is set up by leaving a car at Sycamore Canyon (the end point of the hike) then going 2 miles west to the La Jolla Canyon for the beginning.

Walk downstream toward the ocean from the La Jolla Valley parking lot watching for a trail that crosses the stream and goes up the ridge on the right. The trail goes west, steeply up the point of the ridge toward Mugu Peak. During the 1000' of elevation gain before reaching the trail coming around the south side of the peak, you will have experienced the evolvement of a most spectacular view of the Pacific Ocean imaginable. The trail takes you to the brink of a steep drop to the water below, then continues relentlessly up the mountain.

Upon reaching the trail that contours from the south side of the peak, turn left for just a few minutes until finding an indistinct trail on the right. Five minutes on this and you are on top of Mugu Peak.

Leave the peak by dropping down a steep trail to the north. Turn right onto the trail that contours around the west side of the peak. This trail makes a big sweeping crossing of the upper part of La Jolla Valley. Generally heading northeast the trail loses some

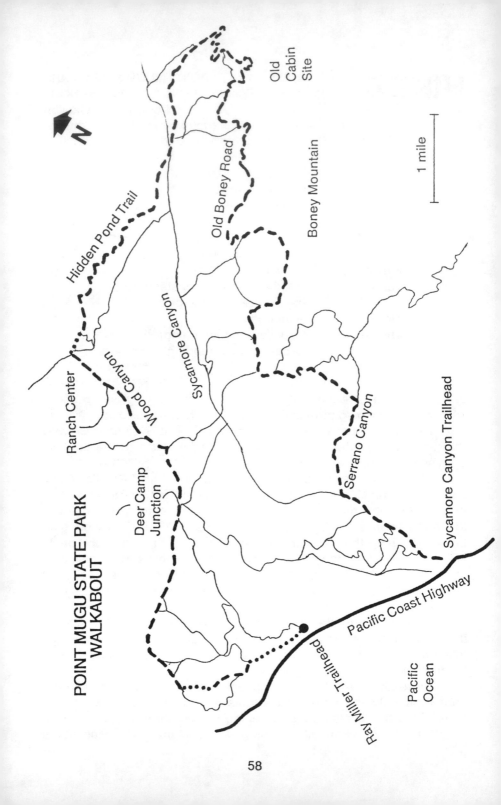

POINT MUGU STATE PARK
WALKABOUT

N

1 mile

Old Cabin Site

Old Boney Road

Boney Mountain

Hidden Pond Trail

Sycamore Canyon

Ranch Center

Wood Canyon

Deer Camp Junction

Serrano Canyon

Sycamore Canyon Trailhead

Ray Miller Trailhead

Pacific Coast Highway

Pacific Ocean

58

altitude, but is almost level for a mile and a half as it goes through an open grassland of native bunch grass, crossing several tributaries of La Jolla Creek. The streams are intermittent this far up and may be dry late in the year. Some springs exist farther down the valley. Continue on the trail reaching the Walk-in Camp on the left in a grove of oak trees. Water and restrooms are available.

Continue northeast on the trail for ten minutes, reaching a saddle on the hill. Several trails branch off at this point; continue ahead going downhill to Deer Camp junction, then turn left. Follow the almost level Wood Canyon Trail, taking 1/2 hour to reach Ranch Center. At Ranch Center climb a ridge due east of the junction of Wood Canyon Trail and Ranch Center Road. This joins the Hidden Pond Trail on the north border of the park, and continues east. You may avoid climbing the steep ridge by walking east on Ranch Center Road to the first saddle. A trail which branches left at the saddle leads uphill to Hidden Pond Trail. In about 2 miles the Hidden Pond Trail joins the paved road along Sycamore Canyon Creek. Follow this upstream until reaching a trail that turns right just before the road crosses the stream. The trail follows Sycamore Creek uphill reaching Old Boney Road in 1¼ miles and gaining 400'. Stop for lunch along the trail.

Turn right on the road and cross the stream going uphill in the shade of Oak and Bay trees. A side trip to the waterfall may be made by going on a trail to the left at the first switchback. The road continues gaining altitude as it switches back and forth on the northeast shoulder of the mountain. When you come to a fork, stay left, on a road. The right fork is Old Boney Road and turns to go up higher on the mountain where you will join it later. The Old Cabin Site is 4/10 of a mile from the fork and is a good rest stop. The cabin is no longer in existence but the 13' high chimney with fireplace and an outline of the cabin foundation show the location. Water is available at a spring near the stream. In the last few years the water has taken on a sulphur taste. I don't drink it anymore.

Continue the hike by following the road past the spring, across the creek and up the hill beyond. After climbing 350' of elevation the road rejoins Old Boney Road, turn left. The Road is at 1800', the highest point of the day, and starts downhill soon. Two trails branch off to the right and join the Sycamore Canyon Trail below. Continue on the road until coming to a junction that would lead to the Danielson Ranch if you turned right; instead, turn left and start to gain 650' as you work your way up a canyon. (There is a large

59

ten foot boulder near the junction that is easily seen.)   At this point you may be out 1½ hours since the Old Cabin Site. Continue on the road going up the canyon making a big right hand turn as the canyon changes direction.

Old Boney Road follows along the north slope of Boney Mountain and ultimately comes to a saddle at the western end of the ridge, looking south into Serrano Valley.   Upon reaching this point, turn left and immediately go downhill on a steep road that levels some, making a left turn around a shoulder of the mountain. The road crosses a stream and turns sharply right, then climbs for a few minutes before levelling off on the shoulder of a sloping grassy ridge.   Go south down the ridge, heading for a prominent Laurel Sumac tree. Look for a trail to the right of the tree and follow it downhill on the ridge. The trail may be overgrown with grass. If you cannot find the trail, stay on the sloping ridge until it levels out, then turn right and look for a break in the chaparral near the old fence line. A trail here goes west toward the stream dropping quickly into Serrano Canyon shaded with luxuriant vegetation. Look for the best stands of Poison Oak to be seen on the hike.

Serrano Canyon is a solid rock gorge connecting upper Serrano Valley with Sycamore Canyon.   The trail is good but has some stream crossings that present a problem when the water is high.

When you reach the Big Sycamore Canyon Trail turn left and have an easy walk to the trailhead.

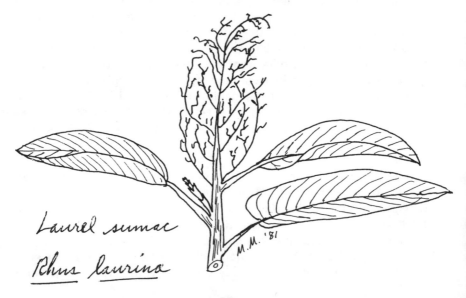

Laurel sumac
Rhus laurina

M.M. '81

60

HIKE 5

Maps:	Point Mugu, topo
	Triunfo Pass, topo
Distance:	8½ miles roundtrip
Elevation:	1100' gain and loss
Terrain:	Steep trail and road
Time:	3-3/4 hours
Trailhead:	Sycamore Canyon

This is a moderate trip taking you through some of the most scenic parts of the center of the Park. Big Sycamore Canyon with its large trees, Serrano Canyon with dense foliage, an open field, a ridge, and a large expanse of chaparral present a variety of plant forms.

Reach the trailhead by driving 20 miles west of the Malibu Canyon Road on the Pacific Coast Hwy to Sycamore Canyon. Park outside the gate.

Walk through the campground and upstream on the Big Sycamore Canyon Trail. A mile and a half after leaving the campground you will pass the Serrano Canyon Trail on the right. That will be the trail that you will come down later. Continue up the gently graded Sycamore Canyon, occasionally crossing the stream. This part of the canyon is wide, and is typical of this outstanding sycamore savannah. Deep grass under spreading trees, deer tracks and on occasion a deer, a couple of acorn woodpeckers sitting on Sycamore branches making short flights if you walk up close, a ground squirrel; all these make this eco-system a vibrant, live and interesting place to visit. One hour after leaving the trailhead you will be near the Wood Canyon Trail junction. Several trails branch out from the main trail in this area; the one that you will be taking is on the right and is a trail, not a road.

The initial view of this trail is shocking after the previous level walking. The trail goes up a steep ridge relentlessly gaining 800 feet before reaching a level area near Old Boney Road. There is some consolation In the spectacular view of Sycamore Canyon.

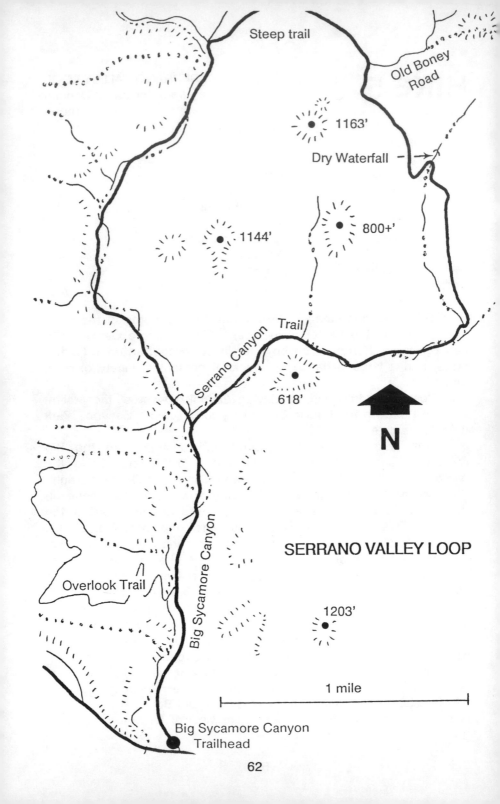

Steep trail

Old Boney Road

•1163'

Dry Waterfall →

•800+'

•1144'

Serrano Canyon Trail

•618'

N

Overlook Trail

Big Sycamore Canyon

SERRANO VALLEY LOOP

•1203'

1 mile

Big Sycamore Canyon
Trailhead

Once on the ridge dividing Sycamore and Serrano Canyons, you can see the grasslands of Serrano to the southeast and Boney Mountain with its many peaks jutting out to the east. A chaparral plant community dominates the ridge and the slope to the north.

Take the road south downhill into Serrano Valley. This road drops 350', then makes a left turn around a shoulder and goes across an intermittent stream coming down from a prominent rock waterfall. After crossing the stream and making a right turn, the road climbs for a few minutes, leveling off on the shoulder of a grassy ridge that slopes to the south. Walk south on the ridge (there may be no trail because the grass grows fast) heading for a prominent Sumac tree. Look for the trail to the right of the tree, but do not be concerned if you can't find it — just continue south on the highest part of the downhill sloping ridge. When the ridge levels out, the trail angles to the right and meets the trail that goes down Serrano Canyon. An old fence line divides the grassland from the chaparral. It is near the fence line that you can pick up the well-defined trail into the canyon.

The trail goes through some chaparral, then very quickly enters the canyon environment of shaded trails, pools of cool water, and luxuriant vegetation. Serrano Canyon is a steep-walled, solid rock, water formed gorge, connecting the higher Serrano Valley with the Sycamore Canyon downstream. The footing is good in most places. Some stream crossings might present a problem, depending upon the level of the water. Some low hanging branches can be a hazard, and keep a lookout for Poison Oak.

Upon reaching the Big Sycamore Canyon Trail, turn left and return to the trailhead.

in Serrano
Canyon

California
Blackberry

July '80

MKM

63

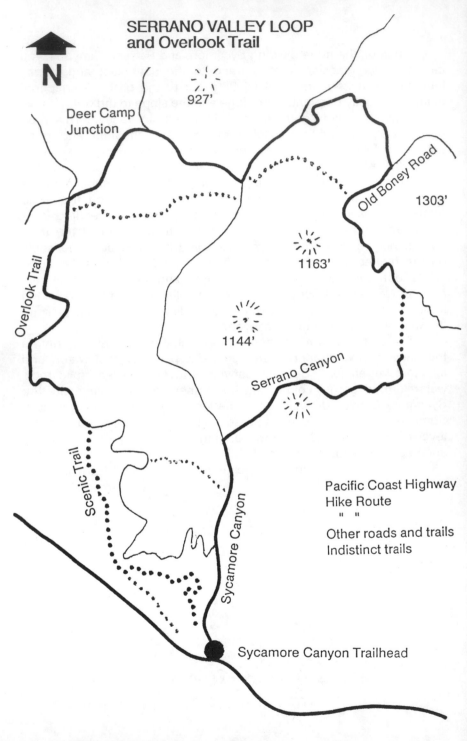

SERRANO VALLEY LOOP
and Overlook Trail

N

927'

Deer Camp Junction

Old Boney Road

1303'

Overlook Trail

1163'

1144'

Serrano Canyon

Scenic Trail

Sycamore Canyon

Pacific Coast Highway
Hike Route
"   "
Other roads and trails
Indistinct trails

Sycamore Canyon Trailhead

HIKE 6

**SERRANO VALLEY LOOP
AND OVERLOOK TRAIL**
from Sycamore Canyon (loop)

Maps:	Point Mugu, topo
	Triunfo Pass, topo
	Point Mugu State Park
Distance:	13 miles roundtrip
Elevation:	2100' gain and loss
Terrain:	Road and trail
Time:	5½ hours including lunch
Trailhead:	Sycamore Canyon

This trip is long for a beginning hiker but might be just the challenge you want. The hike takes you through a wide variety of plant communities: grassland, riparian woodland, coastal sage, and chaparral.   There is a need to follow the map and hiking instructions closely because some of the trail junctions are obscure.

Begin the hike by driving to the trailhead at Sycamore Canyon Campground and park outside the gate. Sycamore Canyon is on the Pacific Coast Highway 20 miles west of the Malibu Canyon Road.

Walk through the campground keeping to the east side, following the well defined Big Sycamore Canyon Trail as it gently ascends the broad floor of the valley. Several trails come in from the west side. Two trails enter the campground on the west and are not seen from the trail; four-tenths of a mile after leaving the campground the Overlook Trail enters; then three-tenths of a mile farther, a seldom used steep trail from the Overlook comes in. Twenty-five minutes after the start of the hike you will come to the Serrano Canyon Trail. Take the right fork and begin a steady climb on a foot trail.   Serrano Canyon is a secluded intimate riparian woodland.   The vegetation is luxuriant, and depending upon the period of time elapsed since anyone has trimmed the vegetation back, some of that abundant greenery that you are brushing against can be Poison Oak. Overhead the trees form a closed canopy, making this a shady and delightfully cool canyon. There are some low hanging branches and a few that must be stepped over. The intention is that the trail not be suitable for horses, so only a minimum removal of trees and branches has been made. This area is truly unspoiled.

Forty minutes after entering Serrano Canyon you will have gradually gained about 300 feet; and after crossing a side stream by going down some rock steps, you suddenly leave the stream and its protective environment to climb a chaparral hillside. The trail makes a sharp turn to the right. (Actually it is now a fork in the trail to the right because many overshoot this turn and have gone up another trail leading into a lot of brush.) So make the turn to the right, going through an old fence line to a grassy ridge. Turn left and go north up the ridge through a large grassy area. An old metal building and a metal tank on the hillside can be used as guides. Stay to the left for the easiest going. You will see a Laurel Sumac tree on top of the ridge — head for it. Stop at the Sumac and look around. Serrano Canyon runs east to west, south of you; to the east is a ranch; and the road coming down the slope to the east is the Serrano Road. It goes to the Park property gate, through the ranch, then the overgrown continuation of the road passes several hundred feet north of the Sumac. You should head for this road by continuing north on the ridge, then turn left.

Follow this road for nearly a mile as it works its way northwest, losing some altitude as it drops down for a sidestream below a prominent rock waterfall, then climbing to the ridge dividing Serrano Canyon and Big Sycamore Canyon. There is a road junction at the ridge. Turn right and follow Old Boney Road northeast for about ten minutes, then take a side road on the left that drops steeply down to Sycamore Canyon, losing 700 feet in a little over one mile. Upon reaching the Big Sycamore Canyon Trail, turn left and walk downstream for 10 minutes until coming to the Wood Canyon Trail on the right. This part of the canyon is a beautiful sycamore savannah — the best example in the Santa Monica Mountains.

Take a look in the stream crossing at the beginning of the trail. In April we saw four common gartersnakes swimming in a deep area of the slow moving water probably hunting tadpoles, their favorite food. One snake stayed on top with his head out of water, flicking his tongue to smell us. I would like to think since spring is mating season, he may have been searching for a mate. Determining that our hiking group wouldn't do, he quickly dove to the bottom.

A gentle fifteen to twenty minute walk upstream along the Wood Canyon Trail will get you to Deer Camp Junction and its restroom, water, and picnic area. This is a good place to eat lunch in the shade of Oak trees by the side of Wood Creek. The trail forks at Deer Camp Junction. The right fork continues up the Wood Canyon Trail to Ranch Center; the left fork leads to the Overlook Trail. Take the left fork and prepare to gain 700' in the next three-fourths of a mile. Upon reaching the ridge separating Sycamore Canyon on the east from La Jolla Valley on the west, turn left on Overlook Trail going south along the ridge.

Time yourself because you will be looking for a not-too-distinct trail on the right in 35 minutes. The Overlook Trail does just what the name implies — it stays high on the mountain presenting views of Sycamore Canyon and La Jolla Valley, and sometimes a look into Serrano Canyon, and of course Boney Mountain beyond. The view of the ocean is special; water as far as the eye can see, and off to the west are the Channel Islands. On a clear day some islands are in view to the south. Mugu Rock isn't In view yet but can be seen later. After 35 minutes on the Overlook Trail and as you come to the saddle north of Peak 1132, Scenic Trail branches off to the south. Take it, and contour around on the west side of the peak. Now you can see Mugu Rock if you look to the west. You will reach a point on the ridge where the trail branches. The right well-used fork is the Ray Miller Trail. It is 2 miles long and switches down to the trailhead in La Jolla Canyon. On this hike we won't drop down to La Jolla Canyon so don't take the Ray Miller Trail but continue toward the ocean along a seldom used trail on the ridge. This rough trail drops down on a ridge to the south, then becomes very steep. Several trails coming up from the campground in Sycamore Canyon are in view. This gives you a selection after you leave the steep area. By staying to the right, you will come close to the "Great Sand Dune." This sand dune has been formed by the prevailing westerly wind picking up sand from the beach and carrying it up against the mountain. Wind is one of the natural forces that can carry material uphill. You will have a view of the dune from above by getting off the trail. At least two routes will take you east down to Sycamore Canyon. You will lose 400 feet in one-half mile and cross the stream. Sycamore campground is downstream.

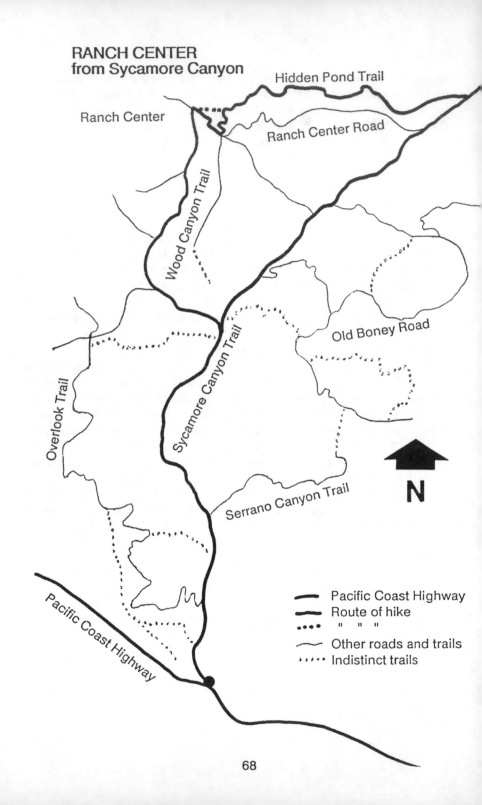

RANCH CENTER
from Sycamore Canyon

Hidden Pond Trail

Ranch Center

Ranch Center Road

Wood Canyon Trail

Old Boney Road

Overlook Trail

Sycamore Canyon Trail

Serrano Canyon Trail

N

Pacific Coast Highway

Pacific Coast Highway

——— Pacific Coast Highway
——— Route of hike
•••• " " "
——— Other roads and trails
····· Indistinct trails

HIKE 7

RANCH CENTER
via Wood Canyon Trail
Hidden Pond Trail and Big
Sycamore Canyon Trail from
Sycamore Canyon Campground
(loop)

Maps:	Point Mugu, topo
	Camarillo, topo
	Newbury Park, topo
	Triunfo Pass, topo
	Point Mugu State Park
Distance:	16 miles roundtrip
Elevation:	1200' gain and loss
Terrain:	Trail and road
Time:	6½ hours, incl. lunch
Trailhead:	Sycamore Canyon

This is a long walk covering a large segment of the Park from the ocean to the northern boundary and back. Most of the trail is of moderate grade and good footing. One segment near Ranch Center is steep but there is an easier optional route.

Drive 20 miles west of Malibu Canyon Road on the Pacific Coast Highway to Sycamore Canyon Campground. Park outside the gate and walk through onto the Big Sycamore Canyon Trail.

The trail goes north, almost level as it gently ascends the floor of the valley. A brisk one hour walk will put you close to the Wood Canyon Trail Junction. Several trails leave the main trail near this point; take the well marked, well travelled one on the left.

After crossing Sycamore Creek, the trail follows Wood Creek and enters an area shaded with oaks and sycamores. The hillsides are chaparral; grass and flowering plants grow along the floor of the valley. The trail forks at Deer Camp Junction; the left fork goes uphill and into La Jolla Valley. Take the right fork continuing on the Wood Canyon trail. Restoom facilities and water are available at Deer Camp Junction. Wood Canyon Trail continues in a gentle climb, shaded most of the way. Ranch Center is the northern terminal of the trail and is on the northern border of the park. Water is also available there.

Leave Ranch Center by going directly up the ridge east of the road and trail junction. This is a stiff 450' climb up a grassy ridge, intersecting the Hidden Pond Trail. An alternate, gentler (but still 450') climb can be taken by going southeast on the paved Ranch Center Road until it also intersects the Hidden Pond Trail on which you go north. Hidden Pond can be a disappointment — it is sometimes dry. The trail winds around some and has short uphill and downhill sections, offering impressive views of Sycamore Canyon and Boney Mountain. Following the trail up the slope is straightforward, but as it drops close to Sycamore Creek, overgrown vegetation presents a route finding problem. Nearing the stream the trail comes down the east edge of a grassy field then turns left, going through light chaparral as it almost parallels the stream, then crosses it and joins Sycamore Canyon Trail (a paved road at this point) a few hundred feet from where the road leaves the stream and goes uphill to the Potrero entrance. Water is available here.

The return trip is downstream on Sycamore Canyon Trail to the parking lot.

Danielson Home in Sycamore Canyon

70

SYCAMORE

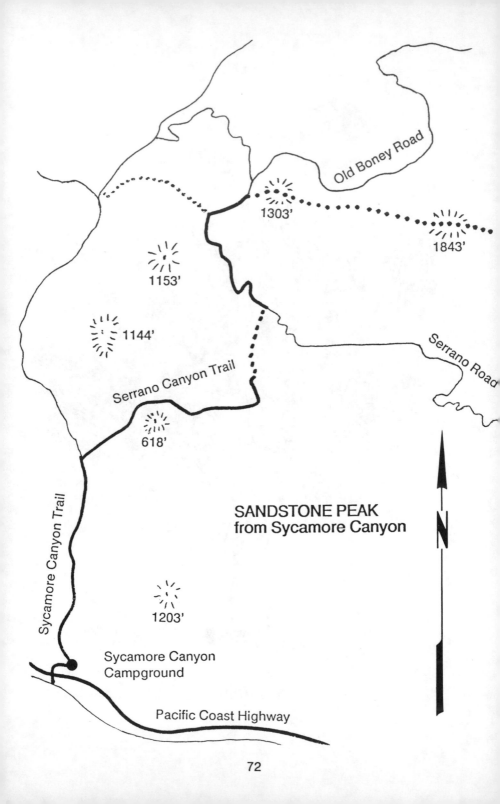

Old Boney Road

1303'

1843'

1153'

1144'

Serrano Road

Serrano Canyon Trail

618'

Sycamore Canyon Trail

**SANDSTONE PEAK
from Sycamore Canyon**

N

1203'

Sycamore Canyon
Campground

Pacific Coast Highway

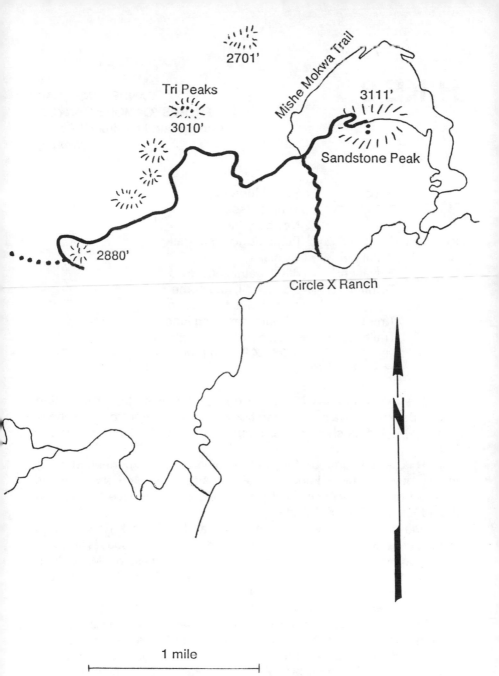

2701'

Tri Peaks
3010'

Mishe Mokwa Trail

3111'

Sandstone Peak

2880'

Circle X Ranch

N

1 mile

HIKE 8

Maps:	Point Mugu, topo
	Triunfo Pass, topo
	Newbury Park, topo
	Point Mugu State Park
Distance:	11 miles
Elevation:	4000' gain, 2300' loss
Terrain:	Road, trail, and some
	off-trail bushwhacking
Time:	7 hours including lunch
Trailhead:	Sycamore Cyn (beginning)
	Circle X Ranch (ending)

The map on pages 72 and 73 does not indicate the new section of the Backbone Trail. The traditional hike has been to bushwhack along the ridge as shown. The bushwhack route is also described in Hike 9.

This is a strenuous trip and is for only the experienced hiker in a group led by a knowledgeable leader. Finding the route is involved, the uphill bushwhacking is difficult, you'll have hot sun on the ridges and Poison Oak in the canyons.

The car shuttle begins by meeting at the Circle X Ranch. This is on Yerba Buena Road, 5½ miles from the Pacific Coast Highway. If you come in from the other direction, drive west on Mulholland Highway until reaching Little Sycamore Canyon Road; turn right and go 5.4 miles to the Circle X Ranch. Yerba Buena Road and Sycamore Canyon Road are the same road -- it is named differently at either end. Check-in with the ranger; then set up the shuttle by leaving some cars at the Circle X, where the trip ends, and driving to Big Sycamore Canyon trailhead where the trip begins. Sycamore Canyon may be reached by going to the Pacific Coast Highway, turn right and go 3 miles.

This hike will go to the top of Sandstone Peak, the highest point in the Santa Monica Mountains at 3111', so an important ritual is to be observed. We shall go from the lowest point to the highest point. To do that we enter the campground, turn left, walk to Big Sycamore Creek and follow it to the ocean, going under the Pacific Coast Highway. Wet your feet in an incoming wave and start the hike by going upstream, through the campground and onto Big Sycamore Canyon Trail. One mile up the trail turn right onto Serrano Canyon Trail.

While you have the opportunity, take advantage of the coolness and shade of Serrano Canyon because you will soon spend a lot of time on exposed ridges and in dry winds. Here is where you will find the Poison Oak I promised. There are some low hanging branches over the trail, and other obstacles, but this is a beautiful place and a pleasant walk — cherish it. After 30 to 40 minutes on the Serrano Canyon Trail it abruptly pulls away from the stream and makes a sharp turn to the right. Actually, it is a fork in the trail going uphill to an old fence line and onto a grassy ridge. Now turn left and go north up the ridge through a grassy area. An old metal building and a metal tank on the ridge are route indicators. The trail goes to the left of them and heads for a Laurel Sumac tree on top of the ridge. Continue a couple hundred yards farther, coming upon an old dirt road. Turn left, following the road as it contours along the hillside then drops down to cross a streambed that features a rock waterfall upstream. The road climbs to the ridge dividing Serrano and Big Sycamore Canyons. At the fork turn right and follow Old Boney Road about a mile coming to a trail on the right. This new trail, completed in 1990, is part of the "Backbone Trail" linking Point Mugu State Park and the National Park Service's Circle X Ranch.

We take this trail and climb east uphill all the way, passing near a split rock. Before the trail was built we went cross-country along the ridge, and by tradition went through the split — a tight squeeze. On cool days this is an acceptable lunch spot. Weather protected areas with more shade are found farther along the trail. The trail contours along the north side of Peak 2880, making some turns as it winds through the peaks on Boney Mountain. The trail eases up somewhat and enters the "Camp Allen" recreation area. During the Boy Scout era of the Circle X Ranch, Camp Allen was location for backcountry camping. At present water is not available and the campground is not open.

A road leads uphill to the south from the rest area. Follow this as it leads to the crest of the ridge overlooking a series of small peaks. About halfway between the rest area and the peak, the road crosses the Mishe Mokwa hiking trail. Note the location.

Continue east on the road, and after a switchback each way start looking for the steep trail that goes to the top of Sandstone Peak. The trail is on the right and takes you to the peak, a rock scramble.

You have now gone from the lowest point in the Santa Monica Mountains to the highest point — a great feeling. You will want to savor the moment by scanning the horizon; south and west is the Pacific Ocean dotted with some islands that are visible on clear days; the Oxnard Plain is northwest, and the Santa Ynez and Topatopa Mountains beyond; in the near foreground are the many peaks of Boney Mountain. Notice the sheer cliffs on the south side of Sandstone; and now look at the rock you are sitting on — it is not sandstone at all, it is volcanic! Between 13½ and 15½ million years ago a period of volcanic activity in the Santa Monica Mountains resulted in a number of outcroppings throughout the range, the highest one being Sandstone Peak, 3lll'.

Retrace your steps as far as the road at the bottom of the steep trail coming down from the peak. You have the option of returning to the Circle X Ranch by three routes: (1) The shortest and quickest way is to turn left and go west on the road for about 10 minutes and upon reaching the trail crossing the road, turn left and drop a thousand feet in about one mile, arriving just opposite the parking lot; (2) The longest way home is to go west on the road back to Camp Allen. Cross the camp area heading northeast. A road leads east, downhill, from a ridge and soon follows along Carlisle Creek. Continue downstream to Split Rock, a prominent rock along a stream in an oak glen. Cross the stream and locate a trail that initially goes southeast as it contours around the shoulder of Sandstone. This Mishe Mokwa Trail leads to a road that intersects Yerba Buena Road one mile uphill from the Circle X Ranch. (3) The other route is to turn right on the rocky road after coming down the steep trail from the peak. Follow the road until it intersects Yerba Buena Road one mile uphill from the Circle X Ranch.

This hike will give you a good workout. You will sleep well.

Point Mugu State Park Headquarters

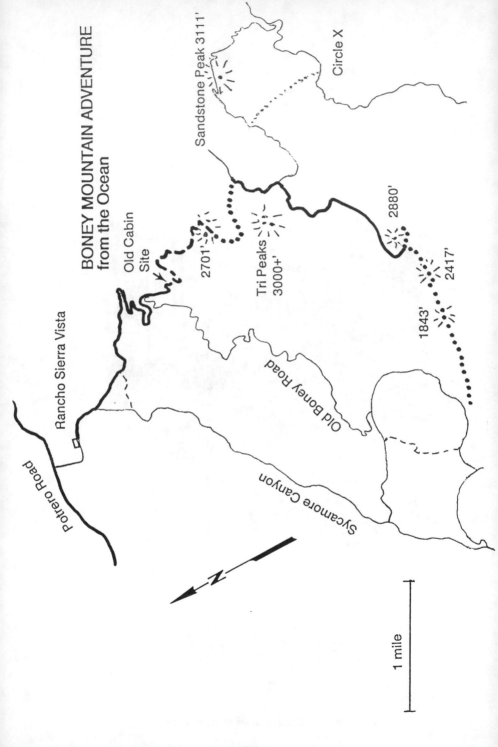

BONEY MOUNTAIN ADVENTURE
from the Ocean

Sandstone Peak 3111'

Circle X

Old Cabin Site

2701'

Tri Peaks 3000+'

2880'

2417'

1843'

Rancho Sierra Vista

Potrero Road

Old Boney Road

Sycamore Canyon

N

1 mile

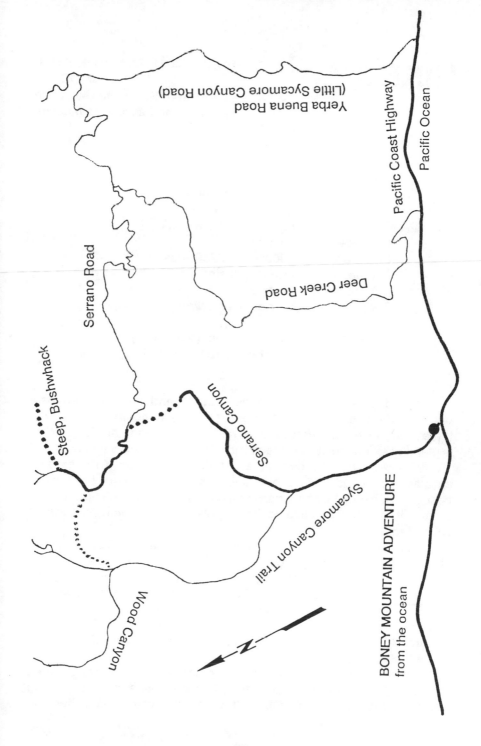

BONEY MOUNTAIN ADVENTURE
from the ocean

Pacific Ocean

Pacific Coast Highway

Deer Creek Road

Yerba Buena Road
(Little Sycamore Canyon Road)

Serrano Road

Steep, Bushwhack

Serrano Canyon

Sycamore Canyon Trail

Wood Canyon

N

HIKE 9

Maps:	Point Mugu, topo
	Triunfo Pass, topo
	Newbury Park, topo
	Point Mugu State Park
Distance:	15 miles
Elevation:	4000' gain, 3250' loss
Terrain:	Road, trail, steep bushwhacking
Time:	8½ hours including lunch
Trailhead:	Sycamore Cyn (beginning)
	Rancho Sierra Vista (ending)

This trip is for the experienced hiker and is even then best done under competent leadership. The route-finding is involved, there is some serious uphill chaparral bushwhacking, the Poison Oak is plentiful along the streams, and the sun is hot on the ridges.

A part of the hike crosses a corner of the Circle X Ranch, and an advance call to the Ranger giving information about the hike is desired. Because this hike passes through some difficult and remote terrain, it is good practice to keep potential help well informed of your intentions.

Set up the car shuttle by leaving some cars at Rancho Sierra Vista, where the trip ends, and driving to Sycamore Canyon Trailhead, where the trip begins. Rancho Sierra Vista may be reached from the west end of Thousand Oaks. Take the Borchard Rd. Exit from Ventura Freeway, and drive south 1½ miles to Reino Road. Turn left and continue two miles on Reino (which becomes Potrero Rd.) to Pinehill Avenue. Turn left and drive to the Rancho Sierra Vista parking lot.

Drive to Sycamore Canyon by going west on Potrero Road, down Long Grade Canyon past the Camarillo State Hospital turning left onto Hueneme Road, next left onto Las Posas Road, then left onto the Pacific Coast Highway. Park outside the Sycamore Canyon Campground, and the hike begins.

Walk through the campground picking up the Big Sycamore Canyon Trail as it gently ascends the broad floor of the valley. Enjoy the less than 100' elevation gain during the first mile because things are about to change. Twenty minutes after leaving the trailhead, and after 2 stream crossings, you will come to a fork in the trail — turn right and go up the Serrano Canyon Trail.

Serrano Canyon is heavily shaded near the stream and offers a cool, pleasant walking trail. A few stream crossings are required, and if done in the spring, this adds a small challenge. Poison Oak grows well in this canyon so watch closely. There are also some low hanging branches over the trail, as this is for hikers only — no horses. In 30 to 40 minutes you will leave the riparian woodland atmosphere and almost suddenly find yourself on a grassy ridge. Turn left at the old fence line and go due north up the ridge for ten minutes. The ridge is dotted by a few isolated Sumacs and a metal water tank. You will join an old road and go left as it contours some, then drops down into a side canyon that displays a prominent rock waterfall upstream. The road then climbs to the ridge dividing Serrano and Big Sycamore Canyons. Turn right on the road and follow it as long as it stays on the ridge, maybe five minutes. The road (Old Boney) leaves the ridge, contouring along the north slope. (When the trail along the

west ridge was built in 1990 this "adventure" became easier. You may elect to use the trail by continuing another half mile along Old Boney Road, but I have left the original bushwhack description in the book for those who want an extra challenge.) Leave the road, staying on the ridge as you climb east. After 1½ hours of climbing through chaparral, over several reddish basaltic peaks, and across an old rusty barbed wire fence many times, you will come to a prominent split rock. Tradition says that the trail goes through the split but it's a tight squeeze and you may not be mentally adjusted to prolonging such a tradition. This is a good place for a lunch stop.

Split Rock

You might want to reflect back on the trail about a half mile to a point where, had you been inclined, you could have looked for the boundary marker that noted a corner of the Guadalasca land grant and the El Conejo land grant. These two Ranchos totalling 79,266 acres were granted by the Mexican government in the 1800's prior to the Mexican-American War that resulted in the United States' acquisition of California.

Continue climbing east on the ridge. After a stretch of the usual chaparral bushwhacking, you come over a rise and are "on a trail!" Ahead and to the left there is a well defined road in view. You will soon be on this road as it circles around to the north side of the peak marked with 2880' altitude, but first continue east to the pass overlooking the upper Little Sycamore Canyon. This should take 45 minutes from Split Rock. The view of the south escarpment of Boney Mountain and Sandstone Peak is spectacular. Immense volcanic cliffs dominate Upper Little Sycamore Canyon and the west fork of Arroyo Sequit. Go west back down the trail a few hundred feet then take the right fork as it starts the circle around the peak. The trail gradually becomes a road and twists around some as it winds among the peaks on Boney Mountain. Twenty-five minutes after leaving the Little Sycamore Canyon Overlook, a large split rock is prominent about 100 yards off to the right. Soon after passing this spot take the right fork in the road. Five minutes later you will reach a gate. Continue on the road, almost immediately turning right on a side road that drops down through a wash, crosses another road and goes uphill joining a good road. The H. W. Allen overnight campground is south of this area. Ten minutes after passing the gate, begin looking left for a cross-country bushwhack route up to the ridge on the north. There is an indication of a trail leaving the road, and actually some semblance of a way through the chaparral. You may miss these small clues and just have to strike out on your own and climb to the top of the rocky peak. It should take 20 minutes from the road. Upon leaving the peak, contour north about 400 yards picking up the trail on the ridge that drops down to the northeast toward Peak 2701. After going through a mini-forest of Ceanothus and Red Shanks, the trail curls around the south side of the peak and drops sharply for a l000' elevation loss, going through one of the largest stands of Manzanita in the Santa Monicas. The trail is steep, but well-defined throughout the descent to the Old Cabin Site and upon approaching this welcome rest stop, the chaparral changes to Oak trees, Laurel trees, and grass.

The cabin is gone but the thirteen-foot high fireplace chimney remains and, along with the outline of a foundation, marks the spot where the cabin stood. Downhill and to the left the spring furnishes a strong flow of cool water from a pipe. Horses have tramped about the spring itself and the water doesn't run out of the pipe as it should. I have stopped drinking the water. The water from the spring flows into a stream that runs down the canyon to the northeast and is a tributary of Big Sycamore Creek. So, in a sense, you have hiked from the mouth of Big Sycamore Creek as it entered the ocean and are now seeing the source of one of many tributaries. Stay here as long as time permits, it is only one hour to the end of the hike.

Go downhill from the Old Cabin Site on a road that soon crosses the stream and heads north. In less than ten minutes you will come to Old Boney Road; take the right fork and continue to contour around the shoulder of the mountain before making switchbacks down to the main stream. Cross the stream and continue on the road as it starts up a slight grade — resist the temptation to follow the shady trail downstream. In a half mile the road comes to a gate. Several trails cross the large field, all leading to the exit road and the parking lot.

"Spring" near the Old Cabin Site

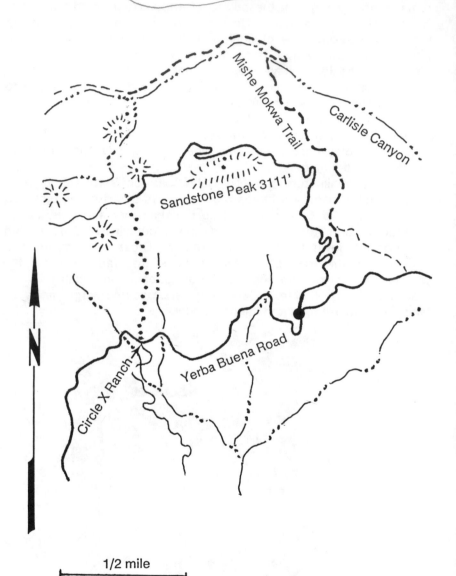

SANDSTONE PEAK by the
Mishe Mokwa Trail

Mishe Mokwa Trail

Carlisle Canyon

Sandstone Peak 3111'

N

Circle X Ranch

Yerba Buena Road

1/2 mile

HIKE 10

Maps:	Triunfo Pass, topo
	Newbury Park, topo
Distance:	7 miles roundtrlp
Elevation:	1500' gain and loss
Terrain:	Road, trail (sometimes rocky and steep) some optional class 2 off trail
Time:	3 hours
Trailhead:	Circle X Ranch

Sandstone Peak and the trails leading to it are on a massive volcanic rock formation called Boney Mountain. Inform the Ranger at the Circle X Ranch of the hike plan, and get any information you need about the current status of trails, before the hike.

The Circle X Ranch may be found by driving west on the Pacific Coast Hwy (State No. 1) 1.1 miles west of the Los Angeles-Ventura County Line. Travel north on Yerba Buena Road 5½ miles to a parking lot on the right at the Ranch.

In the event you are coming from the other direction, drive west on Mulholland Hwy until reaching Little Sycamore Canyon Road on the right. Take this road and drive 5.4 miles to the Circle X Ranch. (Some confusion can exist as to the name of the road — the sign at the ocean end says Yerba Buena Rd; the sign at the east end says Little Sycamore Canyon Rd. Most maps also reflect these two names.)

After checking-in at the Circle X Ranch, go east on the highway, 1 mile to a fireroad on the left. Walk up the dirt road. After 10 or 15 minutes you will see a trail on the right with a sign reading in part "Split Rock." Follow this, the "Mishe Mokwa Trail."

Initially the trail goes through the chaparral, climbing gently with some level stretches as it works its way around the eastern shoulder of the mountain. Take a moment to stop and look back over the rugged expanse of mountains and canyons. The south slope of this mountain presents a panorama of sunlit chaparral. Look for the different shades of green; maybe not noticeable at first, but soon you can pick out the Red Shanks in the chaparral by the yellow tinge in spring, turning rusty by fall. The bright green patches could be Holly-leaf Cherry or Laurel Sumac. Back along the trail you may have seen a lone Peruvian Pepper tree — how this tree came to be growing here far from its native land is anybody's guess. Near the trail, very close to the ground, can be found a small salmon colored flower called "Poor Man's Weather Glass." During spring and early summer a wide variety of flowers intensify the beauty of this trail. Look for Golden Yarrow, Wild Buckwheat, Brodiaea, Sticky Leaf Monkey Flower, Popcorn Flower, and Wild Peony.

Continue along the trail as it enters the canyon coming down from the right and ahead. Looking across the canyon you will see the outstanding geological sight — "Balanced Rock." The rock is volcanic in origin as is most of the rock in the area. How this rock came to be balanced where it is and how it has managed to resist the force of earthquakes and other of the elements is food for thought.

The trail becomes shadier as it nears the canyon, dominated by Oak and Laurel trees. Poison Oak becomes common and Clematis and Humboldt Lilies are seen occasionally. The trail dips into the canyon at Split Rock. Split Rock is a volcanic breccia, split into three pieces. A pathway large enough to walk through goes between two of the pieces. The running stream is shaded by Bay, Sycamore, and Coast Live Oak trees. The Coast Live Oak has a distinctive leaf; it is about 3/4" by 1" and is cupped. If a leaf were placed upside down on water it would float. Another characteristic of the leaf can be seen with a magnifying glass — little tufts of hair are spaced on the upper surface, sort of starbursts. Split Rock is a good place to eat lunch.

To continue the hike, go downstream about 100 yards and turn left onto an old roadbed and follow it upstream. Across the stream on the left is an unusual rock formation, a magnificent cliff that looks something like a giant slab of swiss cheese. A wooden bridge crosses a side stream. Horehound plants grow here, which can be made into cold remedies either in liquid or candy form. The scientific name is Marrubium vulgare; a name that to me has an intriguing poetic balance. Just after crossing the bridge leave the stream on the left by making a right turn to continue uphill. When you crest out and head south into a semi-level area, look for 2 water tanks high on the opposite hill. The trail passes below and east of the tanks. Follow the road east, level for awhile but soon becoming uphill. After two switchbacks look for a trail on the right. This steep trail goes to the top of Sandstone Peak. Upon close inspection of the rock formation, we find that Sandstone Peak is not sandstone at all, but volcanic rock.

None of this detracts from the spectacular view from this highest point in the Santa Monica Mountains. At 3111', Sandstone Peak commands a 360° panorama of the western end of the Santa Monica Mountains. The Pacific Ocean dominates the view of the quadrant in the southwest. To the south may be seen the islands of Santa Catalina, San Clemente, Santa Barbara, and San Nicolas; on the west are the Channel Islands of Anacapa, Santa Cruz, Santa Rosa, and San Miguel. Boney Ridge extends westward from the peak for 1½ miles of rugged rock formations.

The Oxnard Plain is northwest of our position. This relatively flat land is a giant syncline — or downfold of the surface — that has been filled by the material being washed down from the surrounding mountains. The depth of fill including all sediments has been measured at 41,000'. Stratigraphically this is a most interesting valley because it is one of the thickest sections of Tertiary sedimentary rocks in the world.

The mountain range to the north is in the Los Padres National Forest. A significant feature is the Sespe Condor Sanctuary. Condors have not been seen in the Santa Monicas for a number of years and are temporarily missing from the Los Padres Forest. A program of supplying Condors from the San Diego and Los Angeles Zoos is expected to repopulate the Sanctuary.

Go down the steep trail on the north side of the peak to the road. Turn left and follow it for about 10 minutes, watching for a sign on the left " $\circledX$ ". (Signs sometimes disappear so look for the trail.) A trail from this sign goes downhill to the south for about 1 mile, most of the time deep in a canopy of trees. The trail is steep but with good footing, and ends near your car.

Several alternate trails come down from the Peak. One is to go down the steep trail on the north side of Sandstone Peak and upon reaching the road, turn right and follow it back to the highway. This point is 1 mile uphill from the Circle X Ranch.

This trip is one of my favorites. The variety of vegetation from Chaparral to Riparian Woodlands is striking, and the rock formations are spectacular. Since Sandstone Peak is the highest point in the Santa Monica Mountains, there is some charm in just being there.

This may be a good time to review some history of the Circle X Ranch, so I'll pick up the story in the 1940's.

The Exchange Club, a Los Angeles service organization in their search for projects that needed their help, reviewed a number of ideas and decided upon supporting a camp so that boys and girls could learn self-reliance by living with nature. After several years of searching for affordable property, the site finding committee located the Crisp Ranch and the Exchange Club bought it. Most of the 160 acres and the surrounding land was wilderness. The property had several houses, a barn, a corral, a tennis court, and a windmill. The year was 1949; they paid $25,000.

In order that members could donate money and get an income tax exemption, the non-profit Circle X Ranch Foundation was formed as a charitable corporation. (The Exchange Club emblem was an encircled C and X, and this translated to Circle X.) A member designed a Circle X ranch brand, which is registered in Sacramento. When escrow closed, 120 acres was bought by the Circle X Foundation; 40 acres was bought by the Boney Ridge Club, inc. (a separate corporation owned by the Exchange Club members).

The ranch was opened up to all accredited youth organizations with less than an enthusiastic reception. Eventually the Los Angeles Council of the B.S.A. agreed to maintain the property and operate it. In 1951 Circle X Ranch was leased to the Boy Scouts of America for 99 years at an annual rental of $1.

Happy Hollow became part of Circle X in 1953 when the Hollywood Turf Club donated $23,000 to buy 160 acres. A number of gifts of land and quite a few purchases were made. With the purchase of 631 acres in 1954, including Sandstone Peak and Boney Ridge, for $15,000, the Circle X had grown to 1721 acres.

A chaparral fire that started in Newbury Park on 7 November 1955, burned the camping area and all the buildings except the ranger's house. Another fire on 27 December 1956 from the Malibu Creek area burned into the areas missed in 1955, but not any of the new buildings.

Many people were essential in creating Circle X, but throughout the entire period of search, acquisition, building, and financing W. Herbert Allen was totally committed to the project with his energy and money. Without his dedication Circle X would not have become the Scouting training ground that it has. In 1965 a movement began to rename Sandstone Peak to Mt. Allen. A bronze plaque — the one we are looking at if we are on top of the mountain — was cast. A request to rename Sandstone Peak was sent to the Department of Interior, but because of a long standing policy not to approve a geographic name which would honor a living person, Sandstone Peak was not renamed. Undaunted, on 23 August 1969 a large assembly of people gathered atop "Mt. Allen" for the formal dedication. The overflow crowd including 400 Scouts representing all fifteen districts of the Council, were below and heard the ceremony by walkie-talkie. so, to a segment of the hiking community Sandstone Peak is Mt. Allen.

In 1979 the Exchange Club of Los Angeles ceased to function. The Circle X Ranch foundation has deeded its holdings in the Ranch to the Los Angeles Council of the Boy Scouts of America, and continues as a charitable organization. The Boy Scouts placed the property on the market in 1986, and the Mountains Recreation and Conservation Authority bought the Circle X Ranch and assumed management of the property on 1 March 1987.

HIKE 11

Maps:	Triunfo Pass, topo
Distance:	4 miles roundtrip
Elevation:	1500' gain and loss
Terrain:	Trail, very steep
Time:	2 hours
Trailhead:	Circle X Ranch

Leave information about your hike with the Ranger at the Circle X Ranch. Call before driving to the trailhead because the area is often subject to fire hazard closure.

The trailhead is reached by driving west on the Pacific Coast Highway 1.1 miles west of the Los Angeles-Ventura County line to Yerba Buena Road. Go north 5½ miles on Yerba Buena Road to the Circle X parking lot on the right.

The steep trail starts across the road from the parking lot and goes up the south flank of the mountain. The trail is shaded most of the way with chaparral. After a stiff gain of 1000' the trail reaches a saddle west of Sandstone Peak and crosses a road.

Turn right on the road and after two switchbacks look for a steep trail on the right. After some rock scrambling this trail takes you to the top of Sandstone Peak. The peak at 3111' is the highest point of the Santa Monica Mountains. Whoever named the peak must not have gotten very close, because it is the largest mass of volcanic rock in the Santa Monicas.

Return the way you came, getting a different view as you descend.

ARCHAEOLOGICAL COMMENT

Two streams drain the south slope of Sandstone Peak: Arroyo Sequit on the east and Little Sycamore on the west.

An ancient Chumash village was located at the mouth of Little Sycamore Canyon on a promontory on the east side of the stream next to the ocean. The Pacific Coast Highway now cuts through the site, some buildings occupy part of the northern edge of the old village, and the stream has been relocated fifty yards west of its original course to accommodate the highway.

Sample archaeological excavations were made in 1952. The original village is estimated to have covered 30,000 square feet of land. Surrounding the village is twice that amount of land also rich in artifacts. The actual excavation consisted of 500 square feet of the village, a small percentage but believed to be representative of the unexcavated area.

The large number of millingstones and mullers and the scarcity of mortars and pestles indicates that the Indians ground hard seeds rather than acorns for that part of their diet. This trend was evident throughout the life of the village. The millingstone and muller method of grinding was used by the early cultures of the peoples of Southern California and the mortar and pestle method became widely used by the late prehistoric and historic peoples. The millingstone process was always prominent, particularly in areas where acorns were not abundant.

Some projectile points were found, none of which were of a size to have been used as arrow points.

The site could have been initially occupied 7000 years ago and existed for several thousand years.

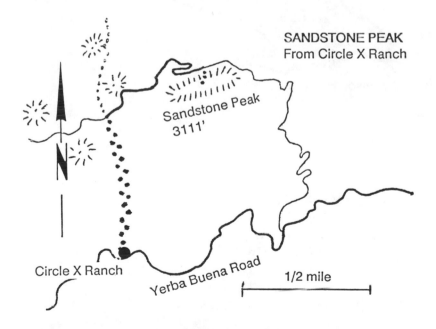

SANDSTONE PEAK
From Circle X Ranch

Sandstone Peak
3111'

N

Circle X Ranch

Yerba Buena Road

1/2 mile

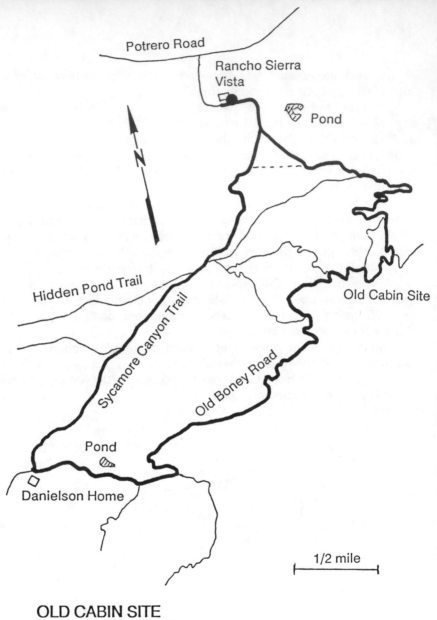

Potrero Road

Rancho Sierra Vista

Pond

N

Hidden Pond Trail

Sycamore Canyon Trail

Old Cabin Site

Old Boney Road

Pond

Danielson Home

1/2 mile

**OLD CABIN SITE
OLD BONEY ROAD
DANIELSON HOME
from Rancho Sierra Vista (loop)**

HIKE 12

Maps:	Newbury Park, topo
	Triunfo Pass, topo
	Point Mugu State Park
Distance:	12 miles roundtrip
Elevation:	2100' gain and loss
Terrain:	Road and trail
Time:	5½ hours including
	lunch
Trailhead:	Potrero Gate

From the Ventura Freeway in the west end of Thousand Oaks turn south on Borchard Road. Follow Borchard 1½ miles until coming to Reino Road then turn left. Drive 2 miles on Reino (which becomes Potrero Rd) to Pinehill Avenue, turn left and drive to the Rancho Sierra Vista parking lot.

Follow the road until coming to a trail that crosses a big field on the left. One-half mile of trail brings you to the beginning of Old Boney Road. Walk on the road uphill for a ways, then downhill and across the stream. The road goes uphill following the stream then makes a hairpin turn to the right. A short side trip from this point takes you to a view of the waterfall. To get there, go upstream on the path, turning right as you come to a sidestream, then upstream to the waterfalls.

After returning to the hairpin turn continue on the road for about 3/4 mile until coming to a fork. Take the left fork and reach the Old Cabin Site in 10 minutes. Other than a rock fireplace and chimney, the only visible evidence of a cabin is a level area with some rocks, indicating the cabin outline and floor. The slope downhill from the site is grassy with scattered oaks shading the soil. A trail on the upper side of the open area leads to the Boney Mountain Ridge. Today's hike, however, continues on the road, dropping down slightly as it passes the spring then crosses the stream.

The next 1/2 mile is up the steep slope on the north side of the stream, gaining 350' altitude before levelling off just before reaching Old Boney Road. Turn left and continue on the road. After 4/10 of a mile a marked trail on the right leads down the slope to the northwest and intersects the Sycamore Canyon Trail. One half mile farther along Old Boney Road another trail leads down the slope, joining the first trail near the bottom of the canyon. Don't take either of these trails unless you want to shorten the hike 3½ - 4 miles. Continue along the road generally in a westward direction but with considerable turning. Most of the grade is downhill, but occasionally some uphill comes along. 2.2 miles after the last trail junction, an old road comes up the streambed from the Danielson Home. There is a boulder near the junction that must be 10' in diameter — a good landmark.

Turn right and follow the road down to and across the stream. 300 yards after the stream crossing, a trail goes uphill on the left. This trail is not distinct and as of now is not marked. Continue on down the road, which can also be indistinct because the winter rains wipe it out. Keep on the west side of the stream, passing by a pond, then down a heavily wooded valley toward the ranch.

Upon reaching the paved road turn right and go upstream. There are restrooms and water one-half mile up the road. Sycamore Canyon is appropriately named. Sycamores dominate the entire valley. Oaks take over on the edges of the valley, and either sage near the coast, or chaparral farther inland predominate on the slopes; but the Sycamores own the valley.

A paved road comes into the Sycamore Canyon Trail on the left about a mile up from the Danielson Home. This is the Ranch Center Road and leads to Wood Canyon. Another 3/4 mile upstream and the Hidden Pond Trail enters on the left. Continue on the road as it gains 300 feet in one mile, then another mile to the trailhead.

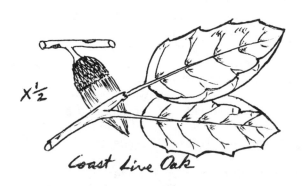

X½

Coast Live Oak

OLD CABIN SITE
Upper Sycamore Canyon near Old Boney Road

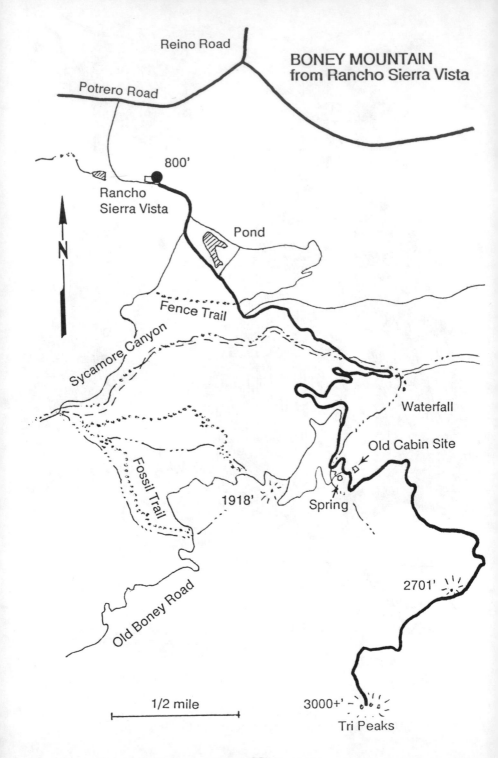

Reino Road

Potrero Road

BONEY MOUNTAIN
from Rancho Sierra Vista

800'

Rancho
Sierra Vista

N

Pond

Fence Trail

Sycamore Canyon

Waterfall

Old Cabin Site

Fossil Trail

1918'

Spring

2701'

Old Boney Road

1/2 mile

3000'

Tri Peaks

HIKE 13

Maps:	Newbury Park, topo
	Triunfo Pass, topo
	Point Mugu State Park
Distance:	12 miles roundtrip
Elevation:	2700' gain and loss
Terrain:	Road, trail, and
	steep trail
Time:	6 hours
Trailhead:	Potrero Gate

From the Ventura Freeway in the west end of Thousand Oaks turn south on Borchard Road. Stay on Borchard about 1½ miles until coming to Reino Rd., then turn left. Drive about 2 miles on Reino (which becomes Potrero Rd.) to Pinehill Avenue. Turn left and drive to the Rancho Sierra Vista parking lot.

Follow the road southeast until coming to a trail on the left that crosses the big field, or continue on the road to a bulletin board and a water tank near the road. The road continues down into Sycamore Canyon but at this point our route makes a 90° turn left and follows a trail along the fence. You will notice that Peonies grow on this ridge. This perennial starts its growth in winter and is blooming by the end of January.

Upon reaching Old Boney Road follow it, and in 1/2 mile notice the trail that branches off to the right and goes downstream. Stay on Old Boney Road crossing the stream and continue uphill under the canopy of overarching Oaks and Bay trees. The road shortly makes a hairpin turn to the right; at this point, you may want to take a 15 minute side trip to the waterfall. If so, leave the road and continue upstream on a path a short distance, following the stream that comes down on the right. Expect some boulder hopping up to the base of the falls. The water tumbles and somersaults down a sandstone cliff in about six cascades. The north side of the wall is covered with fern fronds six feet long, and a Big Leaf Maple forms a canopy overhead. This sculptured verdant recess seldom

97

suffers the blast or touch of wind and sun, so retains a sheltered character of its own.

Go back to the hairpin turn and continue up the road. The road makes two sets of switchbacks allowing your first view of the Channel Islands and the Oxnard Plain. After the last switchback from where you can see the ocean, walk about 1/3 mile and notice that Boney Road turns sharply right and continues uphill; go straight ahead, slightly downhill, and in about 1/2 mile arrive at the Old Cabin Site.

The Old Cabin Site is a good place to take a break. This is a grassy slope in an oak grove. All that remains of the cabin is a 13 foot chimney with fireplace and the remains of a rock foundation of about 12 x 18 feet. The spring is down near the stream; currently, a pipe delivers water into a concrete container.

A trail goes up the hill from the upper side of the site. After a switchback or two the trail heads in an easterly direction climbing along the north shoulder of the mountain, eventually turning south and going up the ridge toward Peak 2701. In the 50 minutes that it takes you to walk 2 miles and to climb 1200 feet, you go through a beautiful stand of Manzanita mixed with some Ceanothus and Red Shanks. This north side of Boney Mountain is an outstanding chaparral forest.

The trail goes along the ridge and weaves through some Ceanothus and down to a small saddle where the trail crosses another trail — turn right. Continue winding through the chaparral and immediately after breaking out of it into an open area, you will see a rocky ridge with a pinnacle on the right end. The trail goes to the ridge, which affords a limited view of the ocean. The canyon on the other side is flanked by massive rock cliffs. The trail cuts left at this point and follows along the ridge. The tendency is to try to walk along the right edge of the ridge; avoid this as the indistinct trail is twenty feet or so to the left. Within ten minutes you will be on a peak with an outstanding view of Mugu, the ocean, and the Channel Islands, as well as the rest of Boney Mountain.

This can be the turnaround point, or you may explore Boney Mountain by working your way to the southwest. There are several very nice peaks along the crest, all at about 2900' elevation.

Return to the trailhead by the same route.

Upper Sycamore Waterfall

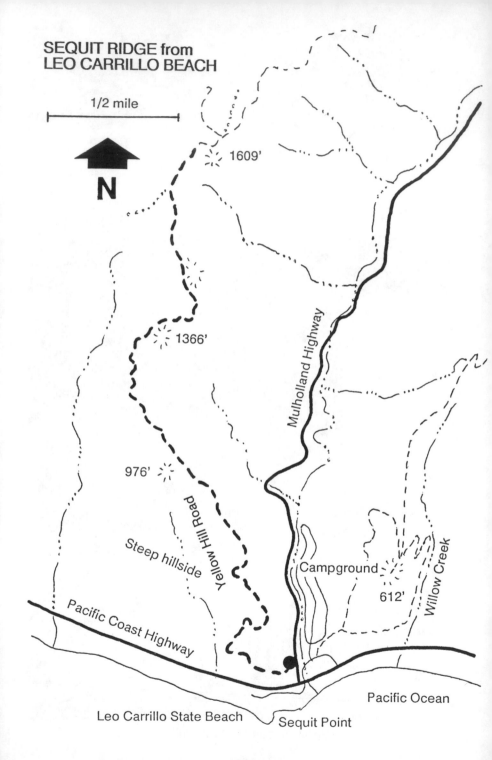

SEQUIT RIDGE from
LEO CARRILLO BEACH

1/2 mile

N

1609'

1366'

976'

Steep hillside

Yellow Hill Road

Mulholland Highway

Campground

612'

Willow Creek

Pacific Coast Highway

Pacific Ocean

Leo Carrillo State Beach

Sequit Point

HIKE 14

Maps: Triunfo Pass, topo
                       Leo Carrillo State Beach
Distance: 6 miles roundtrip
Elevation: 1650' gain and loss
Terrain: Fireroad
Time: 2 hours 45 minutes
Trailhead: Leo Carrillo State Beach

This hike features outstanding views of the Pacific Ocean and an opportunity to look for the boundary markers, if any, of the western property line of the Topanga-Malibu-Sequit Mexican Land Grant grazing concession awarded to Jose Bartolomé Tapia in 1802 or 1804, (the records conflict) and confirmed as a grant by Mexico after independence, then later confirmed by the United States. This 22 mile long land grant had a western boundary near the Ventura-Los Angeles County Line. The map indicates that benchmark 1609 could have been the northwest corner of the property. The land grant marker descriptions usually referred to "a sandstone rock" or "a lone oak" or similar feature of the countryside. I don't know the terminology in this case.

The Yellow Hill Fireroad begins on the west side of Mulholland Highway near the Pacific Coast Highway. Park at Leo Carrillo State Beach (fee) or off the Pacific Coast Highway. The Ranger's residence and maintenance area are close to the trailhead.

The hike begins on the road heading west paralleling the coast and climbing all the way. After one-third mile the route turns inland and works up a ridge still gaining altitude. Occasionally you might want to stop and look at the ocean. On a clear day the Channel Islands of Anacapa, Santa Cruz, Santa Rosa and San Miguel are visible due west. Santa Barbara Island is small and not mountainous, but can sometimes be seen just west of due south.

Initially the hike goes through the Coastal Sage plant community, but farther inland changes to Chaparral. This hike would be more interesting if there were a trail that dropped down to Arroyo Sequit and went downstream to the trailhead. This would then include a segment of a Riparian Woodland plant community, offering a wide spectrum of plant life along the route of the hike. At present this hike follows Yellow Hill Fireroad out and back.

Peak 1609 is the northwest boundary of the Park as well as being the Land Grant boundary, and is a logical turnaround point for the hike. There is some private property in the area outside the Park that should be respected.

Return the way you came.

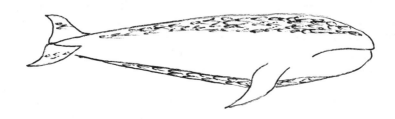

HIKE 15

Maps:	Triunfo Pass, topo
Distance:	7 miles
Elevation:	1800' gain, 2200' loss
Terrain:	Trail
Time:	3½ hours
Trailhead:	3.1 miles from west end of Mulholland Highway

Arroyo Sequit has cut a deep channel in the mountains north of Leo Carrillo Beach, leaving us with a steep hike taking us up the north facing slope of the mountain onto Nicholas Flat. Usually the hike is one way, using a car shuttle to avoid backtracking on the trail. We set up the shuttle by leaving a car in the Leo Carrillo Beach parking lot and driving 3.1 miles north on Mulholland Highway. Parking space is limited and care must be taken to find a spot completely off the pavement.

South of the bridge that crosses East Fork of Arroyo Sequit we find an old dirt road leading uphill to the east. Our hike begins here and continues uphill for the next 2 miles. The old road quickly takes on the appearance of a mountain trail because the vegetation has crowded in and taken over. As we gain altitude a panorama develops to the north and northwest, giving us fine views of Boney Mountain. Along one section of the trail we can look across to the West Fork of the Sequit and in the spring see a double waterfall.

After about 1 hour of steady climbing the trail levels out and then goes downhill a short distance. We look sharply to the right for a trail that branches right and makes a couple of switchbacks, then heads southeast through open grassland, Sage and Sumac to a saddle. We head in a westerly direction as the trail takes us through overgrown Black Sage. After peaking out at 1838' the trail loses altitude and drops down to an old road. We turn left and go southeast downhill 1/2 mile to Nicholas Flat pond.

The pond makes a good setting for lunch. Meadowland on one side and an oak grove, backed with cliff-like rocks, on the other gives us a choice of sun or shade. Everything doesn't come easy;

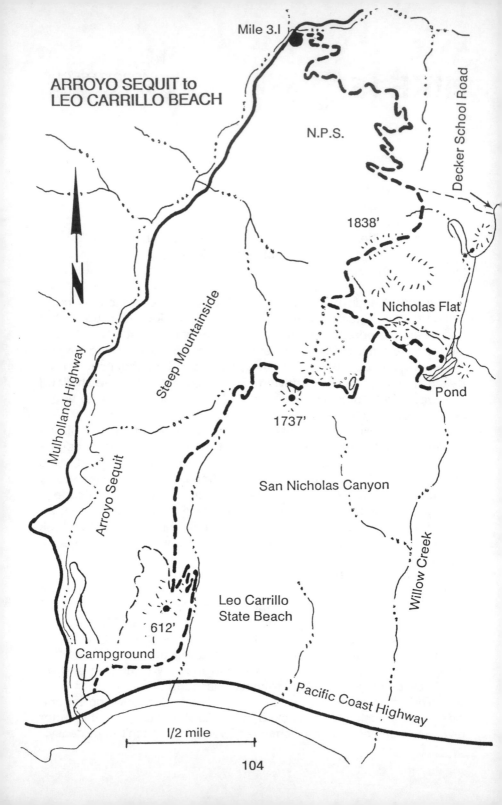

ARROYO SEQUIT to
LEO CARRILLO BEACH

Mile 3.1

N.P.S.

Decker School Road

1838'

Nicholas Flat

Steep Mountainside

Pond

Mulholland Highway

1737'

Arroyo Sequit

San Nicholas Canyon

Willow Creek

612'

Leo Carrillo
State Beach

Campground

Pacific Coast Highway

1/2 mile

N

some Poison Oak hides out in the shady spots. This entire area supports a wide variety of plant life; wildflowers grow well in the meadows and under the oaks. The pond offers an environment for Cat-tails, Arrow-grass, Pondweed, and other moisture loving plants. A hike here in spring is especially rewarding because the plants are madly competing for moisture before the summer drought.

After lunch we leave the pond and follow the same route as described in hike #16. Briefly, we follow the trail uphill to the northwest turning left at the first fork, then turning right at the ridge. The trail continues west, passing north of Peak 1737, going downhill all the way and turning south, staying on a sloping ridge. The trail branches at a saddle on the ridge — either right or left is correct as they rejoin near the end of the hike. Upon reaching the parking lot at Leo Carrillo, get the drivers back to their cars by turning right onto PCH, right on Mulholland and drive 3.1 miles.

LEO CARRILLO STATE BEACH AND NEARBY PARK AREAS
35000 Pacific Coast Highway

The Park features the beach and the back-country. The well-known beach extends for 6600 feet and is divided into two separate areas by Sequit Point, a rocky bluff. both the west beach and east beach have restroom and dressing room facilities. The west beach can accommodate overnight campers in 50 campsites, some for tents, some for RVs — but no hookups. Skindiving, swimming, surfing, fishing, and picnicking are popular.

Two campgrounds are north of the highway. One can accommodate 138 family groups in either tents or RVs. Restrooms and a shower building are available but no hookups. The other is a group campground capable of handling 75 people. It has a restroom and shower.

A nature trail starts at the north end of the campground and makes a loop under the trees and up onto the side of the hill. Also, the streambed makes an interesting hiking area. We must do some rock scrambling and take care to avoid Poison Oak, but exploration along the Sequit is a tradition — the Indians that lived in the village at the stream's mouth used the stream as a corridor for thousands of years.

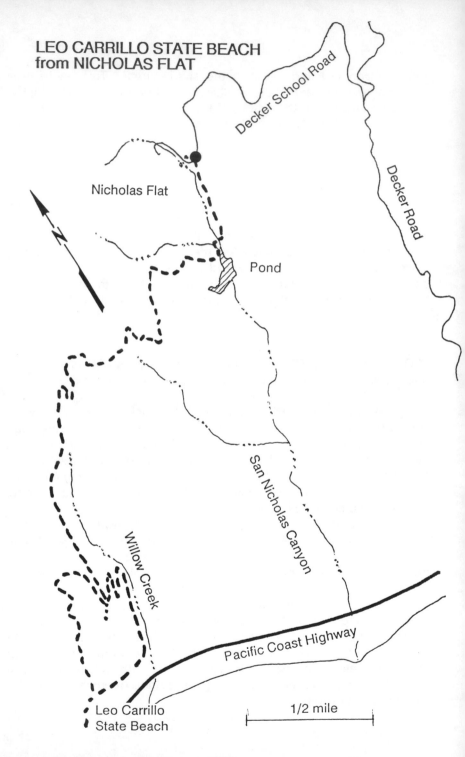

LEO CARRILLO STATE BEACH
from NICHOLAS FLAT

Nicholas Flat

Decker School Road

Decker Road

Pond

San Nicholas Canyon

Willow Creek

Pacific Coast Highway

Leo Carrillo
State Beach

1/2 mile

HIKE 16

Maps:	Triunfo Pass, topo
Distance:	4 miles
Elevation:	250' gain, 1750' loss
Terrain:	Trail
Time:	2 hours
Trailhead:	Nicholas Flat

Hiking trails in the Santa Monicas that actually connect the mountains to the sea are rare, and to find a trail that unrolls scene after scene of new discoveries is rare indeed. The hike can be done as a roundtrip from either end, or by using a car shuttle we make it a one-way trip from Nicholas Flat to the seashore. We can set up the shuttle by letting hikers off at the end of Decker School Road. During the half hour that it takes for the drivers to park cars at Leo Carrillo Beach and return to the trailhead, the main group could walk to the lake and wait.

We begin the hike by going around a rustic gate, then along an oak-tree-shaded dirt road. The watercourse to the right invites exploration, but the Poison Oak discourages any careless dash to the streambed. When we come to a crossroad, we'll turn right, cross the stream, and after about 100 yards turn left, staying on a trail that parallels the stream. The trail leads us into a meadow and then to the edge of the lake. A trail curves around the west side of the lake and enters an open oak grove on the south side. Large boulders and rocky cliffs form a scenic backdrop to the lake. A short walk to the ridge offers a view of the steep canyon below.

When the rest of the hikers arrive and everyone is accounted for we leave the lake by a trail that goes uphill to the northwest. At the first fork in the trail, we angle left and continue uphill. In a few hundred yards the trail levels off and forks right (the left fork leads to a levelled spot on a ridge). We continue hiking west, gaining a little more altitude, and enter a chaparral forest. A small group of Sierra Club volunteers built this trail in 1981. There is something special about a hand-hewn trail because the sensitivity of the workers is reflected in the final result. Unique rock formations are left undisturbed, trees that add to the beauty are preserved, and the usual evidence of "overkill" that accompanies the use of power equipment is precluded.

The trail makes a big sweeping curve around the north slope of the mountain, losing altitude all the time. For awhile we pass through a dense growth of chaparral, mostly Ceanothus. We will vow to come back in March to witness the blooming of this "wild lilac." The ocean comes into view, and we start a long descent down the slope and out onto a broad ridge. The vegetation makes a transition from Chaparral to Coastal Sage Scrub. The canyon to the west is Arroyo Sequit, and the point of land at the ocean is Sequit Point. The Topanga-Malibu-Sequit Land Grant, first claimed by Jose Bartolomé Tapia in 1802 or 1804, took part of the name from Arroyo Sequit. This land grant extended 22 miles along the Malibu coast from Las Flores Canyon to the Los Angeles-Ventura County line and was kept almost intact until the 1930's. Most of the Nicholas Flat Trail is on the old Land Grant land.

We continue downhill toward the ocean, coming out onto a saddle from which two trails branch; one goes east and contours around to the ocean, and the other drops down on the west side. Both of these trails meet again on the south side of the hill near the campground, so we can select either one. Another option is to continue south along the ridge to the top of the hill for a special view of the ocean. Whale watching from this point calls for binoculars.

When we reach Leo Carrillo State Beach, we must remember to get the drivers back to the cars at Nicholas Flat. Driving directions to the trailhead from the beach are: Go east on the Pacific Coast Hwy 2½ miles to Decker Road. Turn left and go 2½ more miles to Decker School Road (an obscure road on the left). Turn left and drive 1½ miles to the end of Decker School Road.

NOTE; Nicholas Flat and the area of the trail burned in a fire of October 1985. The plant and animal life have recovered but it will be several years before the Ceanothus regains its dense forest-like structure. The flowers more than make up the difference.

Nicholas Flat Pond

ARROYO SEQUIT PARK

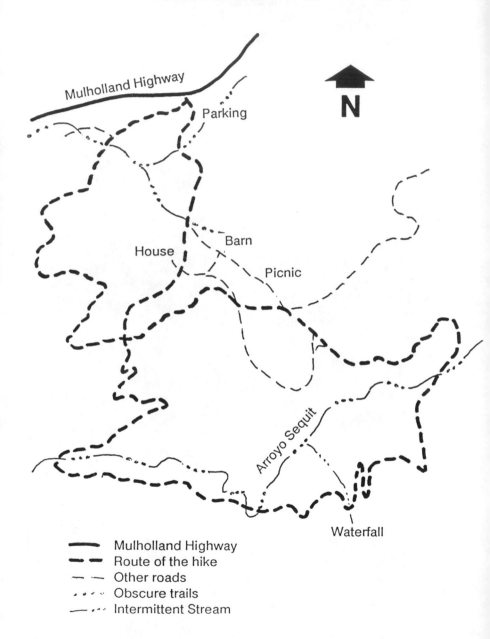

N

Mulholland Highway
Parking
House
Barn
Picnic
Arroyo Sequit
Waterfall

▬▬▬	Mulholland Highway
▬ ▬ ▬	Route of the hike
— —	Other roads
· · · ·	Obscure trails
— ···	Intermittent Stream

HIKE 17

Maps:	Triunfo Pass, topo
Distance:	2½ miles
Elevation:	250' gain and loss
Terrain:	Road and trail
Time:	1 hour
Trailhead:	34138 Mulholland Highway

Arroyo Sequit Park is 155 acres of open meadows and steep canyons. The Santa Monica Mountains Conservancy purchased the land from Dick Mason in 1985 for public recreational use. The ranch has been developed for hiking, picnicking, and wildflower walks. Portable restrooms, picnic tables, parking, and water are available. Future use includes use as an orienteering site, group camping, and as a link for hikes to Malibu Springs, Leo Carrillo State Beach, and Point Mugu State Park.

We drive 6 miles from the Pacific Coast Highway on Mulholland Highway to the entrance at mail box number 34138. Turn right into the driveway and park. The Park is open for day use, weekends only. A paved road leads to the ranchhouse, and we can start a figure-of-eight hike around the property by continuing on the trail south of the house and down into the canyon. Part of the upper Park and all of the canyon burned in the fire of 1985 and for the next few years wildflowers will dominate the area until the brush returns.

Upon reaching the canyon bottom, we turn left and go upstream. Raging in spring with several small waterfalls, the stream dries up in the summer. The climb out of the gorge is on a well-graded trail but significant enough so that we get some exercise, and upon reaching the top heads west, slightly downhill toward the picnic area. Before reaching the picnic area we angle left on a trail that stays to the right of the high ground. About 1/4 mile beyond the fork and after crossing a trail, taking a right fork, and crossing another trail going to the ranchhouse, our route turns north and crosses a meadow and through some chaparral back to the main gate. Other trails are available for exploration if our time allows it. Arroyo Sequit Ranch offers great views of the mountains, comfortable hiking, and adventure for all.

HIKE 18

Maps:	Triunfo Pass, topo
Distance:	2½ miles roundtrip
Elevation:	600' gain and loss
Terrain:	Dirt road and trail
Time:	1½ hours
Trailhead:	Encinal Canyon Road

Charmlee County Regional Park covers 460 acres of rolling meadowland surrounded by rocky ridges and steep mountain slopes. Oak woodlands, ocean views, rocky ridgetops, and fields of wild flowers are features of the Park. The land was acquired by the Los Angeles County Department of Parks and Recreation in 1968 from Charmain and Leonard Swartz. We believe Charmlee was derived from the combined first names.

Facilities include restrooms, drinking water, picnic areas, and a Nature Center. The Park is open 8:00 a.m. to sunset daily.

From the Pacific Coast Highway west of Zuma Beach go north (inland) on Encinal Canyon Road about 4 miles to the entrance on the west (left) side. Drive in and park at one of several designated lots.

We can start our hike at the picnic area by locating the trail on the east side and go south, initially through the oak grove, then up to a rocky outcrop. The main trail skirts the east edge of a meadow and we follow the trail as we pass a couple of oak-sheltered boulder knolls. Any of these spots as well as groves to the east of us make good rest areas. The trail begins to head westerly and we notice a side trail on our left, going to "Ocean Vista" overlooking the Pacific .7 of a mile away and 1250' below. The trail climbs as we head west then north through two switchbacks cresting out near some Eucalyptus trees and a concrete reservoir. A trail takes us northwest to some Oak trees on a knoll — another good lunch spot. From here we take one of several trails northeast along the edge of the meadow until reaching an east-west road, then turn left and go west, uphill.

Several trails and roads become available, but our objective is to stay high and eventually turn north on the ridge that has the watertank. A few hundred yards beyond the watertank we make a turn right and walk down to the Nature Center and the end of the hike.

Many trails criss-cross this Park so you can spend all day exploring.

CHARMLEE PARK

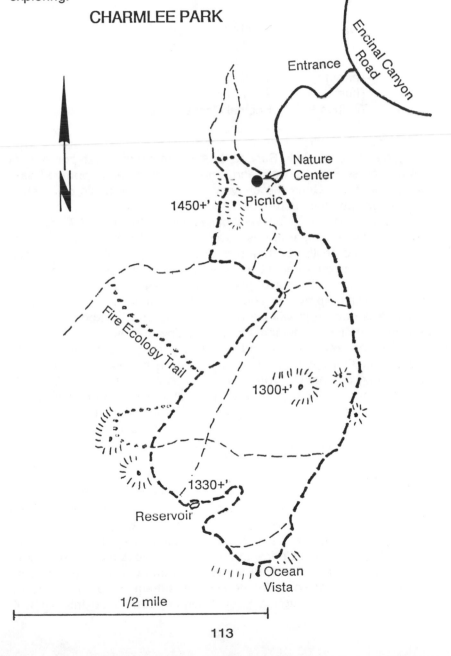

HIKE 19

Maps:	Point Dume, topo
Distance:	5 miles roundtrip
Elevation:	500' loss and gain
Terrain:	Trail and streambed
Time:	2½ hours
Trailhead:	Encinal Canyon Road

The National Park Service has informed me that portions of this trail cross Park Service land, and it has not been approved as a safe public trail. Once the canyon is in complete public ownership, the trails will be constructed for public use.

Upper Zuma Canyon was easy hiking after the 1978 fire but recovery of the Chaparral has been good, and use of the trails has been sporadic so the trails are overgrown. A slight inconvenience to hiking is encountered at the outset in that the people operating the recycling system have placed a sprinkler so that unpleasant smelling water sprays a segment of the trail. Alternate routes around this challenge will develop. In time, the Backbone Trail will be built giving us an additional route into Upper Zuma.

The roadhead is reached by driving west of the Kanan Dume Road on Mulholland Hwy. Go 0.9 mile to a fork in the road. Take the left fork, Encinal Canyon Road, and continue 0.5 mile. There is room to park a couple of cars on the left side of the road near the water recycling pools or at a larger area around the curve.

The Zuma Ridge Motorway is a well used road that goes southeast. A sign says "Buzzards Roost." Do not take this road; instead take an indistinct road that starts a few feet on the east side of the Zuma Ridge M/W, going close to the water recycling pool. This leads you through a shady area covered with luxuriant plant growth, then out into an open burned-over area ablaze with flowers every spring. The road passes near the top of a cascading waterfall, then after two switchbacks, a steep trail leaves the right side and drops down a ridge to the stream. Cross the stream where some cat-tails grow, and turn left following close to the stream until crossing it again. You leave the stream for a few hundred yards as you go through a Rose briarpatch and then into an Oak grassland. The trail along the stream requires some boulder-hopping skill and sometimes the trail disappears. Since the objective of the hike is the top of Big Zuma waterfall, route finding consists mainly of following the stream.

Occasionally it becomes difficult to stay near the streambed; the trail will go up the bank to get around obstacles. Sometimes the trail is steep and care is needed. As the canyon deepens, the sandstone rock formations become prominent and show the typical waterworn formations. Small cascades of water tumble into solid rock basins. At one place a ledge of rock extends from one side of the canyon to the other making a broad waterfall.

The destination of the hike is the top of Big Zuma waterfall — a 25' high spectacular drop. The view into the gorge below is of waterworn grottos at the sides of the canyon near the base of the falls, massive rock walls, and trees farther down. A large flat rock at the top of the falls is a good lunch stop.

Return to the trailhead the way you came. If wildflowers and other plants are your interest, bring a book that will help you identify them because Upper Zuma Canyon puts on a grand display.

UPPER ZUMA CANYON

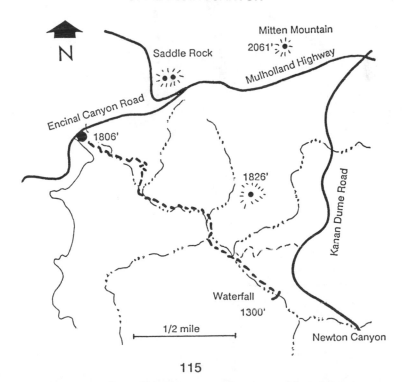

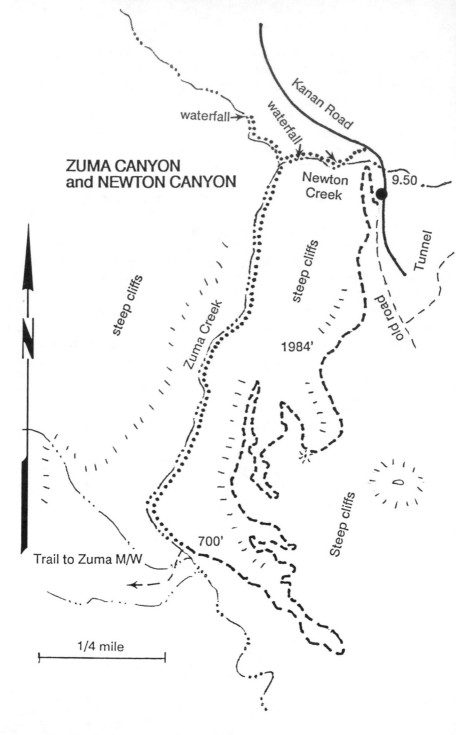

ZUMA CANYON
and NEWTON CANYON

Kanan Road

waterfall→

waterfall

Newton
Creek

9.50

Tunnel

steep cliffs

steep cliffs

old road

N

Zuma Creek

1984'

Steep cliffs

Trail to Zuma M/W

700'

1/4 mile

HIKE 20

Maps:	Point Dume, topo
Distance:	6 miles roundtrip
Elevation:	1200' gain and loss
Terrain:	Road, trail, streambed boulder hopping, and class 2-3 rock climbing
Time:	4 hours
Trailhead:	Kanan Dume Road

The National Park Service has informed me that portions of this trail cross Park Service land and it has not been approved as a safe public trail. Once the canyon is in complete public ownership, trails will be constructed for public use.

This section of Zuma Canyon is a most spectacular combination of stark volcanic cliffs, rugged boulder filled stream, and sheltered recesses beside plunging waterfalls. The only way in is on foot and recommended only for the experienced hiker who has rock climbing ability, and even then should join a group being led by someone familiar with the route.

The parking lot at the trailhead is on Kanan Dume Road (County Route N 9) 1.8 miles south of Mulholland Hwy, and is on the west side of the road just north of the southernmost of the three tunnels on Kanan. A road marker reading "N9 LA 9.50 positively identifies the location.

Take the steep switchback road up the hill west of the parking area. A vigorous 15 minutes of walking puts you on top of the ridge and at a fork in the road. Go straight ahead and start down from the ridge. Almost immediately there is another branch; take the one to the right and go downhill. One can rightfully question the term "road" from this point on because small landslides and stream erosion have reduced the route to a trail.

In the next 10 minutes you will have the opportunity to make two more trail decisions, take the right hand route both times. Going downhill continually and flanked on one side by overpowering volcanic cliffs and by a deep canyon on the other, look for a sharp switchback to the left. Stop for a moment to go to the edge and take in the panorama upstream. Imposing rugged cliffs on the right, a precipitous abyss at your feet, the hint of refuge in the Sycamore sheltered stream below are all exposed to view. Looking to the south toward the ocean, a small rounded bump is seen above the plain. This is Point Dume. Point Dume is made up of sandstone and mudstone on the north side, and on the ocean side volcanics of 14½ million years of age.

Continue down toward the floor of the canyon and in another 15 minutes the trail you are on crosses one that comes in laterally from the left. Continue on down or take the right hand trail, the difference being that the right hand trail reaches the stream 3/4 mile up from the other. In either event sit down by the stream upon reaching it, and as a first order of business take the stickers out of your socks.

Zuma Creek is an amazing stream that rages in spring and trickles in the fall. It plunges and tumbles through a rugged, boulder filled canyon deep in the shade of Sycamore trees. An occasional waterfall that can present a climbing challenge, or Fern covered grottos in the sculptured canyon walls present a continually changing scene in this delightful retreat. Pick your way upstream; sometimes boulder hopping, sometimes crawling between angular rocks as big as a house, but often walking along a pool on hard sandstone. Immense volcanic boulders have tumbled down from the lofty ridges above; some of the gray sandstone exposes the fossils of turritella shells and an occasional pecten; each rock, each turn in the stream, and every pool presents a never ending variety of delight Do not do this trip alone, not because of the danger, but because this place should be shared.

New adventure lies in wait upstream. The gorge cuts deep, and rock walls portend the approach to a waterfall. Thundering after a heavy rain, splashing at other times, the first of a series of falls has hollowed out a gravel lined pool nestled in a sheltered recess graced with moss and ferns.

After negotiating several waterfalls you will notice a major stream coming in on the right (east). This is Newton Canyon and will be the way out, but first visit "Big Zuma" waterfall. It is 200 yards or so up the canyon in which you have been travelling, and in my opinion is the culmination of the grandeur of this canyon. The waterfall drops 25 feet over a massive ledge, and appears to present an absolute barrier to further travel. For this trip it is the turnaround point.

Go back to Newton Canyon. There are two more waterfalls to see on the way out. The first one cascades some 25 feet over a moss and fern covered rock cliff. When the flow of water allows it, this can be negotiated by approaching the base of the cliff on your left and working up a naturally sculptured stairway cresting out on the stream. Rock climbing ability is needed. Another way up is available by a very steep trail on the left before reaching the waterfall. The next waterfall is 200 or 300 yards farther up. There is no practical way up this waterfall so go back downstream a short distance and climb up the hillside on the north side of the stream. Follow the stream then go southeast up a steep bank to the parking lot. Do not take this hike in the rain or when the rocks and soil are wet because the climbing becomes class 3-4 and places this hike beyond the scope of this hiking guide.

ROCKY OAKS

N

Kanan Road

Mulholland Highway

Picnic tables

Parking

Pond

1850'+

1/4 mile

Saddle Rock
Ranch (private)

Mitten
Mountain

2061'

HIKE 21

Maps: Point Dume, topo
Distance: 1 - 2 miles
Elevation: 200' gain and loss
Terrain: Trail
Time: 1 hour
Trailhead: Mulholland Highway
            at Kanan

Until the 1978 Agoura fire burned the barns, sheds, and farm equipment, Rocky Oaks Ranch was a working cattle ranch. The Santa Monica Mountains National Park Service now manages the property. The Park features a pond, a southern Oak Woodland, Chaparral, areas of Coastal Sage Scrub, and Grassland. Facilities include drinking water, restrooms, picnic tables, an amphitheater, and a trail system. The Park is used by walkers and equestrians. The limited size does not lend it to a serious hike but because of an extensive trail system it offers exceptional opportunities for wildflower walks, interpretive sessions, picnicking, and family outings.

Reach the trailhead from the Ventura Freeway by going south on Kanan Road to Mulholland Highway. Turn west on Mulholland and then to the right into the parking lot. It may be reached from the Pacific Coast Highway by going north on Kanan/Dume Road to Mulholland. Parking is free.

A trail leaves the picnic area and goes north to the pond and beyond. Look for Coots swimming along the edge. We might even see a Great Blue Heron, or hear a Bull Frog's "Jug-o-rum." Follow the trail to the north end of the Park and turn left on an old road that contours along the hillside overlooking the pond. In ten minutes you will find yourself climbing steps to the top of hill 1850+'. A good view of the area is gained by the climb. Retrace your steps and turn left at the bottom of the hill. After a downhill walk turn right and continue down to the stream crossing. Look for Watercress in the stream and California Rose along the banks. The trail upstream enters a wooded area with large volcanic boulders near the streambed.

The trail leads to private property, so we turn around and follow a trail to the parking lot.

HIKE 22

Maps:	Point Dume, topo
Distance:	1/2 mile roundtrip
Elevation:	203' gain and loss
Terrain:	Beach, sand and trail
Time:	1/2 hour
Trailhead:	Westward Beach Road

This isn't going to be an all day hike, but is a "change of pace interlude" for a time when you may need something entirely different from the usual rigor of miles of mountain trail.

Point Dume is a point of land that overlooks the Pacific Ocean. It is located by driving on the Pacific Coast Highway about 1½ miles west of the Kanan Dume Road. Turn south toward the ocean on the access road that takes you to either Zuma Beach or Point Dume Beach; then stay left on Westward Beach Road, driving to the end, and park your car.

Trudge across a couple hundred yards of sand, staying near the cliff on the left. A footpath leads up the cliff, branching several times — stay left for the trail, otherwise you will be doing some steep climbing. A number of trails allow exploration to the top of Point Dume, and also out on the scenic point overlooking the ocean. A steep climbing trail goes down to Dume Cove and to Paradise Cove.

This is an ideal place to watch for the migration of the Gray Whales as they head south to Baja, California, on their annual 10,000 mile roundtrip from Alaska. They usually travel in a pod of two or three or more surfacing several times, then with their tails in the air, diving deep for a longer period under the water. The migration route is close to shore at Point Dume, and in the winter the probability of seeing some whales is very good.

Besides the Gray Whales, Point Dume provides other interests such as surfers (farther up the beach) riding the challenging waves, active swimmers, relaxed sunbathers, kites flying, people fishing, boats, scuba divers after Pismo clams and other marine life, and surprises. Plan to spend an hour or two here enjoying this magnificent view.   The sun turns the water into shimmering, sparkling diamonds; and the never-ending splashing of the waves washing ashore makes one reluctant to return to reality.

Geologically, Point Dume consists of three different formations: (I) the Trancas Formation consisting of sedimentary sandstone, shale, mudstone, and breccia;   (2) the Zuma Volcanics: and (3) Monterey Shale composed of clay shale and siltstone.   The peak and the east slope of Point Dume is Trancas Formation; the rest of the point is Zuma Volcanics; and Monterey shale is prominent in the rest of the area.   You may have noticed the layers of Monterey Shale along the cliff where you parked the car.   A sample of volcanic rock taken from a spot near the ocean on the southwest side of Point Dume has been dated radiometrically at 14.6 + million years.   All three formations are of Miocene age.

ARCHAEOLOGICAL NOTE

About one mile northwest of Point Dume near where Zuma Creek enters the ocean there once was an Indian village. Dating as established by the C-14 method shows that the village was occupied from 5000 years ago until the Spanish invasion.   Several nearby sites, or parts of the same village complex, date 7000 years ago with evidence of occupation until about 3500 years ago.

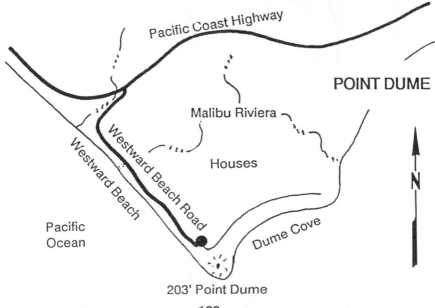

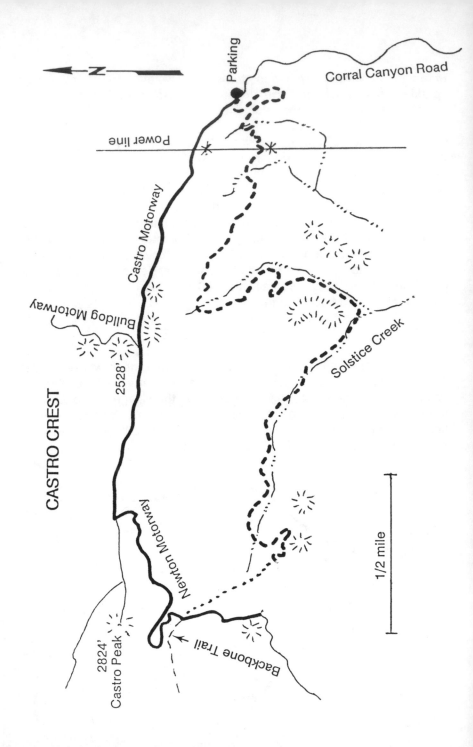

CASTRO CREST

Parking

Corral Canyon Road

Power line

Castro Motorway

Bulldog Motorway

2528'

Solstice Creek

Newton Motorway

1/2 mile

2824'
Castro Peak

Backbone Trail

HIKE 23

Maps:	Point Dume, topo
Distance:	4 miles
Elevation:	1050' gain and loss
Terrain:	Fireroad and trail
Time:	2 hours
Trailhead:	Corral Canyon Road

Castro Crest is National Park Service land in upper Solstice Canyon. The area is adjacent to Malibu Creek State Park and has interconnecting trails. The Backbone Trail follows the east-west ridge on Mesa Peak Motorway and Castro Motorway, and as an alternate route, the Backbone Trail follows the trail in Upper Solstice Canyon. The loop trip described here will be on the Backbone Trail. (See more on pages 282 and 283.)

We reach the roadhead by driving the Pacific Coast Highway to Corral Canyon Road a little over 2 miles west of Malibu Canyon Road. The road marker reads 50.36. Turn north and drive uphill on a paved winding road for about 5½ miles to the end of the pavement and on to a large parking area.

A trail leads down into Solstice Canyon from the west edge of the parking area. After 10 minutes of travel we cross a streambed and walk up to a ridge on the west. An old road comes down the ridge and out to a rise — several service roads still remain from the time the power line was put through the area. The trail temporarily follows the bed of the service road then angles right as the road turns left and goes steeply downhill to a streambed. The trail contours along the slope. As it crosses a stream we can see a 20 foot waterfall (after heavy rain only) upstream.

This entire area was burned in October 1982 during the Dayton Canyon fire — a riot of wildflowers covered the basin five months later. The chaparral will recover in seven or eight years but upper Solstice Canyon will always be a garden. We follow the trail downstream until coming to a fork at the stream junction. We turn right and go uphill — a left turn would take us out of the Park and onto private land. The trail stays close to the streambed as it heads west under a cover of Coast Live Oaks. Two-thirds of a mile from the stream junction finds us on some switchbacks going up the slope at the west end of the basin. On reaching the ridge we turn right onto a dirt road that goes up to Newton M/W. (NPS has scheduled realignment of the trail, eliminating use of the steep Motorway.) At a saddle along the Motorway, we will see the continuation of the Backbone Trail heading off to the west. We continue to gain altitude skirting around the south side of Castro Peak until we reach the crest and Castro Peak M/W, and turn right again. The hike along the crest opens up spectacular views on both sides. Look for Hawkweed plants growing out of the cliffs — blooms in June through the summer. Santa Susana Tarweed and Wrights' Buckwheat are found growing in the sandstone outcroppings. They bloom in late summer and fall.

The motorway is a downhill grade to the parking lot.

GEOLOGICAL COMMENT

Solstice Canyon has an interesting geologic structure. Several faults cross the area, significant of which is the Malibu Bowl Fault downstream of where we will be hiking. Some of the geological features described here are south of the Park property and on private property. Hikers have used the route down the stream for many years, but increased use of the property by owners could cause some restrictions on hikers and equestrians.

Some very important formations are present in the canyon. Most of these can be seen during the usual hike.

First take a look at this diagram to get a feel for the ages we are discussing. The older rocks were formed first, then subsequent layers were built on top until thousands of feet of strata had been built up.

Time in millions of years ago	Periods Epochs	Formations found in Solstice Canyon
	Pleistocene	
3		
	Pliocene	
11		
	Miocene	Volcanics
25		
	Oligocene	Sespe
40		
	Eocene	Llajas?
		Coal Canyon
60	Paleocene	Simi Conglomerate
70	Cretaceous	Tuna Canyon
135		

Starting at the top with the youngest rocks visible and using nomenclature of the stratigraphic succession as used in the publication "Stratigraphic Nomenclature of the Central Santa Monica Mountains" by Yerkes and Campbell, I will briefly describe the formations as we descend the trail.

The parking lot and all of the rock in the immediate vicinity, including the finbacks along the ridge east-southeast, are of a nonmarine sequence named the Sespe Formation. Composed of sandstone, pebbly sandstone, mudstone, and cobbles, Sespe is often reddish colored, but mostly gray here. The 3000 feet of strata dips northeast on a steep angle, in some places 80°. Sespe was formed during late Eocene, Oligocene and early Miocene times, 40-25 mya, when the land was above sea level and an immense flood plain. The first 20 minutes of our hike into the canyon is on Sespe.

400 yards beyond the waterfall and as we drop down into the canyon, we leave the cobbled Sespe Formation and enter the Llajas (?)Formation;, a marine sequence of sandstone, siltstone, and pebbly conglomerate that was laid down during Eocene times, 50-40 mya. Peak 2034' and the rock along the streambed is all on Llajas (?).

The route of the loop hike turns right at the junction with the west fork of the stream, and goes upstream on Llajas Formation. If we elect to go downstream at the junction we will reach the Coal Canyon Formation in about 3/8 mile. Keep in mind that at the present time (1987) the land downstream is privately owned, and even though the trail has been used by hikers for many years, future use and development may change the condition of its use. The Coal Canyon Formation is another marine sequence of sandstone, siltstone, and pebbly conglomerate. This formation was laid down during late Paleocene and Eocene times, 60-50 mya. Marine fossils can be seen in many places along the streambed. Layers of mollusks are clearly seen in the large rock slabs.

After crossing about 1/4 mile of Coal Canyon Formation, the stream flows over 100 yards of Simi (?) Conglomerate. This nonmarine formation is characterized by well-rounded polished cobbles and boulders of quartzite, granitic rhyolite, and gneissic conglomerate in coarse-grained sandstone. The Simi(?) Formation is of Paleocene age, 70-60 mya, and has no fossils.

Downstream of the Simi(?) Formation is found a small exposure of Tuna Canyon Formation, a marine sequence of sandstone, siltstone, and small pebble conglomerate. This sequence is located in a broad triangle not much over 1/4 mile east and west with the south limit at the Malibu Bowl Fault. It is upper Cretaceous in age, 135-70 mya, not exposed at the base in Solstice Canyon and overlaid in part by Conejo Volcanics.

At Baller Motorway the stream crosses a major fault — the east-west trending Malibu Bowl Fault. Conejo Volcanic rock, constituting the upper plate of the fault, is found downstream of this point. The age of the Conejo Volcanics is Middle Miocene, 16-12 mya.

Geologists are not in complete agreement as to nomenclature of the various formations, and the ages are subject to interpretation. I have used Geological Survey Bulletin 1457-E by R.F. Yerkes and R.H. Campbell as a major source of information. A (?) indicates questionable data.

GEOLOGIC FORMATIONS IN UPPER SOLSTICE CANYON

HIKE 24

The first bit of information is that a dam once impounded Triunfo Creek to form a lake, but the dam has disappeared and no lake exists. Drive on Ventura Freeway to Kanan Road and go south 2.8 miles to Troutdale Road and turn left. At Mulholland Highway again turn left, cross a bridge and turn right into the parking lot. Walk back across the bridge and enter the gate into the ranch. Currently the ranch is open for visitors from 11 a.m. to 5 p.m. on the 1st and 3d weekends of the month only. Conducted walks are offered. Restrooms, drinking water, a play area, and picnicking facilities are available.

A hiking trail system introduces us to the Park by taking us on a 3/4 mile loop up onto the chaparral hillside, and back through the shade of Oak Woodlands. This could be a 15 to 20 minute brisk walk, or a 1 hour wildflower walk. Find the trailhead by going between the amphitheater and the aviary, and turning left.

If we care to extend the hike, we should look for a trail on the right after we have walked 10 minutes. The trail goes uphill and is steep in places. Fifteen minutes and nine switchbacks later we will see another trail branching to the right. If we take this option, expect eleven more switchbacks and another ten to fifteen minutes of walking before coming to the end of the trail high on the hill. We can see Malibu Lake a mile to the east of us and 700 feet lower. We are on a massive mountain of fragmented volcanic rock and the ruggedness of the crags and cliffs adds to the beauty.

Coming back down, take a left at the first trail junction, a right at the second, and another left at the third. This should put you in view of the playground area. A number of side trails can be seen. Most of these are no longer used and are so marked with a row of rocks. Two trails lead southeast out of the Park and on to private property.

On your walk look for Woodfern, Maidenhair and Goldback fern. Milkmaids bloom along the Loop Trail in the spring. Four species of Ceanothus can be found; look for Buckbrush at the south end of the Park — it is rare elsewhere in the Santa Monicas but plentiful here. Deep blue to purple flowers of the Hairy-leaved Ceanothus are found during late March and April. Both Hillside Gooseberry and Golden Current — rare elsewhere — are found here.

HIKE 25

Paramount Ranch has been a prominent area of land throughout history. Triunfo Creek comes down to Malibu Lake from the west and Medea Creek from the north. Malibu Creek has its origin at Malibu Lake and is the only stream that cuts completely through the mountains. As a result, the Malibu Creek and its tributaries have been a travel corridor of the Chumash Indians for thousands of years. Paramount Ranch is a few hundred yards north of Malibu Lake and even though the lake is man made, the juncture of Medea Creek and Triunfo Creek took place there, and consequently was the crossroads of trans-mountain trails.

The Spanish invasion by Portolá in 1769 disrupted the Indians' use of their land so that in the early 1800's Spanish horses and cattle were grazing the valley where Paramount Ranch now lies. The El Paraje De Las Virgenes was not a true land grant but was a grazing concession. The King of Spain retained title. Under Mexican rule a land grant was made, recognizing the concession by ownership. The United States later recognized the Mexican land grant.

The 326 acres that constitute the present Paramount Ranch are part of a much larger area that from 1921 to 1946 was used by Paramount Studios as a location for filming scenes for hundreds of movies. All of the sets built by Paramount are gone, but some of the storage sheds they built for storing props are still visible today. People who owned the ranch after Paramount Studios allowed filming to continue and even built a Western Town set using the storage sheds for support. Beginning in the early 1950's the ranch also became the site of large recreational events from square dances and hay rides to scout jamborees and rodeos. For a short time there was a summer camp on the ranch, and an asphalt racetrack was built for sportscar racing. In 1979, the National Park Service acquired the ranch. since then, the Park Service has begun rebuilding the Western Town and making it available for occasional filming of commercials, television shows and movies. One of the storage areas has been turned into a shaded area for group picnics. Nature has reclaimed much of the old racetrack which now serves as hiking and equestrian route through; the northern end of the ranch.

Media Creek flows year round, creating a riparian zone of willows and cat-tails running north to south through the site.

Because of upstream pollution, Medea Creek is unfit for drinking or any kind of contact.

A self-guided nature trail makes a circuit up Coyote Canyon. Walks and guided tours are presented regularly, and evening programs and special events are scheduled.

Paramount Ranch is south of Agoura Hills. From the Ventura Freeway turn south onto Kanan Road and drive 3/4 mile and turn left to Cornell Road (Sideway Rd) and drive 2½ miles south. Paramount Ranch is on the right.

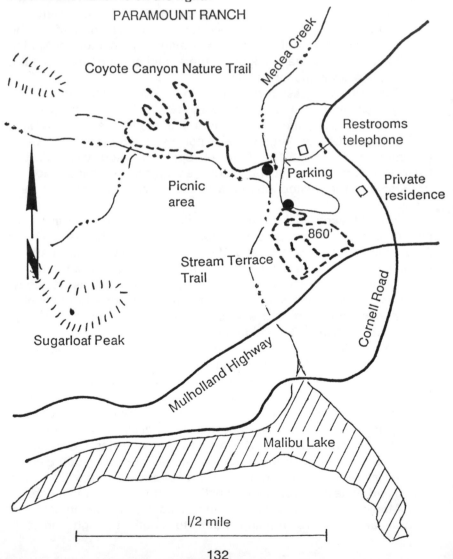

PARAMOUNT RANCH

COYOTE CANYON NATURE TRAIL
Walking time: 25 minutes

The box at the bulletin board will accept your 25¢ donation for a self-guided map of the Coyote Canyon Nature Trail. An abbreviated schedule of stops is included here in the event that the guide is not in stock. Plants die and new ones grow, so expect revisions.

1.   Medea Creek
2.   Western Town
3.   Coast Live Oaks and Valley Oaks
4.   Comparison of north facing slope and south facing slope
5.   Recovery from fire of October 1982
6.   Indian uses of plants: Yucca, Wild Cucumber, Poison Oak, Elderberry, and Mugwort.
7.   Stream has cut a V-shaped canyon
8.   The animals at "Lizard Rocks"
9.   Explore the left trail on your own if you want to
10. Plants adapt to dry summers in many ways
11. Volcanic rock. Sedimentary rock is at the beginning of the trail.
12. Hilltop view

STREAM TERRACE TRAIL
Walking time: 20 minutes

The Stream Terrace Trail begins south of the parking lot just off the "racetrack." The trail circles Hill 860'. Enter the trail in an Oak woodland at the northwest base of Hill 860 and turn east for a shaded walk on a well-graded path. A turn right takes us up an arroyo to a fence near Mulholland. We turn right and parallel the highway, exposed to traffic noise for a few minutes. A trail branches right and makes a loop trip to the top of the hill. Looking north we can see a panorama of the ranch and Malibu Lake to the south. A couple of openings through the trees will allow a good photograph of the "Western Town." Continuing on the trail takes us down to the fence line along Mulholland where we turn right. Turn right again on an old road to return to the starting point.

HIKE 26

Maps: Point Dume, topo
Malibu Beach, topo
Malibu Creek Park
Distance: 3 miles roundtrip
Elevation: 400' gain and loss
Terrain: Trail and some optional
boulder hopping
Time: 2 hours
Trailhead: Reagan Ranch

This trip introduces you to the northwest sector of the Park allowing you to get high on a hill while walking a gently graded trail.

The trailhead is on the SE corner of the intersection of Cornell Road and Mulholland Hwy. Park off the highway and walk into the Park on Yearling Road.

Walk southeast past the building area and get on a trail going past the pond and along the creek. Turn right on the first trail that you come to — the Deer Leg Trail. This will lead onto an oak covered slope. A couple of trails branch right and go uphill. At present, take the second of these trails — the other one is not maintained. Go uphill through an oak woodland. You are now on the Malibu Lake Vista Trail. Enroute you can look east and see the vernal pond and the building area. The trail enters chaparral and turns west just before reaching the ridge for the view of Malibu Lake. This is a turnaround point on this hike. Retrace your steps, then turn right and join Deer Leg Trail going southwest. Follow this as it goes through the picnic area of the Reagan Ranch where the old barbecue pit once stood. The oaks afford good shade, with room enough and rocks enough for a group to stop for lunch.

Continue southeast coming to Udell Creek and a trail intersection. A short side trip can be taken by going downstream to the right. The trail quickly turns to a rock scramble, then to serious rock climbing. Some 8 to 10 foot waterfalls can be seen before the route becomes difficult. Return to the main trail, crossing Udell Creek as you again head southeast. In less than ten minutes the trail leads to a ridge overlooking Century Lake, and Goat Buttes beyond.

Return by going downhill to the northwest and getting on the trail that follows the bottom of the valley back to Park Headquarters. This route passes through an extensive stand of Golden Currant. The open fields along this trail provide a wide assortment of spring flowers: the creek bed and shaded areas support ferns, mosses, and Wild Pansy; the dry hillsides display Baby Blue Eyes and many others including Yucca.

Pass the pond once more; look for ducks as you continue to the end of the hike and the trailhead.

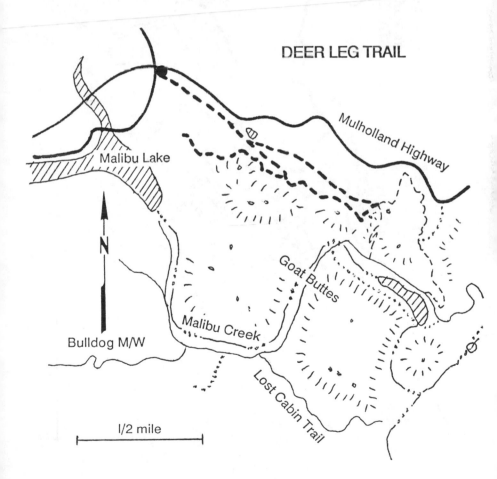

DEER LEG TRAIL

Mulholland Highway

Malibu Lake

N

Goat Buttes

Malibu Creek

Bulldog M/W

Lost Cabin Trail

1/2 mile

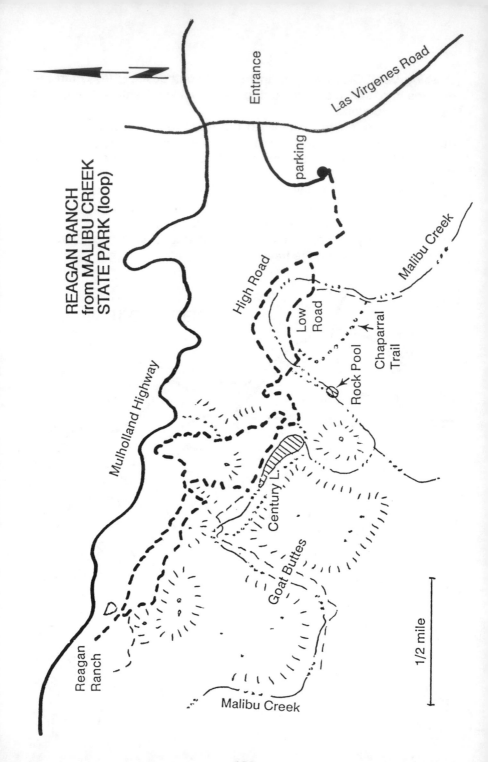

REAGAN RANCH
from MALIBU CREEK
STATE PARK (loop)

Entrance

Las Virgenes Road

parking

Malibu Creek

High Road

Low Road

Chaparral Trail

Rock Pool

Mulholland Highway

Century L.

Goat Buttes

Reagan Ranch

Malibu Creek

1/2 mile

HIKE 27

Maps:	Malibu Beach, topo
	Malibu Creek State Park
Distance:	7 miles roundtrip
Elevation:	500' gain and loss
Terrain:	Trail and road
Time:	2 hours, 45 minutes
Trailhead:	Malibu Creek State Park

The entrance to Malibu Creek State Park is from Las Virgenes Road, 2/10 of a mile south of Mulholland Highway. A fee is required for parking.

This hike will take you along the floor of the valley, then up a hill and down into a valley known as the Reagan Ranch.

Drive through the gate at the attended entrance and go west on the road into the Park. Park in the second lot and start hiking. The first mile is relatively level on a good road. Las Virgenes Creek comes down from the north joining Stokes Creek, which in turn enters Malibu Creek. You will cross Las Virgenes Creek, and in about 5 minutes take a right fork (High Road) along an oak lined lane on the north shore overlooking the creek. Movie sets for "Planet of the Apes" and many other films were built in this area but have been removed so the Park can return to a natural state.

A road comes in from the left after crossing a bridge; keep to the right and start winding uphill. This road tops out in about ten minutes, opening up a view of Century Lake and the Malibu Creek valley to the northwest. Goat buttes on the west of the lake were produced about 15 million years ago under the sea by volcanic action, then later were forced up during the time when the Santa Monica Mountains were formed.

Continue along the road as it starts downhill toward the shore of Century Lake. In a couple hundred yards turn sharply to the right on Lookout Trail. This trail takes you uphill around the south, then the east shoulder of a hill before heading northwest to the ridge overlooking the upper valley. Fifteen minutes after leaving the road you should be on the crest of an oak covered

137

ridge. Turn right and gently drop down an enchanting trail deep in Oaks, Laurel and high Chaparral.

The fire of October 1982 burned the chaparral on this slope, and although the recovery is good, several more years will be needed before the trail is restored to the shaded canopy of trees that it once had.

Look for a clearing on the left; the chances of seeing deer are good. The trail enters a grassy meadow, covered with flowers in spring but very dry in summer and fall. Looking northwest, the grassy strip stretches 3/4 mile and you should see the Park Headquarters buildings near the far end.

The trail passes a small grove of Coast Live Oaks. An Indian mortar once used in the grinding of acorns, can be seen in a flat sandstone rock. The trail keeps to low ground at the edge of the meadow as it gently climbs northwest. Some Golden Currant bushes are growing on both sides of the trail. The plants bloom in late March and April putting on a rare display. A few hundred yards farther along, the trail nears a pond on the right where you may see a few migratory ducks.

Water is available at Park Headquarters, your turnaround point. Return on the same trail until there is an opportunity to go right, and get on the trail paralleling the one you came up on. This trail stays in the shade of Oak trees, passing through the picnic area of the ranch. An old barbecue pit marks the site of earlier outdoor gatherings. Good lunch stops are found along this stretch of the trail where even a large group can relax in the shade of trees or the sun of open areas.

Cross Udell Creek farther along, then a gentle climb of less than ten minutes places you on a ridge overlooking Century Lake.

At one time we walked downhill on the steep "cat track" toward the Lake but serious erosion required rerouting, and during the spring of 1985 a volunteer Sierra Club crew built the Cage Canyon Trail. At the "overlook" turn left and intersect the trail you came in on, then turn right. In about 100 yards turn right again, onto Cage Canyon Trail, which winds down to Century Road near the lake. Turn left and return on the road by which you entered.

Century
Lake

HIKE 28

Maps:	Malibu Beach, topo
Distance:	3 miles roundtrip
Elevation:	550 feet loss and gain
Terrain:	Trail and Fireroad
Time:	2 hours
Trailhead:	Mulholland Highway

We reach the trailhead by driving 1.2 miles east of Cornell Road on Mulholland Highway, and park on the south side off the road. Room for about 10 cars is available off the highway. A narrow trail goes southeast up to a cistern on the ridge. A sloping cement slab catches rainwater and drains it into an underground cistern. No one has explained why the cistern was built or what the plans are for using the water. Matilija Poppies grow on the slopes of the ridge and put on a floral display in late-spring to mid-summer.

Cistern Trail follows the ridge top one-half mile to a cross trail. We turn left and descend on the Lookout Trail. Spectacular views of Goat Buttes and Century Lake make a panorama to the west. You will bring a camera next time. We are soon at the lower end of the trail and at Century Lake. In 1901 a dam was built by the Crags Country Club and impounded water for recreational use. Fishing is allowed but not duck hunting. We can extend our hike by walking along the lake shore to the dam. Drinking water, picnic tables, and a restroom are available.

Walk northwest on the road along the lake. A trail goes through the willows on the left, if we want to take a close look at cat-tails and Wocus. Come back to the road and continue to Cage Canyon where a trail on the right takes us on a steep, winding climb to the trail coming down from Reagan Meadow. At the intersection of the trails, look for Cream Cups, Linanthus, Brown Microseris, and Owl's Clover. March and April are good months for finding flowers.

We are going to turn right and hike back to where we parked, but first let's take a look at a bedrock mortar found under some Oaks about 200 yards to our left. We go west to a grove of Oak trees and leave the trail to look for the mortar. Indians lived here thousands of years before the Spanish invasion, and lived off..the land by hunting and harvesting. Thirty-five hundred, or more, years ago the native Americans discovered that if acorns were ground up and the meal was leached, the water soluble tannin was removed, making the acorns edible. This mortar is now in the shade of Oaks and probably has been for centuries. Several intermittent streams nearby would have been the source of water.

The return trail goes over a low ridge, then contours the south facing slope before crossing a stream and into an Oak woodland. Turn left at the Cistern Trail and climb the ridge.

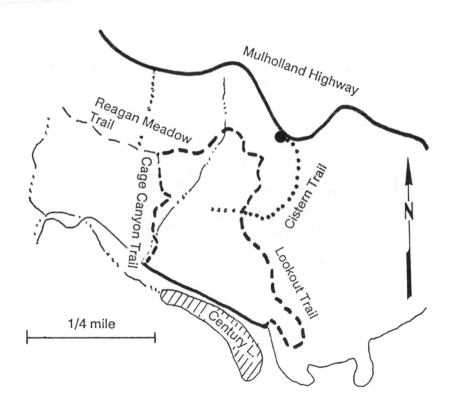

HIKE 29

Maps:	Malibu Beach, topo
	Malibu Creek State Park
Distance:	2½ miles
Elevation:	150' gain and loss
Terrain:	Road and trail
Time:	1 hour
Trailhead:	Malibu Creek State Park

Enter Malibu Creek State Park from Las Virgenes Road, 2/10 of a mile south of Mulholland Highway. A parking fee is required.

This short, almost level hike on a good trail is almost made to order for those days that your time is limited or you just don't feel like a long hike.

ROCK POOL

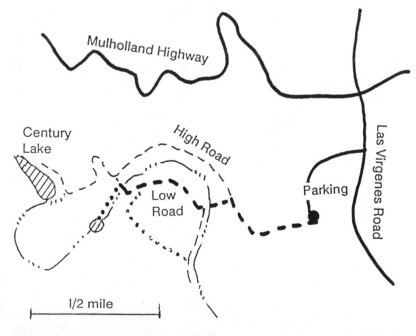

Drive through the main gate to the parking lot. Walk a short way along the road and ford Las Virgenes Creek as it spills across the road on a concrete apron. Usually the water can be measured in inches, but this changes with a good rainstorm. Upon reaching a fork go right and walk along the High Road in the shade of Oak trees that line both sides. This route follows the north side of Malibu Creek until reaching an intersection with a road that crosses the stream on a bridge. Turn left at the intersection finding Gorge Trail near the stream.

Follow Gorge Trail upstream to Rock Pool. Some years the trail becomes washed out by the winter rains and you must do some easy boulder hopping. Rock Pool is at the mouth of the gorge and both the pool and the gorge contain large volcanic boulders. Volcanic cliffs rise from both sides of the pool forming a spectacular setting. When the water is high the pool presents a barrier to further travel unless you care to get wet. Fish can be seen if you are patient. Expect to be scolded by a Scrub Jay or two for intruding into the gorge. Look high overhead toward the mountain to the southwest for soaring Red-tailed Hawks, and perhaps a Golden Eagle. Rock Pool has been the site of television and movie productions. The Tarzan series and Swiss Family Robinson had many of the outdoor sequences filmed here.

Return to the road, turn right and cross the bridge staying on the road as it goes downstream. At the fork turn left, fording Malibu Creek and continue to the High Road. Turn right, retracing your route back to the parking lot.

ARCHAEOLOGICAL COMMENT

Indians lived along Malibu Creek and its tributaries more than 7000 years ago. Several prehistoric village sites and camp areas have been located within Malibu Creek State Park. Some of these areas had been occupied for long periods of time, in one case 2000 years, then died out as a village.

When the Spanish invaded California in the late 1700's, a village named Talopop was found near Las Virgenes Creek. The village survived at least until 1805, when mission records at both San Fernando and San Buenaventura no longer referred to the village. Bartolomé Miguel Ortega received a Spanish land use permit in 1810, for Rancho el Paraje de las Virgenes, a few miles to the west. He had been ranching the land since about 1803, so it is quite possible that the people of Talopop went to work on the

143

ranch. Investigation of the site indicates that people continued to live in the village area for a number of years.

All of the waterways in the Santa Monica Mountains were favored by the Indians as places near which to live. Malibu Creek drains a greater area than any other stream in the mountains. It also is the only antecedent stream — one that cuts completely through the mountain range — and was a convenient transportation network for the Indians.

All of the sites are protected so that only archaeologists under proper permit can excavate. A cultural resource center is planned for the Park so that visitors may better understand the history of the area.

Rock Pool

HIKE 30

Maps: Malibu Beach, topo
Distance: 6 miles
Elevation: 1500' gain and loss
Terrain: Steep fireroad
Time: 2 hours 45 minutes
Trailhead: Tapia Park

Peak 2049 is so named because it is 2049 feet high. Most of the comments that I have heard indicate that an emphasis on the altitude is not misplaced as some uphill stretches are a challenge to one's endurance.

The trailhead is south of Tapia Park on the west side of Las Virgenes-Malibu Canyon Road. The parking lot is south of the bridge. Restrooms are located under pine trees along the trail. Beyond the restrooms look for the trail as it makes a sharp left turn and heads south paralleling the canyon road. In 200 yards make a right turn onto Mesa Peak Motorway. The map (next page) does not show this short trail segment. You could walk south along the highway and turn right at the motorway. I would prefer to get away from traffic as soon as possible so use the trail.

About a half mile farther along the trail, a road branches right and dead-ends at a gate. (On the return trip we may find ourselves wanting to follow that road because it is downhill.) The north slope of the mountain is very steep, and the trail makes a few switchbacks to gain altitude. At one switchback we cross over the ridge and look down into the Malibu Creek gorge, the only stream to cut completely through the Santa Monica Mountains.

Malibu Canyon has been a transportation corridor since the Indians first lived there. The steep canyon is filled with boulders and is difficult to travel through, but as we are about to find out, travel between the ocean and inland over the mountains is also difficult. The highway through the narrow gorge was built during the early 1950's.

The view of Malibu Canyon continues to expand as we gain altitude. The creekbed below is at an elevation of about 300', and

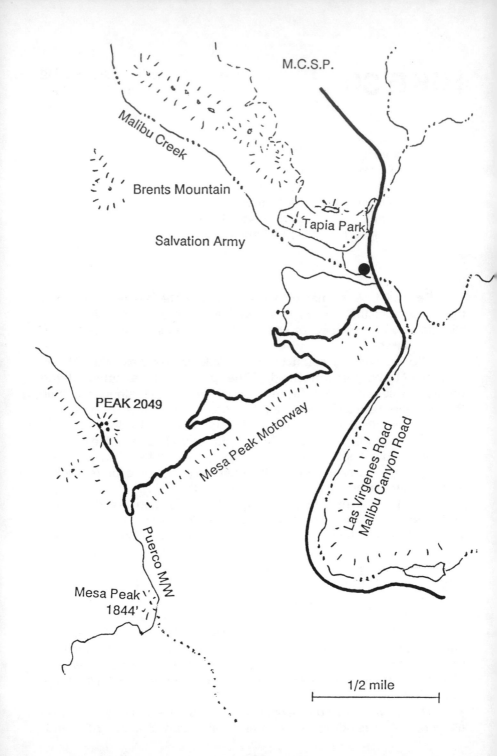

M.C.S.P.

Malibu Creek

Brents Mountain

Tapia Park

Salvation Army

PEAK 2049

Mesa Peak Motorway

Las Virgenes Road

Malibu Canyon Road

Puerco MW

Mesa Peak
1844'

1/2 mile

long before we reach our destination at 2049' it becomes apparent that Malibu Creek has cut the steepest and deepest gorge in the mountains. Climb here on a clear night for a spectacular view of the shore line and the lights of the city below. A group of us did this at night on New Year's Day, 1981, and aside from being chilly after the warmth of exertion, were convinced that being atop Peak 2049 was the place to be.

Before reaching the peak, however, we come to a fork in the road. The left fork drops downhill past Mesa Peak and down through Puerco Canyon ("Pig Canyon") to the Pacific Coast Hwy. The road we have been hiking is Mesa Peak Motorway, and after a right turn at the fork, continues past Peak 2049, and ultimately connects with Castro Motorway and Corral Canyon Road about 2½ miles farther west. One-third mile beyond the road fork, we turn right at a saddle and walk to the top of the peak. We return the way we came.

A persistent notion exists within the hiking community that Mesa Peak M/W should lead to Mesa Peak. This application of logic has caused some confusion when a hiking group doesn't stay together. On at least one occasion a lone hiker ended up at Puerco Beach instead of back at the Tapia Park trailhead. (That hike should be a good car shuttle — if planned.)

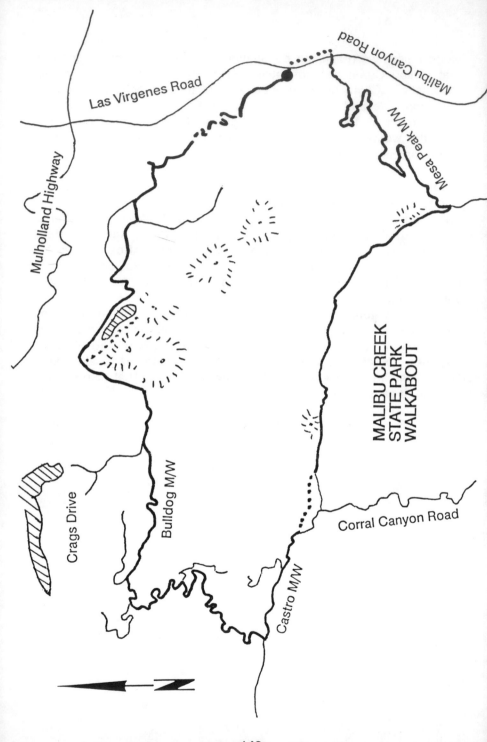

Las Virgenes Road

Malibu Canyon Road

Mulholland Highway

Mesa Peak M/W

Crags Drive

Bulldog M/W

Castro M/W

Corral Canyon Road

MALIBU CREEK
STATE PARK
WALKABOUT

N

HIKE 31

Maps:	Malibu Beach, topo
	Point Dume, topo
	Malibu Creek State Park
Distance:	14½ miles
Elevation:	2000'
Terrain:	Fireroad and trail
Time:	6½ hours
Trailhead:	Tapia Park

This hike takes us on a big loop around the perimeter of the Park, keeping to the ridges where possible. We reach the trailhead by driving on Las Virgenes/Malibu Canyon Road either 4.6 miles north of the Pacific Coast Highway or 4.8 miles south of the Ventura Freeway. The Tapia Park lot is west of the Highway.

We begin the hike at the parking lot of Tapia Park and walk south along the highway, crossing over and back because the sidewalk on the bridge over Malibu Creek is on the east side. Crossing Malibu Canyon Road twice and walking along the shoulder is hazardous. We must exercise a good deal of caution when traffic is heavy.

The trail begins a couple hundred feet south along the road then rises steeply to the west on a fireroad. In time a trail will be built so as to join Mesa Peak M/W without the danger of walking along the highway. The trail eases up after the initial steepness, but then continues the climb, gaining 1500' in 2½ miles.

About 2-3/4 miles from the trailhead, Puerco M/W comes up from the coast and joins Mesa Peak M/W. Continuing on Mesa Peak M/W (which does not pass Mesa Peak) we pass by Peak 2049 on our right. During the next 2½ miles of ridge hiking we walk over an area of turritella fossils, up and down over some little peaks, and to a series of Sespe sandstone pinnacles.

A trail on the right leaves the road and goes along the ridge of rock formations for about 1/2 mile, then intersects Corral Canyon Road. We continue on Corral Canyon Road (or it may be Castro Peak M/W from this point on) for one mile, reaching the intersection with Bulldog M/W, near Peak 2528. Of interest to botanists is a large Santa Susana Tarweed plant, northwest of the junction of the roads. This plant blooms in mid-summer with flowers lasting into fall. Considered rare elsewhere, Santa Susana Tarweed is plentiful along this rocky ridge.

The walk down Bulldog M/W is one that we remember because it is steep and winding — we lose 1800' before reaching level ground again. Several side roads lead to power transmission towers. We continue downstream, around a gate, to the intersection with 20th Century Road. The downhill distance since turning onto Bulldog M/W is about 3½ miles.

After turning right on 20th Century Road we enter the former site of the M.A.S.H. set,(which has been removed) near where the Lost Cabin Trail begins. We continue past Century Lake, and go over a hill to rejoin the stream on the other side at another fork in the road. The left fork, called the High Road, stays left of Malibu Creek. Straight ahead and across the bridge puts us on the low road. They meet again downstream. A short side trip to Rock Pool can be taken by following the Gorge Trail up the north side of the Creek. Before we start down the Low Road, we go to the Visitor's Center in the large white house, then we will take the low road and go downstream to another fork.

The left fork crosses Malibu Creek and joins the High Road, which takes us to the Malibu Creek State Park parking lot.

Upon seeing the parking lot, turn right and follow the road across the bridge. Just after passing a magnificent Valley Oak on the left, look for and take the road on the right that skirts the east side of a large meadow. At the head of the meadow an Oak grove furnishes restrooms and a picnic area. The trail goes to the east of the picnic area and after a short climb heads down into Tapia Park. Cross the park to your car to complete the hike.

Today's hike has been a segment of the "Backbone Trail" system, a hiking and equestrian trail which will eventually stretch from Will Rogers State Historic Park to Point Mugu State Park. Our hike has taken us on the primary route and the alternate route, and I'm not sure which is better.

M.A.S.H. jeep after the fire

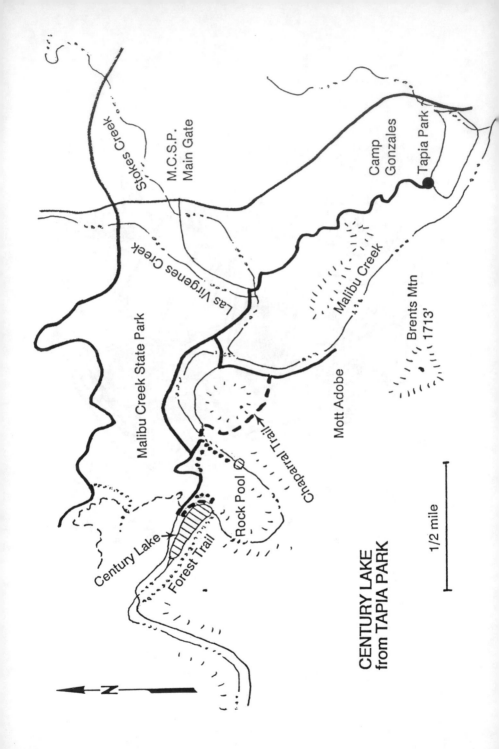

CENTURY LAKE
from TAPIA PARK

Stokes Creek

M.C.S.P.
Main Gate

Camp
Gonzales

Tapia Park

Las Virgenes Creek

Malibu Creek

Brents Mtn
1713'

Malibu Creek State Park

Mott Adobe

Chaparral Trail

Rock Pool

Century Lake

Forest Trail

N

1/2 mile

152

HIKE 32

Maps: Malibu Beach, topo
Distance: 7 miles roundtrip
Elevation: 1000' gain and loss
Terrain: Trail, road, steep trail
Time: 3 hours
Trailhead: Tapia Park

The Tapia Park to Malibu Creek State Park segment of this trail was built by Sierra Club Volunteers before the Dayton Canyon fire of 1982. I've heard comments to the effect that had they known they could have waited, because trail building through chaparral is hard work. The trail is an important link in the Backbone Trail system and is used a good deal by both hikers and equestrians.

The trail begins near the road in the northwest corner of the Park. Upon entering the main entrance to Tapia Park from Las Virgenes Road, turn right and parallel Las Virgenes a hundred yards or so. At the first opportunity turn left and follow the road about 1/4 mile until it goes downhill and you can see a meadow on the right. Park near two oak log segments at telephone pole I 467 294 E. In due time a sign may be placed to designate the trail. We go north across the lower part of the meadow and cross an intermittent stream to enter an Oak Woodland. Watch for a left turn as the trail enters chaparral and goes uphill. After a switchback the trail takes us through a stand of Mountain Mahogany, and soon, after gaining more altitude we can look to our right and see Camp David Gonzales. The rock underfoot to the ridge and beyond is fragmental volcanic breccias that intruded through sandstone about 14 million years ago.

After crossing a saddle, the trail makes two switchbacks in chaparral before dropping down to a large oak grove at the head of a big meadow. Picnic tables, water, and restrooms are available. Look for Goldback Ferns along the trail. A sequence of the movie "Roots" was filmed at the west end of the grove but all props have been removed so the location is completely restored to nature.

An old macadam road skirts the edge of the meadow. Part way down the road, a faint trail goes across the ridge on the right, ending at the proposed RV camp. In May we can find Lilac Mariposa Lilies in bloom on the ridge. Continue down the road until we are in the shade of a magnificent Valley Oak. Having read many articles about the plight of Valley Oaks in southern California, this tree is worth observing. In January 1986 ground squirrels were living under the oak and many mounds of dirt were visible. Some oak seedlings were growing. On 13 July 1986, 614 seedlings were growing under the oak, the tallest of which was 23 inches high. Ground squirrels no doubt hid more acorns than they needed or could find, so many acorns sprouted. These seedlings don't survive because the parent tree takes the sunshine, the nutrients, and the water. This process may not occur every year but my guess is that without interference this oak will at least replace itself.

The route continues across Stokes Creek, turns left near the parking lot, and crosses Las Virgenes Creek then makes a wide turn right and heads northwest. At a road junction we continue ahead on the "High Road" which overlooks Malibu Creek on our left. The High Road is shaded by Coast Live Oaks and is an almost level, pleasant walk for about 1/2 mile. At a road junction we turn right and make climbing turns to the top of a low ridge overlooking Century Lake. Century Lake is impounded by a dam built in 1901 by the Crags Country Club who owned the property during the early 1900's. The lake is gradually silting up because of annual run-off, and in time could become a marsh. The lake is a haven for wildlife: migrant ducks are often seen, coots are regular inhabitants, and occasionally a heron is seen. Fish live in the lake, and this is a popular place for sons to bring fathers to try their angling skills. The route of this hike takes us to the lake shore then left to near the dam — but not on it. An alternate extra 3/4 mile walk is available if time allows. Instead of turning left at the lake, continue ahead until we cross Malibu Creek on a low concrete bridge, then look left for a trail that follows the base of the mountain west of the lake. The Forest Trail is shady and almost level. It ends at the dam so we retrace our steps. Coast Redwood trees were planted along the trail at the turn of the century and some still remain.

A short, steep trail goes uphill from the southeast end of the lake and intersects the road we came in on. We turn right and walk downhill. Before crossing the bridge, we turn right and go a couple hundred yards upstream on a trail and sometimes on rocks, to Rock Pool — a great place for lunch under the Sycamore trees.

After lunch we retrace our steps, turn right and cross over the bridge for a stop at the Visitors Center. Upon leaving the Center turn right and find a trail that climbs up the hill behind the house. We gain about 165' of elevation before reaching a narrow saddle and immediately go steeply downhill to Mott Road. Mott Adobe is a short distance downstream and is the ruins of the original building. A stone fireplace is in place and parts of the adobe walls are standing. Fire and water have taken a toll. Look for the simulated bullet holes on the face of the wall — this was used as a prop in a movie.

After turning around at the adobe our route is upstream until we come to the road that crosses Malibu Creek. We then turn right and retrace our steps to the trailhead at Tapia Park. This hike is flexible to the extent that several side trails are available to us and could extend the hike for as many miles as we feel like walking.

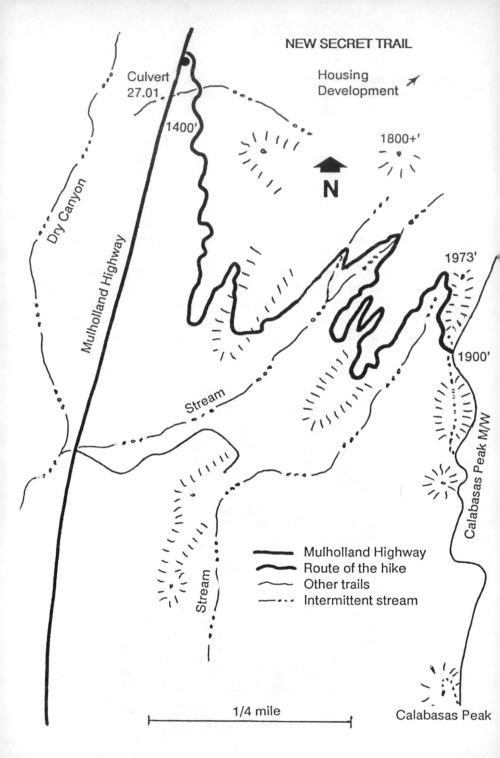

NEW SECRET TRAIL

Housing
Development

Culvert
27.01

1400'

1800+'

N

Dry Canyon

Mulholland Highway

1973'

1900'

Stream

Calabasas Peak M/W

━━━ Mulholland Highway
〜〜 Route of the hike
─── Other trails
·─·─ Intermittent stream

Stream

1/4 mile

Calabasas Peak

HIKE 33

Maps:	Malibu Beach, topo
Distance:	3 miles roundtrip
Elevation:	700' gain and loss
Terrain:	Trail
Time:	1½ hour
Trailhead:	Mulholland Highway

Built by volunteers in 1985 this trail is dedicated to public use by way of an easement given by the owner of their private land. The trail provides access between Mulholland Highway and Calabasas Peak Motorway.

We reach the trailhead by driving 1.9 miles west of Old Topanga Road on Mulholland Highway. A culvert under the highway near roadmarker 27.15 is about 250 feet beyond the trail. Park on the east side. Considerable landform disruption has occurred near the beginning of the trail but within a few hundred feet we are in Black Sage, White Sage, California Buckwheat, Bush Mallow, and other Santa Monica Mountain plant life. The soil at the beginning part of the trail is volcanic, covered in places by clay or silt that has come down the mountain slope. Most of the trail will be over sandstone, some of which contains shell fossils.

Twisting and turning, the trail parallels Mulholland Highway and its sight and sounds for 7 or 8 minutes before making a turn east and away from civilization. Most of the hiking is uphill with a few level or downhill stretches. We will go through Scrub Oak Chaparral while still in view of the highway, and a sloping meadow after making the turn eastward. Plant communities enroute include Coastal Sage Scrub, Southern Oak Woodland, Grassland, Riparian Woodland, Chaparral, and Cliffs. We will be in deep shade at times and exposed to sun and wind at others.

Toward Calabasas ridge the trail makes several climbing switchbacks and works along some massive sandstone slabs. New Secret Trail intersects Calabasas Peak Motorway, opening opportunities of exploring the ridge in either direction or of climbing Calabasas Peak. For the purpose of this hike we turn around at the ridge and return the way we came.

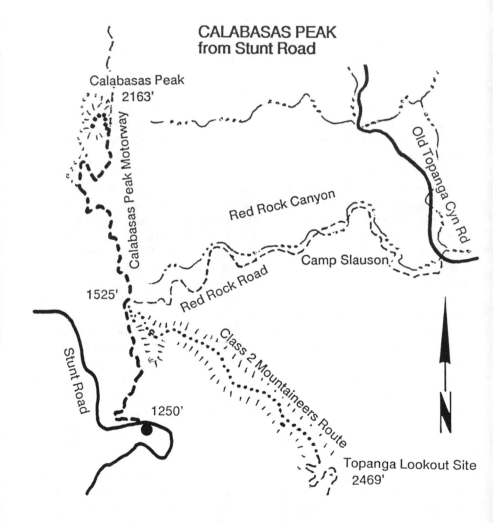

CALABASAS PEAK
from Stunt Road

Calabasas Peak
2163'

Calabasas Peak Motorway

Old Topanga Cyn Rd

Red Rock Canyon

Camp Slauson

1525'

Red Rock Road

Stunt Road

Class 2 Mountaineers Route

1250'

Topanga Lookout Site
2469'

N

HIKE 34

Maps:	Malibu Beach, topo
Distance:	4 miles roundtrip
Elevation:	950' gain and loss
Terrain:	Fireroad and short, steep trail
Time:	1½ hours
Trailhead:	Stunt Road

Reach the trailhead by going west from Woodland Hills on Mulholland Highway to Stunt Road. Turn left and go one mile, parking off the pavement on the right.

Hike up the fireroad to the north. This is steep and rocky giving you an excuse to stop and look around. Cold Creek has its source up the canyon to the south. The porous sandstone stores water from the winter rains, supplying several perpetual springs with clear water. The 530 acre Murphy homestead which includes the springs and the upper part of Cold Creek was presented to the Nature Conservancy by Kathleen Murphy. The year round stream turns west near where you parked your car and enters Malibu Creek downstream from Tapia Park.

Continue uphill on the fireroad. Large slabs of sandstone were tilted on edge when the Santa Monica Mountains were being formed and have weathered to grotesque slanted outcroppings. Upon reaching the saddle you are on "Fossil Ridge." The road to the right drops down through Red Rock Canyon to Old Topanga Road, going through Camp Slauson. On a day when we want to add 3 or 4 miles to the hike, we can go down into Red Rock Canyon as far as the road, then turn around to climb back. On this segment the loss and gain is 550 feet. Now back to the ridge. Stay on the Calabasas Peak Motorway as it continues the climb. Look west to find the profile of "Lady Face Mountain" on the horizon, about 10 miles away. The road switches back making a climb around the south, then east, shoulder of the mountain before heading north, slightly downhill to a saddle.

Upon reaching the saddle leave the road and walk along the bulldozer-eroded area on the left as the trail climbs the bank, then makes a sweeping turn left going steeply uphill. Find a trail through the chaparral and you will soon be on top of Calabasas Peak. Return the way you came, or as an alternate, you may want to continue north on the road as you come off the firebreak from the peak. A few hundred feet along the road and just as you begin to see around the north side of Calabasas Peak, a trail goes west contouring around the peak, rejoining the road below the switchback. This trail doesn't get much use and the chaparral reclaims its own territory with a vengeance, so expect some brush. It would be wise to wear goggles and gloves because each year the trail becomes more overgrown.

"Marmot Rock" near Calabasas Motorway

HIKE 35

Maps:	Malibu Beach, topo
Distance:	4 miles
Elevation:	950' gain and loss
Time:	2½ hours
Trailhead:	Stunt Road

Stunt High Trail is special for several reasons. The variety of plant communities is unsurpassed, the trail takes us along Cold Creek through a beautiful Riparian Woodland, then uphill and across some sloping grassland into an Oak Woodland. The upper trail winds through a magnificent stand of Chaparral. Wild animals frequent the Cold Creek watershed. One of the few mountain lions remaining in the mountains is seldom seen but is known to live in the canyon.

The trail intersects Stunt Road in 3 places; limited off-road parking is available at each place. I will describe the hike that starts at the lower end, makes a roundtrip, and uses the same route back.

From Mulholland Hwy, drive 1 mile up Stunt Road to the main parking area on the right. The trail begins at the east end of the lot. We go around the gate and downhill to Cold Creek, following the old road. The trail crosses the creek then follows downstream on the left bank. We look for ferns in the shade along the stream. About 1/2 mile downstream we branch left at a large rock containing bedrock mortars, and start uphill. To continue downstream would take us onto private property and close to homes, so we must use care and not miss the left turn.

The route leaves Cold Creek and goes uphill through the oaks, then on across a meadow. We parallel an intermittent stream to our right and are out of sight of a large intermittent stream to the left. Spring is the most colorful time to be here — a wide variety of flowers will be found in the oak woodland and in the meadow. We turn left near the top of the meadow.

The Stunt Ranch buildings are in view west of the meadow. A family lives in one of the homes, two of the structures are classified as historical. The building area is not on the route of the hike and should be avoided.

STUNT HIGH TRAIL

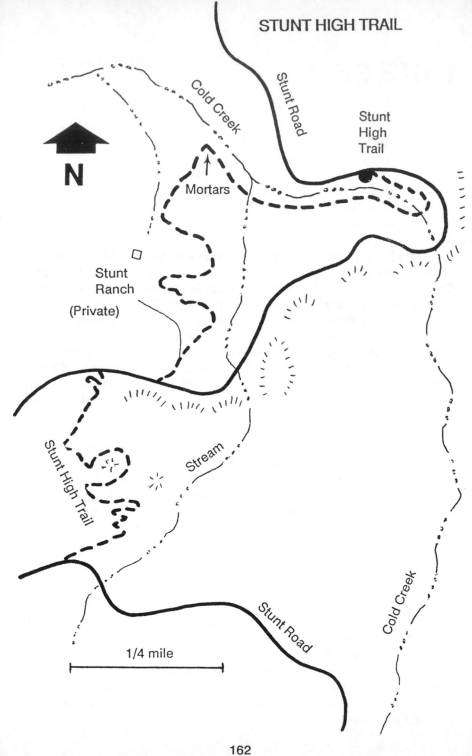

Stunt Road

Cold Creek

Stunt High Trail

Mortars

N

Stunt Ranch

(Private)

Stunt High Trail

Stream

Cold Creek

Stunt Road

1/4 mile

After turning left at the top of the meadow, the trail gains altitude and climbs into a chaparral forest. After a couple of switchbacks the trail intersects the Stunt Ranch entrance road. We turn left and walk to Stunt Road, then turn right and walk uphill along the road about 400 yards. A parking lot has been graded along Stunt Road near the ranch entrance road. It is expected that this lot will be used by people attending naturalist activities.

After the short walk along Stunt Road we look for the continuation of the trail on the south side. The entry to the trail is through a riparian plant community of Ferns, Poison Oak, and Oaks. After a couple of quick switchbacks we enter a forest of Chaparral — a mixture of Ceanothus, Chamise, Scrub Oak, and Redshank. The trail passes some sandstone formations including one in the shape of a seal called "Seal Rock." The trail turns often and is of a gentle grade even when ascending the steep hillside, before reaching the road and the end of the trail.

The Santa Monica Mountains Backbone Trail comes down the north slope of Saddle Peak. We can access the Backbone Trail by walking a few hundred feet downhill on Stunt Road to a trail on the left. This .3-mile-long trail leads to an intersection. We may then turn right to go west, or left to go east on the Backbone Trail.

We turn around at Stunt Road to retrace our steps. Car shuttle options can add variations to this hike. The return hike offers beautiful views of the Cold Creek watershed and Stunt Ranch. The high ridge east of us looks down upon Hondo Canyon and the Topanga watershed beyond. Calabasas Peak and its massive tilted sandstone outcroppings is on the north. Malibu Creek is several miles west.

The land over which the trail has been built was operated as ranches into the 1970's. The Stunt Ranch was homesteaded in the late 1800's, the Murphy Ranch in 1909. Kathleen Murphy donated her 530 acre ranch to the Nature Conservancy who developed it as the Ida Haines Murphy Preserve (Cold Creek Canyon Preserve), an outstanding pristine area. The Mountains Restoration Trust — a nonprofit land trust dedicated to preserving public access opportunities in the Santa Monica Mountains — has recently assumed responsibility for management and preservation of the Preserve. The Stunt Ranch has been purchased by the Santa Monica Mountains Conservancy. A Nature Trail is planned for the lower part of Stunt Ranch and will be available as a self-guided tour. A brochure is being prepared.

MURPHY PRESERVE
(UPPER COLD CREEK TRAIL)

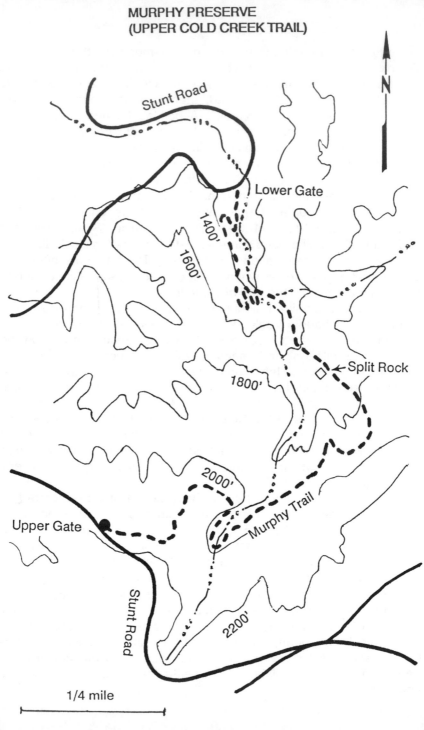

HIKE 36

Maps:	Malibu Beach, topo
Distance:	3 miles
Elevation:	500' loss and gain
Terrain:	Trail
Time:	2 hours
Trailhead:	Stunt Road

The 530 acre Cold Creek Canyon Preserve was a gift to the Nature Conservancy made by Kathleen Murphy. The Murphy Ranch will preserve a part of the Santa Monica Mountains in its wild state for all time to come.

A written permit is required for entry. Apply by calling The Mountains Restoration Trust.

The entry to the Preserve is reached by driving 3.38 miles on Stunt Road from Mulholland Highway.

The trail into the area follows the old driveway to the Murphy home. The grade is gentle and the footing is good. The entire area burned in 1970, but the chaparral has reclaimed the area effectively. The trail is well maintained, a major task because the chaparral is vigorous and has been growing well since the fire.

The outstanding feature of the trail is the variety of plant life. I will comment on some of the plants to be found but leave it to you to spot them along the trail. Chamise and its close relative Red Shanks are both plentiful here, Chamise blooming in May, the Red Shanks in August. California Buckwheat starts blooming in May, lasting well into summer. By looking closely at the flower you can find the Ambush bug, an insect with clawlike pinchers simulating the small Buckwheat flower, waiting for an unwary fly to land and be captured.

Two types of Manzanita are found in the Santa Monica Mountains; both are plentiful along the trail. Eastwood Manzanita sprouts from the root crown after a fire, so it can be identified by looking for the old burned branches with new growth all around. The leaves have a sticky feel. The Bigberry Manzanita does not root crown but grows only from seeds.

Two types of Sumac bushes are found along the trail: The Sugar Bush and Laurel Sumac. They are somewhat similar in appearance but can be distinguished by their leaves. The Sugar Bush has thick shiny, waxy leaves that fold like a taco and are pointed at one end; the leaves of the Laurel Sumac are longer, pointed, have smooth edges, and some fold. A close relative, the Lemonade Berry, is not found in the preserve but can be found closer to the ocean. It has a flatter, oval shaped leaf. Another prominent member of the Sumac Family is Poison Oak. It is evident throughout the area.

Ceanothus is an important chaparral plant found in the preserve and is represented by several species. *Ceanothus megacarpus,* or Big Pod, has white blossoms. It blooms in January-February and sets relatively large seed capsules by May; Redheart (greenbark), *Ceanothus spinosus,* has pale blue or white blossoms, a small seed capsule, and the leaves are larger and shinier, but thinner than the Big Pod Ceanothus. Hairy Ceanothus has larger leaves that are shiny on top and dull underneath; and the Chaparral White Thorn, *Ceanothus leucodermis,* is wicked. There are but a few places in the Santa Monicas where it is found.

Farther down the trail you will pass by an old pick-up truck, burned and rusted; proof that this trail was once a road.

The trail quickly drops down to an area of dense vegetation. Woodwardia and Bracken ferns are plentiful; Bay trees and large Oaks shade the trail and the canyon; a bed of Iris, introduced in the 1950's is crowding out the native plants in the marshy spot below the spring. The massive layers of sandstone that form this mountainside absorb the water from the winter rains and release it throughout the year.

A large split sandstone rock near the spring was used as the walls of a cabin. Notches cut into the rock show where the beams were. The foundation of the main ranch house which burned in the fire of 1970 is farther up the hill.

Travel downstream becomes difficult beyond the cabin site because storms have damaged the trail. This is the turnaround point of the hike, so return by the same trail to the entrance.

The trail downstream was rerouted in 1985 to make the route passable. It is steep and is still subject to landslide activity. I'll describe the route below the split sandstone rock: From this point to the lower gate we add 1 mile each way and 400' loss of altitude. The lower gate is locked so some arrangement needs to be made in advance if we intend to leave the Preserve at the lower gate.

From the split rock we drop down on a steep section of the trail. The north facing slope is deep in shade and supports the growth of Bay Trees, Snowberry, Crimson Pitcher Sage, Woodferns, and Humboldt Lilies. We cross a marshy area near a community of Yellow Flag, then get near the creek on the left. A couple of Bigleaf Maples can be seen from the trail.

After another steep section of trail we cross a small wooden foot bridge. On the right we see a small waterfall that displays a calcium carbonate buildup. Nearby, Venus-hair fern grows on the side of a cliff. The trail eases up a bit, then continues downhill and crosses the creek, then soon makes some switchbacks going uphill to avoid a steep landslide area. The trail soon leads downhill and after some steep parts, comes to a branch. Turn right and go upstream to a waterfall and Stream Orchids; turn left and go to the lower gate.

Some shell fossils are in the sandstone rocks on the property. Examples may be seen near the display board at the entrance. This Fernwood Member of the Topanga Canyon Formation was deposited during the middle Miocene epoch when the land was under a shallow sea.

HIKE 37

Maps:	Malibu Beach, topo
Distance:	3.2 miles one way
Elevation:	1600' loss, 400' gain
Terrain:	Trail (and bushwhack until the trail is completed)
Time:	Unknown
Trailhead:	Stunt Road/Piuma Road

Saddle Creek Trail is a segment of the Backbone Trail. Built in 1987 by crews of California Conservation Corps and Los Angeles Conservation Corps, the trail had been flagged (route determined and marked with flags) in 1986. Prior to trail construction and going back to the 1970's, a small group of us hiked the entire trail every year. This particular segment demanded that we wear goggles, gloves, and other protection to get through the chaparral. The trail is now a pure delight. The north and west shoulders of Saddle Peak are steep, rugged, chaparral covered slopes offering views of a large expanse of the Malibu Creek watershed.

I will describe the hike as a one way trip requiring a car shuttle. The beginning trailhead is on Stunt Road 2.8 miles from Mulholland Highway; the ending trailhead is on Piuma Road 1.4 miles from Malibu Creek Road. Park a car at the ending trailhead near the first switchback on Piuma Road. Drive back down Piuma Road to Cold Creek Road, turn right and go to Mulholland, turn right and go to Stunt Road. Follow Stunt Road and park on the left opposite a gate with sign "Backbone Trail."

An old road leaves Stunt Road on the south side and almost immediately makes a left turn to go uphill. At the turn, leave the road to follow a trail going west that will intersect the Backbone Trail in 3/8 mile. Initially the Backbone Trail neither gains or loses much altitude as it winds westerly, but soon it begins a gentle downhill character, losing about 500 feet per mile, with an occasional short uphill section.

Saddle Creek Ranch is a short distance north of the trail — far enough away that the dogs don't bark when we walk along. For the rest of the hike we don't come close to habitation until the end.

After leaving the Saddle Creek watershed the trail crosses a ridge and heads west crossing a meadow before making some switchbacks down the upper part of an intermittent stream that eventually joins Cold Creek.

The trail contours around the north side of a mountain in dense shade before coming to a western exposure and the beginning of a series of switchbacks, dropping us 800 feet on a constant downhill grade. We cross Dark Creek in the shade of a number of White Alders and climb a 100 foot high chaparral ridge before the last downhill walk to the end of the hike.

This trail can just as easily be an out and back from either trailhead and going as far as you care to. In the next couple of years, and long before this book goes out of print, the Backbone Trail segment to the top of Saddle Peak will be complete. This will add an exciting option for exploration.

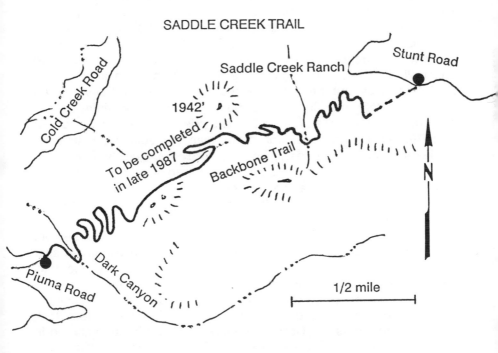

SADDLE CREEK TRAIL

HIKE 38

Maps:	Malibu Beach, topo
Distance:	2¼ miles
Elevation:	100' gain and loss
Terrain:	Fireroad
Time:	1 hour
Trailhead:	Saddle Peak Rd and Stunt Rd.

This is another short walk that gives you a chance to stretch your legs when driving the local mountain roads. The lookout tower is gone but the view remains.

The trailhead is at the junction of Schueren Road, Saddle Peak Road and Stunt Road at the crest of the mountains (3 airmiles from the ocean). Coming from the San Fernando Valley go west on Mulholland highway turning left on Stunt Road and continuing to the crest of the mountains. Park off the road on the north side and walk east onto Topanga Ridge M/W. This is an almost level road that goes out the ridge overlooking Topanga Canyon. An inactive military site is on the peak to the right; entry is not authorized. The entire area on the left side of the road was burned in 1970, leaving no vegetation other than the standing blackened trunks of bushes and trees. The land recovered quickly, first with a riot of flowers the following spring, then with a profusion of other plants that had been waiting for room to grow. The chaparral is now back with impenetrable thickets of Ceanothus, Chamise and Manzanita, so very little evidence of the fire remains.

Nothing remains of the lookout tower other than the cement foundation. Coyotes and deer walk the road, red-tailed hawks soar the updrafts by the hour, and of course lizards scurry about all summer long. Nature is reclaiming the lookout site.

A sandstone ridge leads to the northwest. A mountaineer's route follows the ridge down to the saddle where the Red Rock Canyon road meets the Calabasas Peak M/W; but is not included in this hike. The view to the east is into Topanga Canyon. The steep gully leading down from the southeast slope of the lookout site is Hondo Canyon. Return the way you came.

TOPANGA LOOKOUT SITE

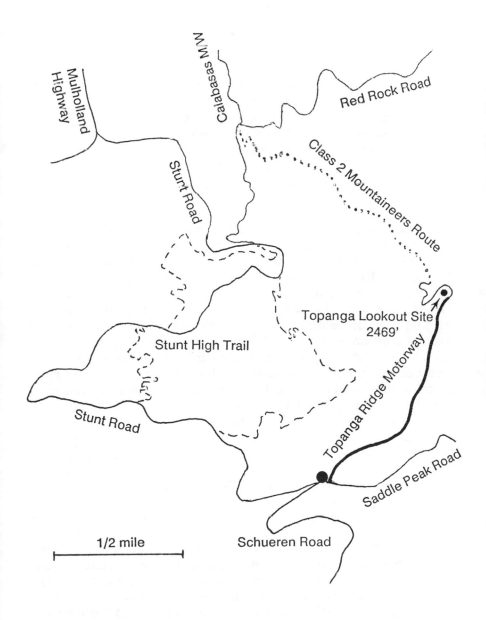

Mulholland Highway

Calabasas M/W

Red Rock Road

Stunt Road

Class 2 Mountaineers Route

Topanga Lookout Site
2469'

Stunt High Trail

Topanga Ridge Motorway

Stunt Road

Saddle Peak Road

1/2 mile

Schueren Road

HIKE 39

Maps:	Malibu Beach, topo
	Calabasas, topo
	Canoga Park, topo
Distance:	8 miles
Elevation:	1750' gain and loss
Terrain:	Trail and fireroad
Time:	3¼ hours
Trailhead:	Adamsville Avenue,
	Woodland Hills

This trip is unusual in that it starts by going downhill and ends by going downhill. Get to the trailhead by driving west on Mulholland Hwy in Woodland Hills to Eddingham Avenue; turn left and go to Adamsville Avenue; turn right and go 2 blocks to the end. This is in a residential area with limited parking so you may elect to park a few blocks away and walk in. As it is in an area of housing development you may want to take a look at the start of this trail in advance of the hike to see if it still exists.

A steep trail drops down beyond the last house on the right. This goes to a north running intermittent stream. Turn right upon reaching the streambed and begin looking for a trail that branches left, going up a gully to the west. This steep trail makes a turn left working up onto a ridge. Stay on the trail until reaching the "Summit-to-Summit" fireroad, then turn right. Go west as you stay close to the ridge. You will cross Old Topanga Canyon Road at its high point and continue west going around a fireroad gate, then uphill. A private road leading to Deer Creek Ranch branches left and should be avoided.

The next segment of the hike is about 2 miles long and gains 550 feet in a series of uphill climbs interspersed with level stretches. The route stays well up on the ridge as it makes a left hand sweep from a west to south heading. Nearing Calabasas Peak you will lose some altitude, then make a left turn and gain 200 feet going around a shoulder to the right and up a grade with the peak on the right. When the roadcut dwindles, cut back to the right and

172

walk along the trail that goes up a bulldozed area to the peak. A break in the chaparral near the top indicates where the trail goes through. A steep, but short, climb puts you on top. At 2163' Calabasas Peak overlooks everything close by. Only the east-west backbone to the south, dominated by Saddle Peak, is higher. The view one mile west is of Stokes Canyon and Stokes Ridge. Beyond is Malibu Creek State Park distinguished by the volcanic Goat Buttes. Climb this at night to see the lights of the Thousand Oaks area and the Ventura Freeway.

Return on the same road you came; cross Old Topanga Canyon Blvd. and continue east. Pass the ridge by which you came up to the road, continuing about 1/2 mile, reaching a 4-road intersection. Stay left going uphill, reaching another road fork after leveling out on the ridge. Turn left and start the final downhill stretch of about 2/3 mile to the trailhead. This area is being developed so expect houses and pavement.

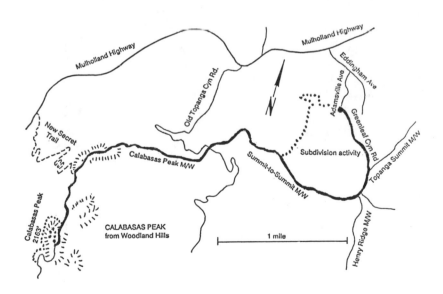

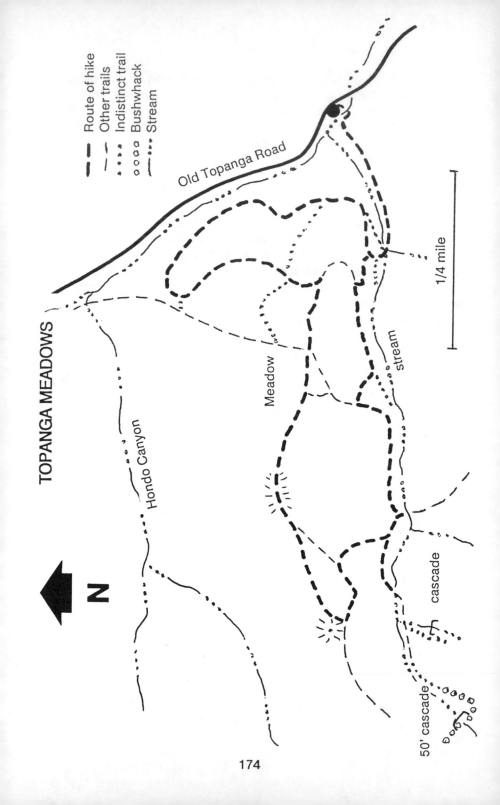

TOPANGA MEADOWS

N

Old Topanga Road

Route of hike
Other trails
Indistinct trail
Bushwhack
Stream

1/4 mile

Meadow

stream

Hondo Canyon

cascade

50' cascade

HIKE 40

Maps:	Topanga, topo
Distance:	4 miles
Elevation:	850' gain and loss
Terrain:	Road and trail
	(some steep)
Time:	1-3/4 hours
Trailhead:	Old Topanga Cyn Rd.

Topanga Meadows presents an opportunity to explore. There are many trails in the area — some that are known to have been used by the Indians for centuries. Exploring the several streams leading down to Old Topanga Canyon Stream is interesting, and the meadows lend themselves to independent investigation. This hike can take an hour, or it can last all day, depending on how much you want to see. You need to recognize Poison Oak when you see it as there's a lot of it here.

The trailhead is one-third mile north of Highway 27 on Old Topanga Canyon Road, a few hundred feet beyond the bridge. Park on the west side of the road and walk down to the stream and cross it to the trail on the other side. The Backbone Trail will go through here in the future; the land has been acquired, the general route of the trail established, and we should expect to see the trail in a few years, so modify this hike at that time.

For now turn right at the west bank of the stream and follow the trail as it goes through a California Rose briar patch and makes a sweeping left turn as it heads up to an intermittent side stream. The trail crosses one of the streams coming down from the west; a cement apron has been built here to control erosion, as the trail once was a road. Another trail comes down from a meadow to the right. Continue ahead on the trail as it leaves the stream and turns right going steeply uphill along the edge of a meadow. Upon reaching an old road, (now a trail) continue ahead (east). Our trail is almost level for a few hundred yards as we turn left and enter a Southern Oak Woodland. Old Topanga Creek is on the right but out of sight. This section of the hike gives us an opportunity to see wildflowers and ferns that grow in oak groves. Spring is the best time for viewing but some plants will be in bloom at all times of the year. Look for Milkmaids, Crimson Pitcher Sage, Sweet Cicely, Miner's Lettuce, California Buttercup, and more. We continue the loop of this segment and gain some elevation. Several trails will lead us west, uphill, all of which will lead us up to the ridge. The route shown on the map is well used. We turn west and go uphill on the edge of a large sloping meadow. Just before cresting out we see an oak grove on the left that has sandstone rocks that invite a rest stop, or a lunch stop. Farther west along the grassy ridge look for Golden Stars and Mariposa Lilies in the spring.

Continue along the crest and merge with the Backbone Trail. The Trail (not shown on map) heads west, crosses the ridge overlooking Hondo Canyon to the north, and contours into the upper part of Hondo Canyon to the "cabin." This segment of trail built by the Los Angeles Conservation Corps in 1991 was funded by money raised by the Santa Monica Mountains Trails Council and Corral 63 of Equestrian Trails Inc., and matching funds of the Santa Monica Mountains Conservancy. The walk to the cabin and back will add at least 2 miles to the hike.

Come back out of Hondo Canyon and at the ridge a right turn will take you onto a trail that goes west uphill about 1/2 mile. At one time several areas had been bulldozed for house foundations, but the project was discontinued.

Another option from Hondo Ridge leads south downhill. On this steep road look for a planked retaining wall. A shady, delightful trail branches right just beyond the planked wall. This trail once went to a waterfall but is now completely overgrown at the upper end. Try it.

We go downstream back to the shady, delightful lane and turn right on a dirt road, go a short distance and turn left. This trail is also shaded and we are able to see the stream down in the canyon on our right. After a left sweep around a sandstone cliff a right fork in the trail takes us downhill steeply. Two more right turns and we are on the trail back to the trailhead.

Take this hike in the spring and see a beautiful display of flowers. Look for Humboldt Lilies, Chocolate Lilies, Monkey Flowers, Chinese Houses, Blue-eyed Grass, Roses, Paint-brushes, Golden Stars, and more.

HIKE 41

Maps:	Roadmap
	Canoga Park, topo
	Topanga, topo
Distance:	12.2 miles one way
Elevation:	600' gain, 1500' loss
Terraln:	HIghway
Time:	Don't walk this one;
	go by bicycle or car.
Trailhead:	Ventura Blvd and
	Topanga Cyn Blvd.

This drive is designed to give a geological view of the Central Santa Monica Mountains by traversing the range north to south on State Highway 27. Several stops are needed to see the features described. Unfortunately some "no parking" areas are in conflict with this plan, so some walking is required.

The trip begins in the San Fernando Valley on State Highway 27 near the Ventura Freeway. The mileage log starts as you leave Ventura Blvd. so set your odometer at zero if you can, otherwise keep a record. You will start at the top of the geological formations and take a journey through time, seeing the youngest rocks in the valley and oldest rocks near the coast.

mile 0.0   Ventura Blvd.   Go south on Topanga Canyon Blvd. Pass Mulholland Drive and start up a slight grade as the road heads for the mountains.

mile 1.5   A large roadcut on the left just beyond Cezanne Avenue displays tilted layers of Modelo shale and sandstone. The Modelo Formation is largely composed of diatomite and clay shale formed 8-12 million years ago when the land was under a deep sea. Layers of this formation can be seen in roadcuts all the way to the summit.

mile 2.9   Summit. Park in the area to the left then cross the highway to inspect the shale at close range. The "Summit-to-Summit" Motorway begins here, goes west, and is a major access trail into the area as far as Old Topanga Road.

mile 4.2   Stop and park just beyond Entrado Road. Across the road on the left is a loop of the old road. Walk around the loop and look for the contact area between the Modelo Formation and the Topanga Group. The actual contact here is an angular unconformity; that is, a part of the underlying formation is missing. What shows is Modelo shale on its base of pebbly sandstone and conglomerate, overlying the Calabasas Formation of the Topanga Group.

mile 4.8   Beyond road marker 7.50 the road makes a sharp turn to the right as it crosses a branch of Topanga Creek. A dark brown outcropping of volcanic basalt is on the right and a few hundred yards down the road a basalt pinnacle can be seen on the left. The volcanic activity in the Santa Monica Mountains began about 15½ mya and lasted for 2 million years.

mile 5.6   Bridge across Garapito Creek. Some rock slides are in this area on the east side of Topanga Creek. The Calabasas Formation of sandstone is hard and weather resistant, but when the strata dips to the west as it does here, the slides can occur along the plane of the rock layers. Over the centuries Topanga Creek has cut away at the lower edge of the bedding plane and with a little help from builders doing the same, a good rain can trigger a slide.

Cheney Drive follows up Garapito Creek and leads to an entrance to Topanga State Park.

mile 6.7   The sandstone cliffs on the right side of the stream are layered almost horizontally and indicate good resistance to weathering. Volcanic rock appears on the left of the road and continues in view to Entrada Road. Many rock walls have been built because of its availability.

mile 7.3   Entrada Road on the left leads to the Trippet Ranger Station at the entrance to Topanga State Park. The sandstone from here down to the business section of the town of Topanga is the Cold Creek member of the Topanga Canyon Formation.

mile 7.7   Intersection with Old Topanga Road, Topanga Post Office, and business buildings.

mile 7.9   Bridge.   Marine fossils have been found in the Cold Creek member sandstone in this area, dated as early or middle Miocene.   Just beyond the bridge is an east-west division of the Cold Creek member above and the Fernwood member below, both of the Topanga Canyon Formation.   This Fernwood, brackish water sandstone forms the cliffs on the east side of the stream to about the 1100 foot level, and on the west of the stream goes to the top of the ridge beyond Fernwood. The dip of the strata is generally east, accounting for the stability and steepness of the cliffs on the east side of the stream.

mile 8.8   The steep bank on the right is composed of dark intrusive rock (diabase) that weathers out and occasionally rolls down onto the road.   On the left is a limited area of Sespe sandstone (Oligocene epoch).   This is pebbly, and a nonmarine formation that is quite often red colored.   Visually above the Sespe Formation is a fault separating the Sespe from the light brown Topanga Formation.   The fault is almost vertical and is near the base of the Topanga sandstone cliffs.   Actually, the Sespe and Topanga sandstone lie side by side.   There is a layer of white colored fresh-water limestone in the lower Sespe Formation.   Also notice the prominent thick dikes in the roadcut.

mile 9.6   You abruptly leave the black intrusive rock on both sides of the road and enter a steep walled canyon made up of the Coal Canyon Formation.   This cliff-forming rock is mostly pebble-cobble conglomerate and siltstone.   Formed in a shallow, tropical sea during Paleocene and Eocene epochs (40-70 mya) it contains marine fossils.   The layers are tilted and massive.   At mile 9.8 a small canyon and roadcut on the right affords a close view.   During times of heavy rain the cascades of water coming down the east escarpment present a spectacular view for this normally dry cliff. Falling rocks and landslides, along with washed-out roads, accompany the heavy storms so one must temper a desire to see this event with caution.

mile 10.2   The east wall shows a division of the Coal Canyon Formation above and the Tuna Canyon Formation (Upper Cretaceous, 70 mya+) below.   The Tuna Canyon Formation is made up of beds of coarse-grained sandstone and minor conglomerate deposits.   The Tuna Canyon thrust fault is discernable on the east wall and can be seen again dipping steeply to the south at a roadcut at mile 11.4.

mile 10.4 Bridge.

mile 10.6   The thrust fault can be seen on the west wall of the canyon.

mile 11.2   Roadcut.   South of here for the next .8 mile the Coal Canyon conglomerate dominates the east wall again.   The Tuna Canyon Formation is found on the west of the road.   The canyon soon broadens, and landslide activity covers most of the base rock.

mile 12.0   Tuna Canyon Formation rock forms the base to the coast even though much of it is covered over with alluvium.

mile 12.2 Pacific Coast Highway.

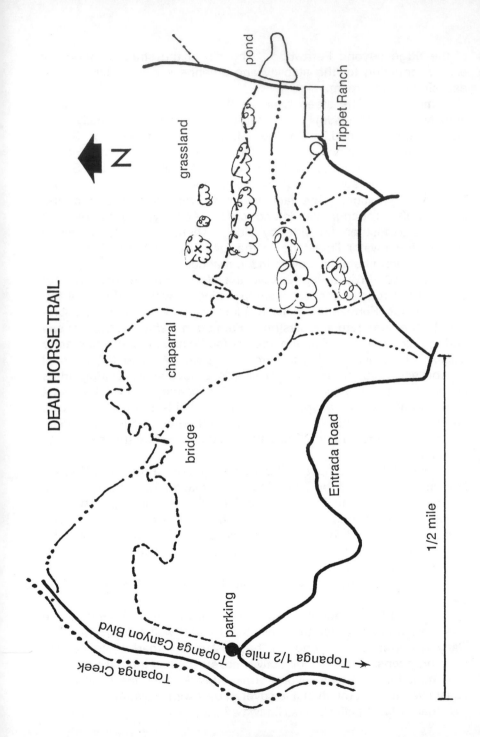

DEAD HORSE TRAIL

N

pond

grassland

Trippet Ranch

chaparral

bridge

Entrada Road

1/2 mile

parking

Topanga Canyon Blvd

Topanga Creek

← Topanga 1/2 mile

HIKE 42

Maps:	Topanga, topo
Distance:	2½ miles roundtrip
Elevation:	400 feet gain and loss
Terrain:	Trail
Time:	1 hour
Trailhead:	Dead Horse parking lot on Entrada Road

A short hike — but an interesting hike — the Dead Horse Trail takes us on a tour of the western approach to Trippet Ranch in the west end of Topanga State Park. We will be introduced to dense streamside shade, grasslands, chaparral and oak groves. This particular area was burned in 1925 and 1948. The major fires of recent years have bypassed the area.

The hike begins at the Dead Horse parking lot, 200 yards from Topanga Canyon Boulevard, 1/2 mile north of the Post Office in the town of Topanga. We must take care driving to the parking lot — the turn onto Entrada is sharp and steeply uphill. The turn into the parking lot is on a blind curve. At present the parking lot is free. The gate is locked at night. The trail heads north through chaparral. Except for the imported gravel on the path up from the parking lot, the initial stretch of trail is on solid basalt, a fine grain volcanic rock. Later we will be on sandstone. After 10 minutes on the trail we cross Trippet Creek on a beautiful, rustic, wooden bridge. It was installed in 1986 without so much as disturbing a blade of grass — a highly responsible care for the environment. The streambed is interesting for those who would climb around on rocks and risk some Poison Oak. Sweet Cicely, Geranium, Grape, and 4 species of fern grow along the banks.

Cross the bridge and soon enter a Chamise chaparral forest. The trail contours along the south and west facing slope of a broad ridge. As the trail heads east we enter an oak woodland on the right and a meadow on the left. Upon reaching a road near the pond, turn right and walk across the earth and rock dam that impounds the water. California Roses have become established on the dam. Trippet Ranch is the Park headquarters. A ranger lives in

181

the house south of the parking lot. Restrooms, drinking water, pay phone, picnic area, parking, and park Personnel are available.

We can return the way we came or locate a trail west of the parking lot that crosses a meadow and continues down the south side of the stream. In about 1/4 mile the trail intersects an east-west trail, which if followed north will join the Dead Horse Trail where we turn left and return to our cars.

HIKE 43

MUSCH RANCH TRAIL
in Topanga State Park

Maps: Topanga, topo
Distance: 4 miles round trip
Elevation: 600' gain and loss
Terrain: Trail and fireroad
Time: 1-3/4 hours
Trailhead: Trippet Ranch

We can make a loop hike using a fireroad for half the trip and trail for the other half. Most of the area of the hike was burned during the Topanga Canyon Fire of 1977, then again by a prescribed burn in June, 1984. This hike will duplicate a part of the Eagle Spring Loop trip but will go in reverse order and with more detail.

Reach the trailhead by turning east onto Entrada Road from Topanga Canyon Boulevard just north of the town of Topanga. Once on Entrada Road turn left at every street intersection and drive 1.1 miles to the entrance of Topanga State Park. Park in the lot; a fee is required.

From the east end of the parking lot go north on the macadam road near the left side of the pond. In about 100 yards, as the road goes over a little rise, turn right onto the trail. After crossing the east end of the meadow the trail quickly enters an enchanting riparian woodland of Oak, Laurel and Sycamore trees. The trail winds through the densely wooded area then comes out for a short glimpse of chaparral before dipping into the next streamside area of Fern and Scarlet Monkeyflower. The trail turns north and heads into chaparral before coming to the Musch Ranch area — which can be distinguished by a stand of Eucalyptus trees. An overnight campground, drinking water, restrooms, picnic tables, and horse corrals are available. Fires are not authorized. Check with a State Park ranger before planning to stay overnight.

Several branching trails may cause some confusion but keep in mind that the trail leads uphill to the east. Shortly after leaving the Musch Ranch area a side trail goes downhill from a low ridge at a point where we angle right and go uphill. The trail again forks farther along and either fork is suitable, as they rejoin in a few

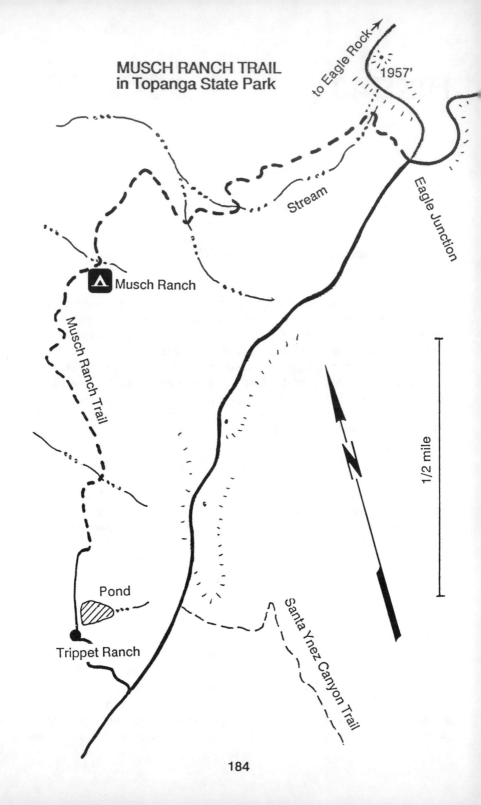

MUSCH RANCH TRAIL
in Topanga State Park

to Eagle Rock →

1957'

Eagle Junction

Stream

▲ Musch Ranch

Musch Ranch Trail

1/2 mile

Pond

Trippet Ranch

Santa Ynez Canyon Trail

hundred yards. The trail from this point on is generally to the east and after two more stream crossings begins a serious climb.

The Topanga Canyon fire of November 1977 swept down this slope and thoroughly burned the chaparral, then again when a prescribed burn was set. The chaparral is recovering nicely because many plants sprout on the root-crowns of burned plants and many seeds that have lain dormant in the topsoil sprout after a fire. The composition of the plant community is temporarily disrupted by fire — maybe for a 7-10 year period. Many flowers that normally do not thrive in chaparral have a few years of glory until they are again crowded out. We look for Bush Poppies as we climb up after the last stream crossing. These 8-10 foot high shrubs are scarce in chaparral but plentiful along this trail. The yellow blossoms appear in February and bloom for three months. Before smelling a blossom, I think "Watermelon," and with a little imagination it smells like watermelon. A stand of Bush Lupines dominates the area farther up the trail. A trip along this trail in February, March, or April will be remembered for the beautiful blue blossoms and the delightful scent.

After a vigorous climb we crest out on a fireroad at Eagle Junction and turn right. The walk on the fireroad stays high on the ridge. Topanga Canyon watershed is on our right and Santa Ynez Canyon on our left. We soon are able to look down on Trippet Ranch to the right and identify the pond, the buildings, and the parking lot. The goat pens can be seen north of the beginning of the Musch Ranch Trail. Goats were used in Topanga State Park as a means of reducing vegetation on the firebreaks. The program was discontinued several years ago. About 1/2 mile from Trippet Ranch the Santa Ynez Trail branches left. The hill southwest of this junction is of volcanic basalt that intruded into the sandstone about 14 million years ago. We keep to the right at road junctions in order to reach Trippet Ranch parking lot.

Trippet Ranch facilities include: picnic area, restrooms, drinking water, and bulletin board information center.

EAST TOPANGA FIREROAD

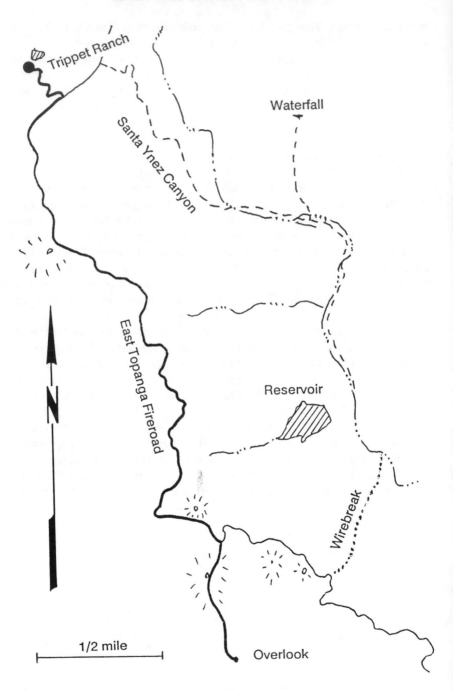

HIKE 44

Maps:	Topanga, topo
	Topanga State Park
Distance:	6 miles roundtrip
Elevation:	1500' gain and loss
Terrain:	Fireroad
Time:	2-3/4 hours
Trailhead:	Trippet Ranch

This trip is high on a ridge and gives an opportunity to look down into the deepest parts of both Topanga Canyon and Santa Ynez Canyon.

Reach the trailhead by turning east onto Entrada Road from State Hwy 27 just north of the town of Topanga. Once on Entrada Road turn left at every street intersection. Drive 1.1 miles to the entrance to Topanga State Park.

Leave the east end of the parking lot and go uphill on a fireroad. This road intersects a road that runs along the ridge at "the Latitude." Turn right and start a gentle climb along an oak shaded road that quickly crests out on the ridge between Topanga Canyon on the west and Santa Ynez Canyon on the east.

Notice the rock underfoot. Since leaving Trippet Ranch the base rock has been sandstone. Now you are on volcanic rock and have just crossed the east-west trending Topanga Fault. Volcanics intruded into the existing sandstone about 15 million years ago during a period of volcanic activity in the Santa Monica Mountains. For the next two miles most of the rock along the route is volcanic with a few areas of sandstone.

This east Topanga ridge gives breathtaking views of the lower part of Topanga Canyon and one can sense the power of the stream that has cut this gorge through the mountains to a depth of more than 1000 feet. Periodically Topanga Creek demonstrates this force by cleaning out some of the man-made structures such as roads. bridges, and buildings that impinge upon the creek bed. The hillside housing on the west side of the canyon is the Fernwood tract of Topanga.

The Santa Ynez Canyon view is equally spectacular with its network of ravines, and massive sandstone slabs of tilted rock. Two trails drop down from the fireroad to Santa Ynez Creek. One, about a mile and a half from the start of the hike, leaves the road near Peak 1629. (This is a sandstone knoll west of the road.) The trail is east of the road and is difficult to pick up because of bulldozer activity destroying the first couple hundred feet about 1978, and the trail has not been used since. The trail is steep, going through a beautiful chaparral forest, and bottoming out through a lot of Poison Oak just before reaching the stream. The other trail begins about 450 yards farther south on the road and is really overgrown. These trails are not part of this hike and are mentioned only for those with a strong urge for adventure. When the land for Topanga State Park was being purchased for what is now the second largest urban park in the United States and the largest wildland within any city in the world, lower Santa Ynez Canyon was not included. This effectively blocked what could have been the main entryway for the people of greater Los Angeles. The housing development in Santa Ynez Canyon is Palisades Highlands.

Continue south along the ridge until coming to a road on the right about 2½ miles from the trailhead. This road turns to a firebreak as it follows a sandstone ridge out to "the Overlook," a high point with an exceptional view of the Pacific Ocean. Return the way you came.

HIKE 45

EAGLE SPRING LOOP
Musch Ranch Trail
from Trippet Ranch

Maps:	Topanga, topo
	Topanga State Park
Distance:	7 miles roundtrip
Elevation:	900' gain and loss
Terrain:	Combination fireroad
	and trail
Time:	2-3/4 hours
Trailhead:	Trippet Ranch

On Highway 27 just north of the town of Topanga, turn east on Entrada Road. Once on Entrada Rd, turn left at every street intersection, 1.1 miles to the entrance of Topanga State Park.

Take the trail up the hill from the parking lot. This intersects with a fireroad. A sign reads: "Eagle Spring 1.6 mi., Mulholland 4.6, Will Rogers State Historic Park 9.2." Turn left at this intersection and walk up a gentle grade, initially in the shade of Coast Live Oak trees — later along an open ridge. (You will pass the trail on the right leading to Santa Ynez Canyon.) Continue on the road for about 1 mile to a fork, Eagle Junction; go left and continue uphill, noting the view of Eagle Rock ahead. Later, from the backside of Eagle Rock, it is possible to take a short side trip, climbing to the top.

Continue east on the road, passing Penny Road entering from the left, until reaching an intersection with three roads, called "The Hub." Just before reaching this junction there is a high point on the left. If you were to walk to the top you would be at the apex of three watersheds. To the south is Santa Ynez Canyon with its intermittent stream draining into the ocean near Sunset Blvd. To the east is Rustic Canyon with its drainage outlet near Chautauqua Blvd. To the north is Garapito Canyon which joins with Topanga Canyon and the drainage is then south to the ocean, just west of where Hwy 27 meets the Coast Highway.

At "The Hub" are three other roads. First is Fireroad 30 on the left which goes 2 miles north to Mulholland Dr. The next road which appears to be a continuation of Fireroad 30, is named

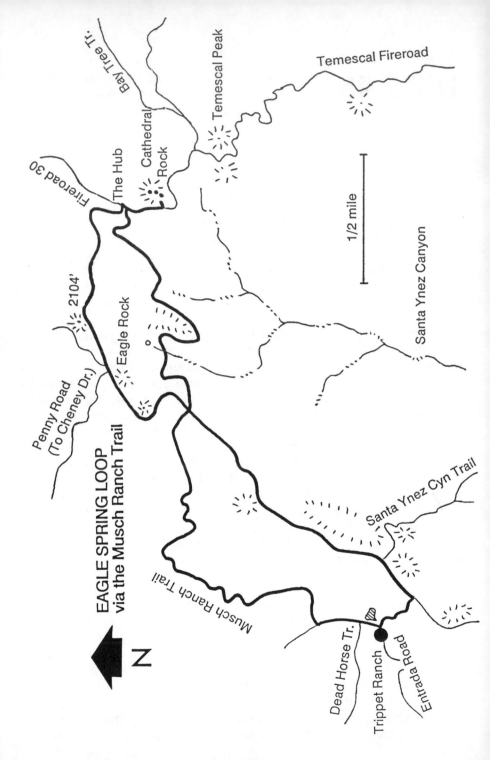

EAGLE SPRING LOOP
via the Musch Ranch Trail

N

Temescal Fireroad

1/2 mile

Santa Ynez Canyon

Temescal Peak

Cathedral Rock

Bay Tree Tr.

The Hub

Fireroad 30

2104'

Eagle Rock

Penny Road
(To Cheney Dr.)

Santa Ynez Cyn Trail

Musch Ranch Trail

Dead Horse Tr.

Trippet Ranch

Entrada Road

Temescal Fireroad at this point and goes south along the north-south ridge, separating Santa Ynez and Upper Rustic Canyons. The third road which goes to Eagle Spring, we'll take later.

This hike goes south on Temescal Fireroad about 1/2 mile to the intersection with Rogers Road on the left. Continue a short distance south of this intersection, leave the road and climb Temescal Peak, the highest point in the Park, 2126'.

Return to "The Hub" the same way you came. A nice lunch stop is at Cathedral Rock to the east of the road a few hundred yards before getting back to the junction and the road to Eagle Spring. Climb into Cathedral rock — there is room for 25 people — or maybe 50 good friends. At "The Hub" turn left to go to Eagle Spring. Three large wooden tanks store water from the year-round spring. (Second edition note: one tank has fallen apart and has been removed.) (Fourth edition note: the second tank has fallen apart and has been removed.) A short walk up the stream locates the spring, protected by abundant stands of Poison Oak.

Eagle Spring Water Tanks

Continue west on the road until coming to Eagle Junction. Cross the road to the west side where you will find the trail that goes down the slope through an area that burned in the November 1977 fire. This is the Musch Ranch Trail, so named because of the ranch at the base of the hill. Continue south on the trail heading down through the chaparral. The chaparral quickly gives way to quiet oak glens, moss covered rocks, and a stream that flows after each rain. Signs indicate the trail location in places. Cross a little meadow, pass the pond, and you have arrived at the parking lot.

The Old Footbridge on Musch Ranch Trail

HIKE 46

Maps:	Topanga, topo
Distance:	8 miles roundtrip
Elevation:	1700' gain and loss
Terrain:	Trail, firebreak and fireroad
Time:	3¼ hours
Trailhead:	Trippet Ranch

On Highway 27 just north of the town of Topanga turn east on Entrada Road. Once on Entrada Rd turn left at every street intersection. It is 1.1 miles to the entrance of Topanga State Park. This is where you will park your car.

The hiking trail goes uphill from the east end of the parking lot. Turn left upon reaching the "Latitude," a point on the fireroad along the saddle. This road leads gently uphill through a grove of Coast Live Oaks. About 300-400 yards after leaving the Latitude there is another saddle that allows a good view of Santa Ynez Canyon on the right. Take the trail that crosses over to a little ridge then, after a left turn, drops down into Santa Ynez Canyon. The upper part goes through part of the area burned in the fire of November 1977 and for a few years will be covered with wild flowers every spring until the chaparral returns. Starting down the trail presents a continuing change in the panorama of the lower canyon. Dense stands of Chamise, Ceanothus, Sumac and Toyon can be seen on the slopes to the west; massive sandstone can be seen on ridges below; and on a clear day the ocean is framed by the mouth of the canyon.

After dropping 700' rather steeply, the trail enters a cool riparian woodland shaded with Oaks and Sycamores. The trail makes a sharp turn left and becomes almost level as it gently follows the stream. Blackberry vines, Humboldt Lilies, and a myriad other plants carpet the banks of the stream. Farther on down, just before the stream we are following joins with the Santa Ynez north fork, an old cabin site is off to the left in amongst some Poison

SANTA YNEZ CANYON
EAST TOPANGA FIREROAD
via the "Wirebreak"

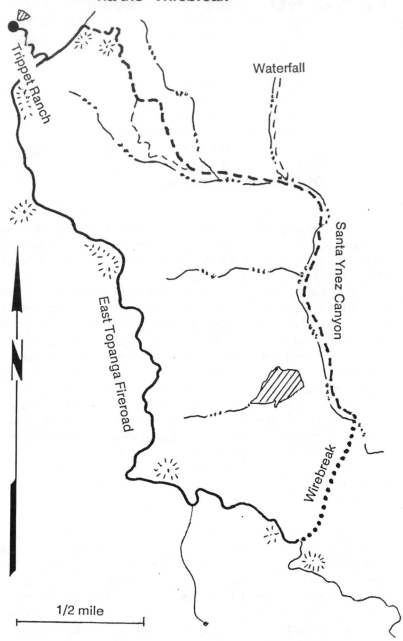

Trippet Ranch

Waterfall

Santa Ynez Canyon

East Topanga Fireroad

Wirebreak

N

1/2 mile

Oak. About all that is visible now are two rock chimneys, one with a fireplace.

Continue downstream for a good 3/4 mile more and come to a large culvert which you walk through. This is in the area of a housing development but if you stay down along the stream, none of the sense of the primitive is lost. Come out of culvert on the left side of the stream and continue for about 1/4 mile, at which time look very closely for the trail on the other side of the stream that leads up to the firebreak. A help in locating this is a power line that goes up the middle of the firebreak.

The "wirebreak," so called because of the power line nearby, is 800 feet of elevation gain in less than 1/2 mile — just continuous uphill misery. Once on top, however, the road that you find is level by comparison. Turn right and follow this East Topanga Fireroad for about 3 miles to a junction where the road drops down to Trippet Ranch.

This section affords a view overlooking both Topanga Canyon on the west and Santa Ynez Canyon on the east as well as an ocean view to the south.

The variety on this hike is emphatic: oak grassland, chaparral, and riparian woodland; pristine wilderness bordered by a housing development; canyon depths and lofty ridge viewpoints; strenuous exertion and relaxed enjoyment — a full range of experience.

SANTA YNEZ CANYON WATERFALL

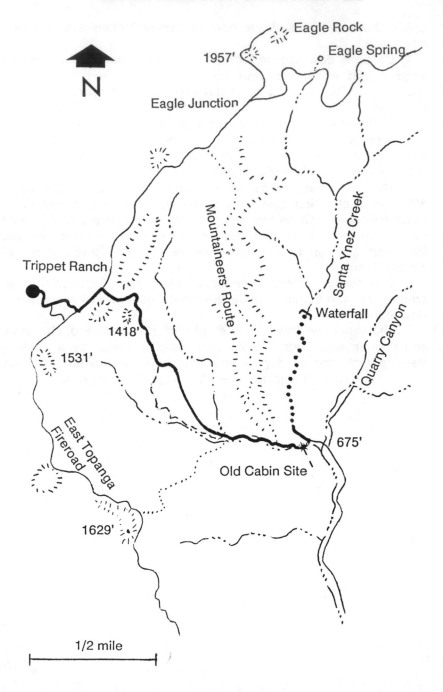

Eagle Rock

Eagle Spring

1957'

Eagle Junction

Mountaineers' Route

Santa Ynez Creek

Trippet Ranch

Waterfall

1418'

1531'

Quarry Canyon

East Topanga Fireroad

675'

Old Cabin Site

1629'

N

1/2 mile

HIKE 47

Maps:	Topanga, topo
	Topanga State Park
Distance:	6 miles roundtrip
Elevation:	1100' gain and loss
Terrain:	Combination fireroad,
	trail, and steep ridge
Time:	3 hours
Trailhead:	Trippet Ranch

On Highway 27 just north of the town of Topanga, turn east on Entrada Road. Once on Entrada Road turn left at every street intersection, 1.1 miles to the entrance of Topanga State Park. Park your car.

From the east end of the parking lot take the trail past the right of the white brick building. Turn right on the Nature Trail and wind uphill through the woods. This trail goes across a grassy area that has a succession of attractive flowering plants every spring: Blue-eyed Grass, Owl Clover, Brodiaea, and Violet.

At the top of the hill turn left on the fireroad and continue uphill until the basalt knoll on the right is passed, then turn right and start down into Santa Ynez Canyon. This section of the trail is in the area burned over in November 1977, and as a result the chaparral has temporarily been replaced by other vegetation. Mustard, Morning Glory, Filaree, Horehound, Wild Cucumber, Bush Lupine, Tree Tobacco, and many other flowering plants can be seen along the trail. About half mile down the trail start looking for a side trail on the left, just after coming down a steep grade on a reddish-tinged sandstone. (It isn't well-marked and can be missed.) Take this side trail and descend along a rocky ridge.

Soap Plant (Amole) is everywhere along the ridge. Six foot tall plants bloom in May and June, the flowers opening in late afternoon. Farther down the trail, the ridge is covered by deerweed, which grows very thick after a fire. As the chaparral returns, the deerweed disappears to a great extent. The sandstone

197

ridge dips steeply to the west, about 45°. The south end of the sandstone ridge has a number of round sandstone inclusions.

A couple of trails leave the ridge and drop down to the trail in the canyon to the west, or we may continue south on the ridge.

Upon rejoining the original trail down in the canyon, turn left. You are instantly in a new environment of Oak, Sycamore, and Walnut trees; Blackberries and Currants line the trail. About 500 yards down the trail are some caves in the cliff on the right. The wall of the canyon is very steep in this part of the Santa Ynez. If you look to the right you will see beautiful examples of conglomerate rock. To the left in about 200 yards and obscured by chaparral are two rock chimneys, all that remain of an old cabin site. The trail forks farther downstream. Take the left fork and go upstream.

Follow a trail upstream for about 3/4 mile. You will cross the stream several times — and may even run out of trail on occasion, because every storm brings down new sand and gravel and makes a few changes. By staying close to the stream you will come to some waterfalls. That is the objective of this segment of the hike. Eventually, rock-climbing ability and equipment are needed to proceed. This is a good place to turn around, retracing your steps to return to the roadhead.

A couple of variations in the route are available: (1) Instead of taking the ridge trail above the sandstone cliff, you can stay on the main trail and follow it all the way to the fireroad that leads to Trippet Ranch. (2) A bushwhack trail goes steeply up the ridge to the north, starting just a few yards west of the two chimneys. (3) An indistinct trail branches from the main trail about 400 yards west of the two chimneys and goes uphill on the left, heading southwest. This overgrown trail starts through a thick stand of Poison Oak, gains 900 feet, and tops-out on the East Topanga Fireroad. The trail is almost impossible to find because of the overgrown vegetation.

Santa Ynez Waterfall

EAGLE SPRING, TEMESCAL FIREROAD, SANTA YNEZ CANYON LOOP

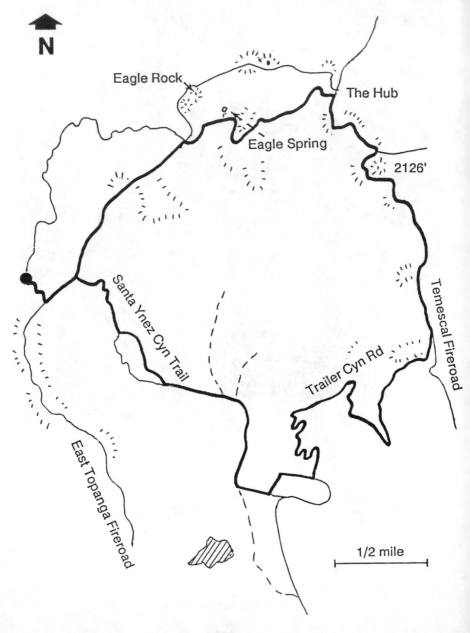

N

Eagle Rock

The Hub

Eagle Spring

2126'

Santa Ynez Cyn Trail

Temescal Fireroad

Trailer Cyn Rd

East Topanga Fireroad

1/2 mile

HIKE 48

Maps:	Topanga, topo
	Topanga State Park
Distance:	10 miles roundtrip
Elevation:	1800' gain and loss
Terrain:	Fireroad and trail
Time:	4 hours 20 minutes
Trailhead:	Trippet Ranch

On Highway 27 just north of the town of Topanga turn east on Entrada Road. Once on Entrada Road, turn left at every street intersection. It is 1.1 miles to the entrance of Topanga State Park. Park your car.

From the east end of the parking lot follow a trail up the hill on the right. Go a quarter mile to an intersection called the "Latitude" to a sign labelled "Backbone Trail." Turn left onto the Eagle Spring Road, go 1½ miles to another road junction (Eagle Junction), take either road. The road to the left gains some elevation right away and gets up on a ridge overlooking Garapito Canyon on the north and Santa Ynez Canyon on the south. The road to the right drops down to Eagle Spring. Either the upper road or the lower road is the same distance between Eagle Junction and "The Hub" — 1.4 miles. Four roads join at The Hub — Fireroad 30 coming south from Mulholland Drive, north loop Eagle Road, south loop Eagle Road, and Temescal Fireroad. If this loop trip is to take 4 hours and 20 minutes you should reach The Hub in 1 hour from the start of the hike, and are due for a ten minute rest. An interesting resting spot is in the "Cathedral Rock" area two minutes south on Temescal Fireroad.

Cathedral Rock may be reached by going past it on the road, then by cutting to the left and back, going up a steep slope to a gap in the rocks. The atmosphere within Cathedral Rock is one of feeling snug, serenely comfortable, secure. You can quickly change his aura by going to the edge of the cliff and looking onto Rustic Canyon. The view of Rustic is an unusual display of steep chaparral covered slopes in a near primitive state, wild and beautiful country that will be seen closer on other hikes.

The junction with Rogers Road is 10 minutes south on Temescal Fireroad. 100 yards farther is a firebreak on the left that goes up to Peak 2126, the highest point in Topanga State Park. Continuing on, there is a short spur road on the right that goes to Peak 2036. a sign nearby states "T.S.P. 4 miles." Continue south on Temescal Fireroad another half mile, leaving the Park property. Almost immediately a road junction appears. The fork on the right is Trailer Canyon Road, and is the way down into Santa Ynez Canyon.

Trailer Canyon Road winds around a lot on the way down to Santa Ynez Canyon and drops 1300'. The road bottoms out in a housing area.

Overlooking Rustic Canyon from Cathedral Rock

Turn right on Michael Lane, following it several hundred yards until reaching a cross street, Vereda De La Montura. Turn right and follow it to the streambed.

A well-used trail goes upstream, gently for awhile, about a mile. There are several caves in the sandstone cliffs on both sides of the stream. a trail forks to the right going up quarry canyon. Stay to the left at this fork and the next one also. The trail follows the west fork of the stream through a dense riparian woodland until it makes an abrupt right turn and goes uphill steeply. Within 100 feet the trail is out of the canyon environment and in chaparral. The trail is steep uphill for an 800' gain in about a mile.

Upon reaching the Eagle Spring Road, turn left and return to the parking lot.

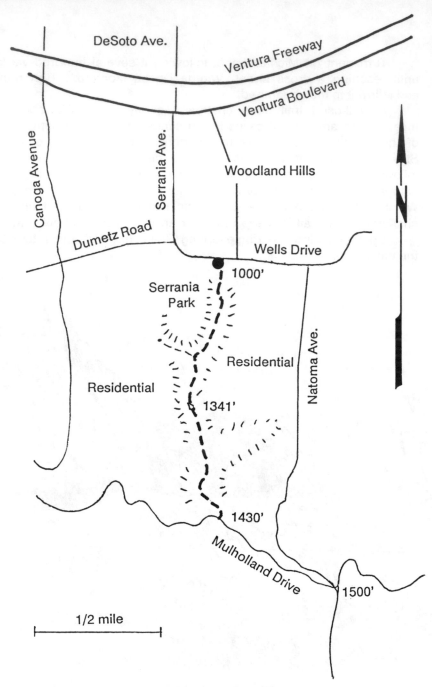

SERRANIA RIDGE

HIKE 49

Maps:	Canoga Park, topo
Distance:	2½ miles roundtrip
Elevation:	500' gain and loss
Terrain:	Road and trail
Time:	1 hour
Trailhead:	Serrania Park

This short hike is suitable for all degrees of hiking ability. It doesn't take you completely away from the city but does give you an opportunity to absorb some of the feeling of open space.

In Woodland Hills drive south of Ventura Blvd. on Serrania to the end to Wells Drive; park on the right.

The hike starts by going south along the ridge at the east side of Serrania Park.

Follow the fence along the east side of the Park until you come to a break. Leave the Park through the hole in the fence and continue south. The initial climb is rather steep, then the trail follows the ridge with some ups and downs. About ten minutes out puts you on a knoll that has a trail coming up from the left. Continue on, until reaching another cross-trail on a ridge. At this point go left, staying on the ridge as it changes direction occasionally, until reaching Mulholland Drive — the turnaround point. The trail splits two times on this section of the ridge, but in both cases rejoins.

After turning around, return the way you came. It is possible to get on the wrong trail coming back so pay close attention going out.

EAGLE SPRING LOOP
by way of Fireroad 30

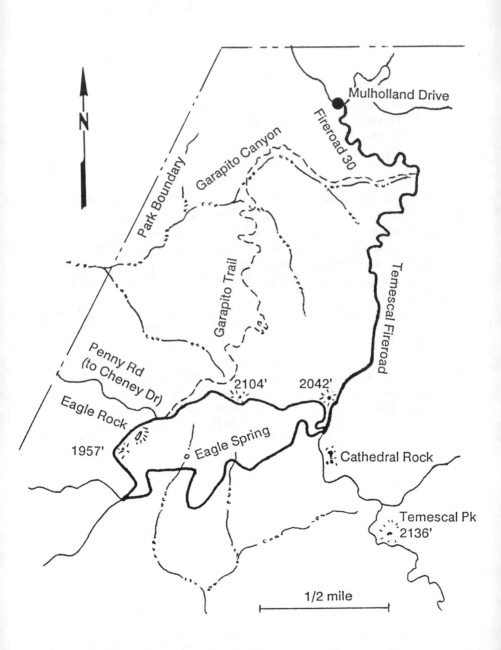

N

Mulholland Drive

Fireroad 30

Park Boundary

Garapito Canyon

Garapito Trail

Temescal Fireroad

Penny Rd
(to Cheney Dr)

2104'

2042'

Eagle Rock

1957'

Eagle Spring

Cathedral Rock

Temescal Pk
2136'

1/2 mile

HIKE 50

EAGLE SPRING LOOP
by way of Fireroad 30
from Mulholland Drive

Maps:	Canoga Park, topo
	Topanga, topo
	Topanga State Park
Distance:	7 miles roundtrip
Elevation:	1000' gain and loss
Terrain:	Fireroad
Time:	2-3/4 hours
Trailhead:	Mulholland Drive

This is a trip in Topanga State Park that is on a fireroad all the way and although steep in a few places is a good introductory hike.

Drive to the beginning of Fireroad 30 on Mulholland Drive. This point is 4.0 miles east from Topanga Canyon Blvd. and 6.4 miles west of the overpass at the San Diego Freeway.

Walk around the fireroad gate south onto Fireroad 30 and go two miles until coming to "Hub Junction," an intersection of four roads. Of the three choices available take the one on the immediate right and go uphill. You will soon be on an east-west ridge that separates Garapito Canyon on the north from Santa Ynez Canyon on the south. On a reasonably clear day you may see Santa Monica Bay and the coast line all the way to Palos Verdes Peninsula. If you have a compass and can use it for sighting, Santa Catalina Island is 180° true (165° magnetic) from the ridge. On the clearest day of the year you might see the rather small Santa Barbara Island and San Nicolas Island farther out.

Continue west along the ridge. Penny Road comes in on the right and is another way of entering Topanga State Park. Just beyond this road but on the left is Eagle Rock, overlooking upper Santa Ynez Canyon. A short side trip will take you to the top of the rock, its sculptured caves, and the impressive view of the valley below.

Continue on the fireroad going downhill until reaching Eagle Spring Junction. Turn left and continue downhill toward Eagle Spring. Eagle Rock looms high overhead, dominating upper Santa

Ynez Canyon with its imposing mass and exposed cliffs. Eagle Spring is announced by two large wooden water storage tanks. (As of this 4th edition, only one tank remains.) The spring itself is upstream a short distance by trail. A pipeline comes down from the spring to the wooden tanks. Enough water leaks out to keep the ground wet. Beautiful patches of Poison Oak thrive in the area. A portable "Andy Gump" restroom is currently alongside the road.

Continue on the fireroad as it contours through the chaparral toward Hub Junction. The elevation gain is moderate, 400 feet in a little more than a mile. As you near Hub Junction you can see a lofty crag on the ridge to the right. "Cathedral Rock" holds a sheltered recess within its protective walls that makes an excellent lunch stop. This is south on the Temescal Fireroad and not on the loop of this hike, but does make an interesting short side trip.

At The Hub go north on Fireroad 30, retracing your steps for the two miles back to the roadhead. The walk is pleasant along this ridge road with the isolation of Rustic Canyon to the east and Garapito Canyon to the west.

Eagle Rock

HIKE 51

Maps:	Canoga Park, topo
	Topanga, topo
Distance:	6½ miles roundtrip
Elevation:	1200' loss and gain
Time:	3 hours
Trailhead:	Mulholland Drive

Garapito Canyon is steep, rugged and beautiful. Sierra Club volunteers began building a trail from Fireroad 30 in 1985 and completed it late in 1987.

Drive 4 miles east of Topanga Canyon Boulevard on Mulholland Drive into the northern part of Topanga State Park, and park on the right without blocking Fireroad 30. Walk around the fireroad. gate and go 1/2 mile to a point where some power lines cross. The trail into upper Garapito Canyon is on the right and begins here. Cross a small meadow then abruptly 'enter dense chaparral. The entire canyon last burned in 1961 and the chaparral has had time to fully recover. Trail building in l985 opened sunlit corridors so that dormant seeds that have lain in the duff since the l961 fire recovery period, could sprout. The spring of 1986 ushered in a riot of Giant Phacelia, Mustard Evening Primrose, Contorted Evening Primrose, White Pincushion, Yellow Monkey Flower, and other fire-following plants along the trail.

In the more than 500 feet of elevation loss, the trail takes us through a lot of Chaparral and occasional patches of Coastal Sage Scrub. Whenever we are near the streambed we will see Sycamores, and at one place several Cottonwoods. Geologically, the streambed and ravines are the Coal Canyon Formation, a marine sequence of sandstone, siltstone, and pebbly conglomerate that was laid down during late Paleocene and Eocene times, 60-50 million years ago. The trail follows side stream channels at times, allowing us the opportunity of getting our feet wet during and after storms. The trail crosses the main streambed, goes up and around a shoulder, and back down to a stretch along the stream to an oak grove. At this point we have walked about 1-3/4 miles from the trailhead — take a

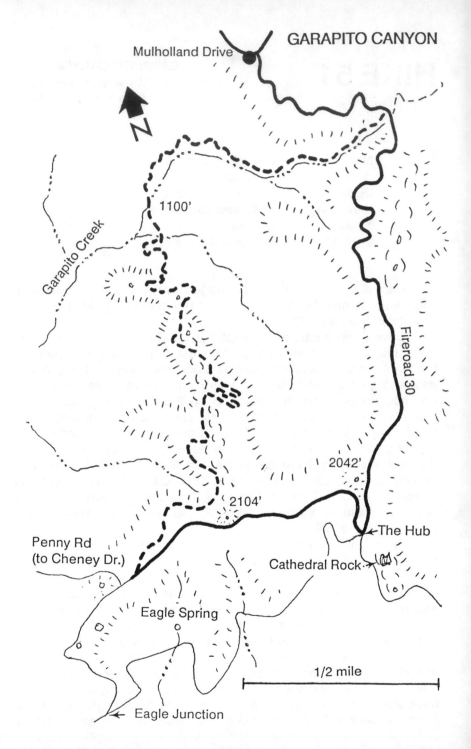

GARAPITO CANYON

Mulholland Drive

1100'

Garapito Creek

Fireroad 30

2042'

2104'

Penny Rd
(to Cheney Dr.)

The Hub

Cathedral Rock

Eagle Spring

1/2 mile

Eagle Junction

rest — we are about to start uphill, gaining 700 feet in the next mile and a half. A massive buttress, or ridge, drops down from Peak 2104 to our present location in the canyon. The trail works its way up the ridge at a comfortable walking grade, making switchbacks as it goes. Along one section of the lower trail we look across an arroyo at a spectacular conglomerate cliff. Later on after a couple of switchbacks, we find ourselves above and near the edge of the cliff. This hike offers lots of excuses to stop and rest. The panorama below unrolls continuously as we climb through the most dense mature Chaparral in the area. (I was going to say "in the world" but that may not be true.) We continue upward and get an idea that the crest is near when we go through some open spaces of California Buckwheat.

Upon reaching Eagle Spring Loop road, turn left. We might elect to go on a short side trip to the top of Eagle Rock from this point. If so we turn right, walk slightly uphill 650 feet, then walk over a rise on the east and climb the backside of Eagle Rock. The view of Santa Ynez Canyon, to the south, and the ocean is dramatic. The fireroad toward Trippet Ranch and East Topanga Fireroad are visible and so is more of the southern half of the Park. Look for Silver Lotus plants in bloom from March through June, growing in cracks in the sandstone of Eagle Rock.

The route out is east to the "Hub," about 1 mile from where Penny Road intersects Eagle Spring Loop road. Enroute we pass the highest point on today's hike near Peak 2104. Look at the road near the peak; the pattern of the rock is caused by the slow cooling of molten lava as it intruded through cracks into the sandstone about 15 million years ago. This lava is called diabase — we've given it the common name "Onion Rock" because it exfoliates concentrically somewhat like an onion would. At the Hub, turn left and walk 2 miles to Mulholland Drive and our cars.

UPPER RUSTIC CANYON
and BAY TREE TRAIL

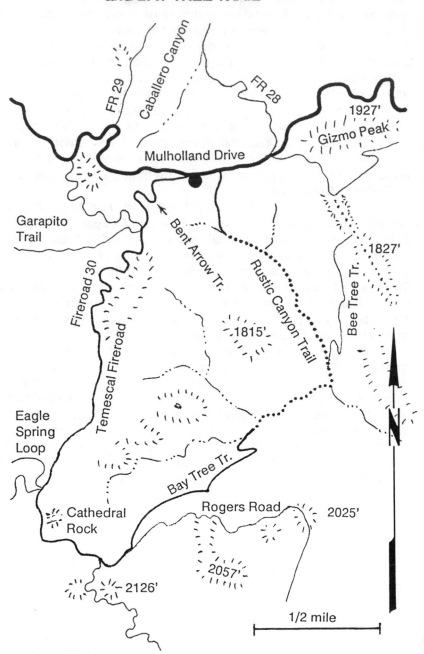

FR 29

Caballero Canyon

FR 28

1927'

Gizmo Peak

Mulholland Drive

Garapito
Trail

Bent Arrow Tr.

Rustic Canyon Trail

1827'

Bee Tree Tr.

Fireroad 30

Temescal Fireroad

1815'

N

Eagle
Spring
Loop

Bay Tree Tr.

Cathedral
Rock

Rogers Road

2025'

2057'

2126'

1/2 mile

HIKE 52

UPPER RUSTIC CANYON
via Rustic Canyon trail,
Bay Tree trail, Rogers
Road, Fireroad 30, and
Bent Arrow Trail from
Mulholland Drive (loop)

Maps:	Canoga Park, topo
	Topanga, topo
Distance:	6 miles roundtrip
Elevation:	1200' loss and gain
Terrain:	Trail, streambed, and
	fireroad
Time:	2-3/4 hours
Trailhead:	Mulholland Drive

This "Rustic Ramble" presents a challenge to your trail finding ability in getting out of the canyon. You should expect to spend some extra time looking for the trail, so it's best to do this hike on a day when you are not on a precise schedule.

The beginning of the hike starts on a trail that leads down from the south side of Mulholland Drive 4.8 miles east of Topanga Canyon Blvd. There is parking space for 3 or 4 cars on the south side of Mulholland Drive at a bend in the road — between Fireroad 28 and Fireroad 29, both of which intersect with Mulholland on the north side.

After parking your car, walk east on Mulholland (about 150 yards) and take the indistinct trail that drops down steeply through the chaparral on the south side of the road. Across the road is a telephone pole with the number 112509M. Upper Rustic Canyon, being rugged and isolated, is seldom visited so you'll be walking along a trail overgrown with brush, and rough spots underfoot.

After about 500 yards of very steep, "brushy" trail you will reach a streambed where you will turn left. Get ready for some boulder hopping. Rustic Canyon is full of rocks that resemble small "blackboard slates," "giant speckled eggs, " some "concrete" rocks, but no "spaghetti" rocks. Also look for tracks made by raccoon, coyote, and deer. Common with most streambed travel in these mountains is the fact that every storm changes the terrain so that last year's sandy trail can be this year's mosaic of boulders. The

213

elevation drop along this intermittent stream is gentle and presents few hazards to travel. Twenty-five minutes after first reaching the stream you will come to another streambed entering from the right. This West Fork is the first major stream joining from the west, and although it is a significant stream it is possible to pass it by because of the trees and brush growing in the canyon.

Turn right and go upstream in the bed of the West Fork for nine minutes. At this point on the left (south) a trail goes up the steep hillside and heads southwest. As the beginning of this trail may be difficult to spot, I'll give my clues. It is about 750 yards from the fork in the stream where you turned right (but seems much farther). You will have passed an overgrown arroyo that enters from the north. The trail shows up soon after we make a right turn coming up the streambed. Two rows of rocks on the left give a hint of the trail and it seems enough. Overshooting is no problem — just come back. A crew of volunteers on maintenance work renamed it the "Bay Tree Trail," and it is justly named.

Follow the trail up through Sycamore, Oak, and Bay. Oh, that Bay!! If you have never experienced the clean pungent smell of fresh Bay leaves, you are due for a treat. Some call it Laurel. In Oregon it is Myrtlewood, but by any name you will long remember the scent of Bay. Take a deep breath because this trail will gain over 800 feet in not much more than a mile, mostly under a verdant canopy of leaves. Soon you will pass a spring — not gushing, but more of a seepage. Once a cup hung on the tree and the water was drinkable, but the cup is gone and leaves have settled into the small basin. We leave the water for coyotes. Later you will discover a sheltered recess that is sanctuary for a trickling stream. The vegetation changes as elevation is gained, and the charm of sylvan enchantment gradually shifts to views of rugged terrain. In fall and winter, dotting the slopes across the canyon are orange-red splashes of Toyon berries on a palette of green chaparral. On the skyline to the west the craggy outline of Cathedral Rock comes into view. Embracing the trail on either side, and adding to its enchantment, are the Holly-leaf Cherries, commonly called Islay. This big-seeded sweet cherry ripens late in the summer along this trail and is a favorite food of the coyotes. It is rare but there is also some Chaparral Currant along this trail. During the summer the Chaparral Currant drops its leaves in order to conserve moisture; but watch what happens a couple of weeks after the first fall rain — look for bare twigs with rose-colored flowers. Thanksgiving is an interesting time of year to be on this trail. The Chaparral Currant is pushing spring — and fall is hardly over.   Now, continue climbing the trail until reaching Rogers Road, then turn right.

As you are heading west on Rogers Road, notice the beginning of Temescal Canyon on the left.   Only a small part of Temescal Canyon is in view, but I mention it because on this hike you will be at the headwaters of five different watersheds: Temescal, Santa Ynez, Garapito — which drains into Topanga — Caballero, and Rustic. After a short uphill walk on Rogers Road the route joins Temescal Fireroad at the crest of the ridge.   You should then turn right and walk north.   A third of a mile northwest on this relatively level fireroad, look to your right for an imposing rock formation. "Cathedral Rock" dominates this part of the ridge and is an ideal lunch stop.   The easiest way is to walk up the steep southwest slope through a gap in the rocks into a sheltered amphitheater that can comfortably hold a group of 25-50 people (if you're very good friends).   The view to the east from this massive hard coarse conglomerate rocky crag is spectacular.   The entire panorama of the first part of the hike is spread out below and the ruggedness of upper Rustic Canyon is impressive.

Now that your hunger has been satisfied, and your pack lightened a bit, continue north on the fireroad and upon reaching Hub Junction go straight ahead toward Mulholland Drive.   The road stays on the ridge separating Garapito Canyon on the west from Rustic Canyon on the east.   After 1½ miles of easy walking, watch for the beginning of the Bent Arrow Trail on the right and follow it around as it contours over to Mulholland Drive and the end of your day's memorable hike.

GEOLOGICAL COMMENT

On this trip there are a variety of geological features that could be of interest to the casual observer as well as to the serious geologist.

With the exception of the first part of the hike coming down to the streambed, all of Upper Rustic Canyon and the trail to the Temescal Fireroad is on Santa Monica slate, a dark-gray to black rock that was formed 150 million years ago during the jurassic epoch.   Subsequent granitic intrusions into the Santa Monica Slate are not in evidence in the canyon but some granite boulders could have eroded from the granitic outcropping just east of Gizmo Peak (Pk 1960).

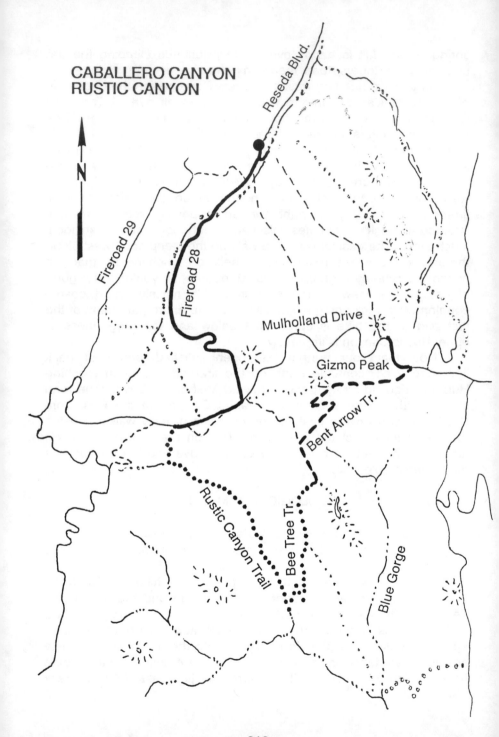

CABALLERO CANYON
RUSTIC CANYON

N

Reseda Blvd.

Fireroad 29

Fireroad 28

Mulholland Drive

Gizmo Peak

Bent Arrow Tr.

Rustic Canyon Trail

Bee Tree Tr.

Blue Gorge

HIKE 53

CABALLERO CANYON
RUSTIC CANYON
from Tarzana (loop)

Maps:	Canoga Park, topo
	Topanga, topo
Distance:	7½ miles roundtrip
Elevation:	1700' gain and loss
Terrain:	Trail, streambed, and
	fireroad
Time:	3½ hours
Trailhead:	Reseda Blvd.

In Tarzana, drive south on Reseda Boulevard nearly to the end and park your car along the street or in a lot. As of 1991 construction is making changes in our parking pattern.

This hike from the San Fernando Valley over the mountains and back is both a good physical and mental workout. There are some steep trails, brush, and streambed travel. Mentally, you will be presented a challenge — first, in finding the way up the ridge out of the valley; second, in locating the trail down into Upper Rustic Canyon; and third, in stumbling on to the trail out of the canyon.

From near the end of Reseda Boulevard walk east, cross the stream and follow the trail south. Upon seeing a steep trail going up a ridge on the left, get into low gear and start uphill.

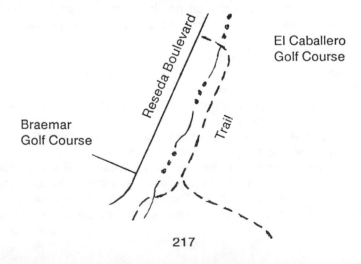

217

The rock underfoot is Modelo shale; the vegetation is Chaparral and Coastal Sage Scrub; the large plants are Black Sage, Purple Sage, Bush Monkey Flower, Chamise, and Scrub Oak. Caballero Ridge Trail is steep, without switchbacks, and only sporadically trimmed so we expect a few hardships. Quite often we are deep in the chaparral and the view is of the trail at our feet, and of the Chamise, Toyon, Ceanothus, and Holly-leaf Cherry on both sides and above. Periodically, breaks in the chaparral allow spectacular views of the San Fernando Valley to the north, Encino Reservoir 3/4 mile east, and the Santa Monicas all around. The trail is steep in places and rocky on occasion; but after one hour we should have gained 900 feet, walked a little more than 2 miles, and have arrived at Mulholland Drive. The trees on the left at the end of the trail are toyon, or "Christmas Berry" or "California Holly" from whence the name Hollywood.

Turn left and walk a couple hundred yards southeast on Mulholland Drive to an area that allows the first glimpse of the Pacific Ocean and the beach. Spectacular as this view is, do not spend much time here because by going west on the fireroad past the fireroad gate (you are now in Topanga State Park) the next 1/2 mile is on the crest of the Santa Monicas with so much scenery in all directions that it's hard to decide where to look.

Walk to the crest of this ridge and descend the south slope on the Bent Arrow Trail, coming out on a firebreak. Travel the south firebreak for about 1/4 mile. On the west side is a trail (Bee Tree Trail) that drops down to the streambed in Rustic Canyon. The trail is easy to find if you know where it is, but difficult to spot otherwise. I use several landmarks: (1) Before coming to the real trail you might notice an old trail on the right that angles down the slope. Don't take it. (2) As you approach, but before you reach a low place along the firebreak with the last high knob up ahead, look for a cleared area on the right. Go to the edge of the clearing and look down into Rustic Canyon. (3) The trail goes straight down from the west edge of this clearing.

The trail is steep, dropping 600 feet in a half mile. Although the chaparral predominates, it gives way somewhat to Oak and Sycamore as the stream is approached. Upon reaching the stream, have lunch in the grassy spot under the oaks.

The next segment of the trip is upstream. There is no trail along the streambed. You will pick your way carefully, avoiding the dense brush areas, occasional downed trees, and Poison Oak now and then. Once more your intuition will be called upon to find the trail that leads up from the streambed. About 20 minutes after leaving the lunchstop you will come upon a small side canyon on the right. Keep your eyes peeled for an obscure trail on the right about 100 feet into this side canyon. It is possible to miss this side canyon entirely; and if you find that you are heading more to the west, and up ahead there is a steep light-colored slide, then you've gone too far. It is also possible to turn into another side canyon below the correct one. A trail does not lead out and any attempt to try to bushwhack would be extremely difficult.

Once on the trail out of the streambed there is a steep, but short, climb to Mulholland Drive, gaining about 300 feet in 500 yards or so.

Upon reaching the road turn right (east), walk a few hundred yards to the fireroad down into Caballero Canyon. This road leads to Reseda Blvd., the end of the hike.

California sycamore

HIKE 54

CABALLERO CANYON
FIREROAD 29
from Tarzana (loop)

Maps:	Canoga Park, topo
	Topanga, topo
Distance:	5 miles roundtrip
Elevation:	850' gain and loss
Terrain:	Fireroad, trail, steep
	washed-out trail
Time:	2 hours
Trailhead:	Reseda Blvd.

NOTE: This hike has appeared in all previous editions of this hiking guide. I have elected to retain it as a hike because when construction is complete on the west ridge, we may still be able to hike the route, but on pavement. Before hiking, ask around to see if the established route down the ridge is still open.

Start the hike by going south on Reseda Blvd. in Tarzana to the end of the pavement, and park your car.

Go through the opening at the fireroad gate and follow the road as it parallels the stream. You are now on Fireroad 28, a 2 mile road that winds up the canyon, ending at Mulholland Drive. Every year the rains wash out about 1/2 mile of this road. The canyon bottom supports the growth of Sycamores and Mulefat, but the chaparral dominates the slopes. Caballero Creek runs full and strong after a rain, but being intermittent, dries up in the summer.

Upon reaching Mulholland Drive turn right, then cross the road picking up the Bent Arrow Trail a few feet to the south of the crest. Follow the trail right as it contours around on the south slope through a dense stand of chaparral, mostly Ceanothus. The trail returns to Mulholland Drive in about 1/3 mile, at which time follow the road as it gains several hundred feet in the next 1/2 mile. At this point Fireroad 29 goes right (north) from Mulholland Drive dropping down along the east Caballero ridge.

Two-hundred yards down the ridge, the road forks right and goes around the east side of the hill, then along a ridge for a ways before passing along the west side of another hill. On top of this hill is a Toyon tree that is one of my candidates for the largest of its kind in the Santa Monicas. Continue on down the road until reaching the upper part of the golf driving range of the Braemar Country Club. This point is one mile from Mulholland Drive.

A trail on the right drops down into Caballero Canyon. This is steep, and rough in places; but within 10 minutes you will reach Fireroad 28. Turn left and return to the trailhead.

An alternate bushwhack trail comes down from Fireroad 29. 8 minutes after leaving Mulholland drive, just as the road passes the first hill on the left, look for the beginning of a trail on the right. The trail cuts aback sharply to the right on a relatively level bench. The route is indistinct for 200 feet then goes straight down to the left — and I do mean down. My guess is that this trail was made by coyotes travelling from the ridge to the stream below. The trail disappears at the bottom so you are on your own to do a few hundred feet to the road.

Caballero Canyon is in the path of subdivision. The wild state of the land may not last.

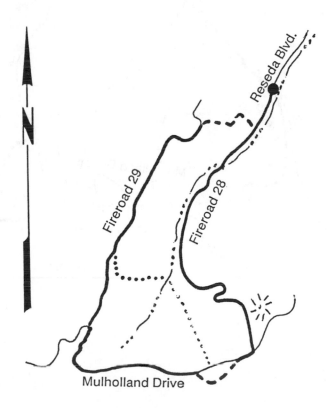

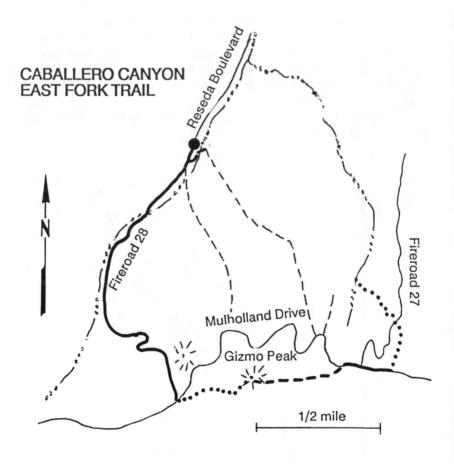

CABALLERO CANYON
EAST FORK TRAIL

Reseda Boulevard

Fireroad 28

Fireroad 27

Mulholland Drive

Gizmo Peak

N

1/2 mile

HIKE 55

Maps:	Canoga Park, topo
Distance:	5 miles roundtrip
Elevation:	1100' gain and loss
Terrain:	Trail, steep firebreak and fireroad
Time:	2+ hours
Trailhead:	Reseda Blvd.

In Tarzana drive south on Reseda Boulevard nearly to the end. Park your car before coming to the Braemar Golf Club entrance. For now this may be somewhere on the street or in a lot when and if provided. Because of construction on both sides of Reseda Blvd., parking is changeable.

From the east side of Reseda Blvd. take the trail across the stream and go south as it parallels the stream. You will see a trail going up a ridge on the left; take it. The East Ridge Trail is steep, the tread is rocky, and in places erosion has made deep gullies. The lower part is exposed because chamise, buckwheat, and sage give little shade. Later we enter chaparral and along some parts of the trail have some shade. This is real uphill — anytime a trail gains nearly 900 feet in 1½ miles you will notice it.

Upon reaching Mulholland Drive, turn left and follow the road until coming to your first glimpse of the ocean. Turn right and head west on the Gizmo Peak ridge. Go around the gate, following the road west for about 1/2 mile until coming to the end of the ridge. A steep firebreak drops 400' in elevation ending at Mulholland Drive. (If the firebreak looks bad to you, an alternate route is available. A few hundred feet back on the ridge, a trail goes south down to the firebreak, crosses it and continues west to Mulholland.) Continue west on Mulholland for 100 yards or so until coming to Fireroad 28 on the right. Go downhill on Fireroad 28, back to the roadhead.

HIKE 56

Maps: Canoga Park, topo
Terrain: Steep trail
Trailhead: Reseda Blvd.

Because of urban expansion on both sides of Caballero Canyon, the hiking community must make some adjustments. Fireroad 29 has disappeared, the old East Ridge Trail has been bulldozed and so has the East Canyon Trail. Caballero Canyon is centrally located on the southern edge of the San Fernando Valley. It is the gateway to the northern entry to Topanga State Park and in time will become an exceptional corridor to the largest urban park in the United States. The loss of three important trails needs alleviation and until such time as a new trail system can be designed and built we must do the best we can to make use of the canyon.

Some trail remnants remain. I'll briefly describe some possible hikes, in addition to those already described. Hike to Mulholland by either the East Ridge Trail or Fireroad 28. Turn left and walk east on Mulholland Drive. (Distances to trails, along the road, are shown in the chart. West to East:

Fireroad 28	to	East Ridge Trail [on north]	1 mile
	to	Fireroad 27 [on north]	1.2 miles
	to	Fireroad 26 [on south]	1.5 miles
	to	San Vicente Park [on south]	2.2 miles
	to	Encino Reservoir Overlook [on north]	2.6 miles

Eighty-five feet east of the East Ridge Trail a trail heads north on a ridge. This spur goes about 1/4 mile then nears the future housing area. The trail ends here.

Fireroad 27 begins at a locked pipe gate and heads north losing altitude all the way. Encino reservoir is in view to the east. A steep trail drops down into the canyon to the left of the road and now ends at the building area. A colony of rabbit-brush (*chrysothamnus nauseosus*) once grew in the canyon bottom but has been eliminated by construction. This was the only known habitat of this plant in the Santa Monica Mountains. The fireroad ends at a locked gate so turn around before then.

The Encino Reservoir Overlook is reached by a trail heading north beyond a locked pipe gate. You can get a good view of the reservoir without leaving Mulholland but a short walk down the trail leads to a level spot. Although the ridge beyond has been bulldozed, it is steep and seriously eroded. You may not want to proceed.

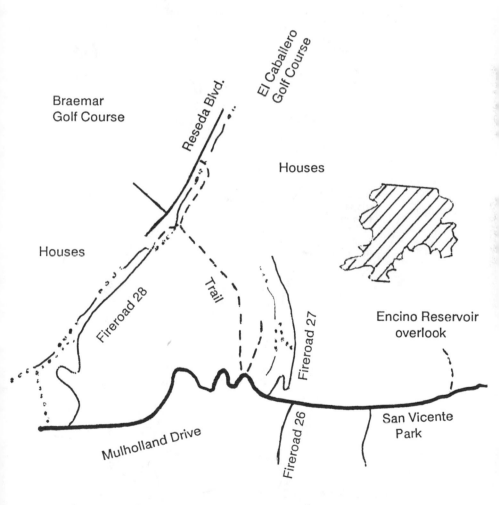

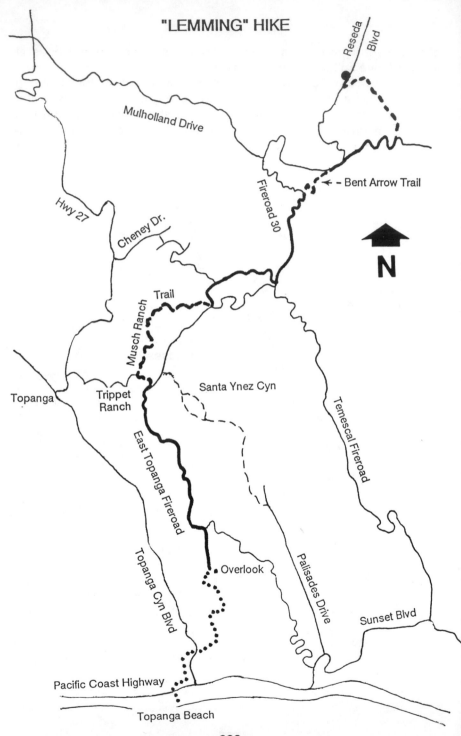

"LEMMING" HIKE

Reseda Blvd

Mulholland Drive

Fireroad 30

← – Bent Arrow Trail

Hwy 27

Cheney Dr.

N

Trail

Musch Ranch

Topanga

Trippet Ranch

Santa Ynez Cyn

Temescal Fireroad

East Topanga Fireroad

Overlook

Palisades Drive

Topanga Cyn Blvd

Sunset Blvd

Pacific Coast Highway

Topanga Beach

HIKE 57

"LEMMING" HIKE
San Fernando Valley to the
ocean via Caballero Canyon,
Bent Arrow Trail, Eagle
Rock, East Topanga Fireroad,
and a chaparral ridge
(shuttle)

Maps:	Canoga Park, topo
	Topanga, topo
Distance:	15 miles one way
Elevation:	2000' gain
	2900' loss
Terrain:	Trail, fireroad,
	streambed, chaparral
	bushwhacking.
Time:	7 hours
Trailhead:	Reseda Blvd.

The concept of a "Lemming hike" is rather lightly based on the lemmings' mad dash to the sea where they swim out and drown. There are no lemmings in the Santa Monicas, but the hike simulates the senseless rush to the sea that lemmings might take, were there any.

Several challenges are presented: finding the way requires close attention to the directions; 15 miles on a variety of terrain requires physical stamina; and dropping down through a dense, virtually impenetrable chaparral while losing 1600 feet of altitude is no picnic. A difficult hike.

This is a one way trip so a car shuttle is necessary. You should leave some transportation at Topanga Beach, where the hike ends. Proceed to the beginning of the hike by crossing the mountains on Highway 27. Upon reaching Ventura Blvd, turn right and drive east into Tarzana; turn right on Reseda Blvd. and travel south to the end where you will park your car.

Walk down the road southeast to the streambed. Turn left and head northwest and 150 yards after crossing the stream start looking for the trail that goes uphill on the ridge. There is some confusion of trails and roads at the beginning, but keep climbing the ridge and eventually they all merge into one trail on the top of the ridge.

This trail is steep and if done briskly will give you a good workout. In about 2 miles and 900' elevation gain you will happily crest out on Mulholland Drive. This trail is often deep in the chaparral which is unusually high on this north facing slope. Chamise, Ceanothus, Holly-leaf Cherry and Toyon are prominent.

Turn right and walk along Mulholland Drive about one mile until arriving at a stretch of the road that allows a clear view, to the left, of upper Rustic Canyon and, on a clear day, a view of the ocean. At this point start looking on your left for the Bent Arrow Trail that in places parallels the road. Take this trail as it turns and contours along the steep south slope of a peak until reaching Fireroad 30, where you should turn left and walk south on the fireroad along an easy grade that gains less than 400 feet in 1½ miles. Garapito Canyon is on the right, Rustic Canyon on the left. About 1/2 mile along the road after leaving the Bent Arrow Trail the road goes through an area of basaltic rock. This is crumbly and not like lava, but was deposited as a result of volcanic activity that began 15½ million years ago. More of this Conejo Volcanic rock will be evident along the East Topanga Fireroad.

Upon reaching Hub Junction, turn sharply to the right and go uphill. This east-west segment of the trip is high on a ridge and affords some spectacular views of Santa Ynez Canyon to the south. The road passes close to Eagle Rock, a mighty sandstone sentinel. A short side trip to the top is well worth the 10 or 15 minute diversion.

The Eagle Rock segment of the road is about 1-1/3 miles long and is joined by the road coming in from Eagle Spring on the left. At this exact point look to the right for the beginning of the Musch Ranch Trail. Take the Musch Ranch Trail down into a canyon on the west. This starts out in an open chaparral area that is recovering from a fire. Down in the canyon the vegetation becomes dense and the trail is in a verdant canopy of shade for much of the way into Trippet Ranch. Trippet Ranch is headquarters for Topanga State Park and offers a picnic area, good drinking water and restrooms. Steady walking will take about 3 hours from the beginning of the hike to this point so if your hike started in the morning this would make a good lunch stop.

Leave the picnic area by going up the road to the south. Upon reaching the "Latitude" (the spot on the road on the crest of the saddle) turn right on East Topanga Fireroad and walk along in the shade of Coast Live Oaks. The road follows along the crest of the ridge east of Topanga Canyon and presents a precipitous view of the angular rock canyon 1000 feet below. Santa Ynez Canyon is on the east side of the ridge and offers a view of massive sandstone slabs tilted on edge down in the canyon next to the stream. The trail leading through Santa Ynez Canyon is visible from above and can be traced through the isolated area. Farther south where the canyon broadens out there is a well-planned community of homes.

Continue south on East Topanga Fireroad until reaching a branch road or firebreak on the right. Take this road to a prominence locally called "The Overlook," aptly described as it overlooks the ocean and the canyons to the south.

It is worthwhile in terms of future comfort and peace of mind to carefully scan the terrain to the south and plan the route, because later when deep in chaparral, your attitude may lack the serenity and composure that is possible now. The route down from this point is on a deer trail that begins at a high point about 100 yards northwest of the Overlook. The route heads 200° magnetic for about 1/4 mile, at which point there is a choice of dropping down to one of the two ridges. Nearly always we turn too soon and find ourselves on an extremely steep slope that drops down to Parker Canyon — a place we want to avoid. Force yourself to continue on the 200° heading and when reaching a somewhat level area look for a trail on the left. By heading 120° magnetic you will drop to the left ridge. Between these two ridges is a canyon that is going to be the exit route to Highway 27 and the sea. There is a semblance of a trail on the left ridge, so head for it and expect to find it at the base of the steepest part of the slope just as the ridge becomes gently sloping. Follow the trail south along the top of the ridge watching very closely for a trail on the right that cuts back sharply and heads down to the creekbed. The trail disappears so we bushwhack. This area has been completely overgrown in the last year or two making it impossible to follow a trail. Getting to the creekbed is a matter of staying on the high part of the small ridge leading to the stream but the chaparral is severe and you are tired. An escape route exists: get back to the north-south ridge where some trail is more or less available, and follow it south to the community of Parker Mesa. A steep down climb will put you on Shoreheights Drive if the hole in the cyclone fence hasn't been repaired. Otherwise you may have a fence climbing chore. Don't go through anyone's yard — the dogs are nervous and the people are sensitive. Continue south to Coastline Drive, turn left and upon reaching Pacific Coast Highway turn right. It's 3/4 mile to the parking lot.

If you don't use the escape route, once in the creekbed continue downstream until reaching Highway 27, then cross the road and head for the beach.

The only rule left for all true "lemmings" is that you must enter the water to some degree. It is not necessary that you go all out and try to swim someplace; you may just take off your boots and wade a little.

Complete the car shuttle — don't leave any stragglers on the beach — and you have completed another great, long day!

HIKE 58

GIZMO PEAK
from Mulholland Drive

Maps:	Canoga Park, topo
Distance:	1 mile roundtrip
Elevation:	100' gain and loss
Terrain:	Fireroad
Time:	30 minutes
Trailhead:	Mulholland Drive

On Mulholland Drive go to a large parking area on the south side, across from Fireroad 27. This is 6.4 miles east of Topanga Canyon Blvd. and 3.8 miles west of the San Diego Freeway overpass.

Walk around the fireroad gate, then west along a one-half mile long ridge. There are steep firebreaks to the west and to the south. The west firebreak leads down to Mulholland Drive in a very steep 400' drop. The south firebreak follows a ridge separating two forks of the stream in upper Rustic Canyon. The Bent Arrow Trail has its beginning below the south crest of the ridge about 300 yards from the west end.

The view from Peak 1927 and Peak 1960 at the far end of the ridge is worthwhile. The San Fernando Valley stretches out to the north and on a clear day or night is really spectacular. Caballero Canyon is below, and on the other side of the ridge to the northeast is Encino Reservoir, a part of the municipal water system. The immediate few south is of Rustic Canyon. Beyond is the ocean, the beach cities, Palos Verdes, and Santa Catalina Island. The view west shows some of Mulholland Drive and part of the Bent Arrow Trail. some exceptional sunsets can be seen from here.

This short side trip can be conveniently taken when driving Mulholland Drive between Sepulveda Blvd. and Topanga Canyon Blvd.

GIZMO PEAK

N

Mulholland Drive

← Topanga Cyn Blvd 6.4 mi.
San Diego Freeway 3.8 mi. →

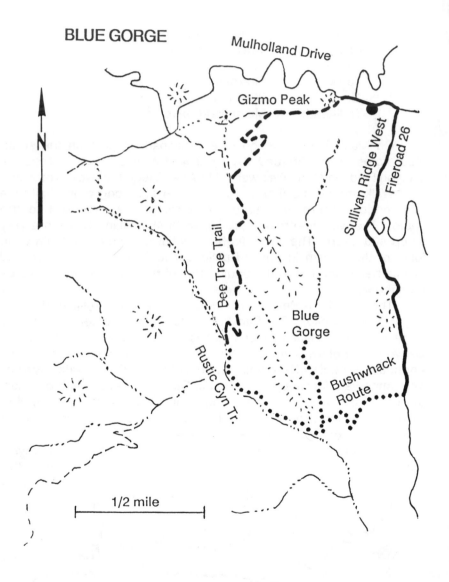

BLUE GORGE

Mulholland Drive

Gizmo Peak

N

Sullivan Ridge West

Fireroad 26

Bee Tree Trail

Blue Gorge

Bushwhack Route

Rustic Cyn Tr.

1/2 mile

HIKE 59

Maps:	Canoga Park, topo
	Topanga, topo
Distance:	5 miles
Elevation:	1250' gain and loss
Terrain:	Fireroad, bushwhack,
	class 2 rock, streambed,
	trail
Time:	3 hours 15 minutes
Trailhead:	Mulholland Drive

This hike presents several challenges: finding the route requires very close observation; the bushwhack down a wild ridge is unnerving; and there is enough Poison Oak to keep you scratching for a week. But Blue Gorge is such a surprise that it could be worth it. The best time for this outing is in the spring, or after a good rain.

This is a loop trip starting at Mulholland Drive just 3.6 miles from the San Diego Freeway overpass. Park along Mulholland somewhere between Fireroad 26 — the start of the hike — and Fireroad 27A — the end of the hike.

Walk around the fireroad gate, at Fireroad 26, south onto Sullivan Ridge west. After 25 minutes of walking, look for a pipeline marker on the right. You will get a good view of the ocean from here. Most of the hike to this point has been on the ridge; the road goes on the east side of a small peak, then around on the west side of the next small peak. Look for the pipeline sign and a ridge dropping down to the west. Follow down the ridge to the west through Deerweed, Buckwheat, and Laurel Sumac. In ten minutes — about a third of the way to the canyon — there is another pipeline sign; the ridge turns 45° left at this point and the route becomes steeper as you go through a plant area of Lupines and Brown Sugar plant. In six or seven minutes the route comes to the end of the clear area and levels off a bit. Turn right and contour north along what could almost be called a trail for seven or eight minutes until reaching some old high chaparral, mostly Sumac, that

233

allows you to go downhill without much trouble. Allow twenty minutes for this part as you want to pick your way carefully, aiming toward descending just on the right flank of the ridge rather than the point. 45 minutes after leaving the road you will be down on the stream — probably you could cut the time in half if you went all-out.

The stream you are on is East Fork. If you happen to come off the ridge at the point or left flank, you would come out onto the mainstream. In any event, go upstream on East Fork, boulder hopping along for about ten minutes and prepare yourself for Blue Gorge. The stream becomes steeper with small rapids swirling around the rocks. The canyon narrows to about fifteen feet. You easily climb over a three foot waterfall, continuing another one hundred feet when almost suddenly, a dark blue-gray, thirty-foot-high rock wall appears ahead. Your feet may get wet, but the lower five foot waterfall that blocks the narrow entry to the gorge can be climbed. You are then in a narrow flat area about fifteen feet long with another five foot waterfall ahead. Above you the gorge narrows to four feet in one place but is generally six to eight feet wide.

Moss and ferns grow from the walls. A part of the rock on the east side is covered with a layer of limestone that has percolated down and changed the dark shiny stone to a light textured pattern. The blue-gray base rock is the oldest geological formation in the mountains. Santa Monica Slate was formed 150 million years ago when this area was under water. The dark rocks are water-worn and smooth; many small grotto like caves have been carved in the walls giving a never ending change to the pattern. There is a particular quality of cool serenity about this place. In a way I am glad that there is some difficulty reaching it.

Overhead, with roots in solid rock, grow a half dozen Maple trees — one with a diameter of more than twenty-four inches. The leaves are 5-lobed, and some are nearly a foot wide; the winged seeds start development early in spring and drop in the fall with some hanging on into winter after the leaves have fallen. Big Leaf Maples in a verdant microcosm, surrounded by chaparral — it's unbelievable!!!

Climb the next waterfall and the gorge widens. Three waterfalls, each about one and a half feet high, with pools at their base are in immediate view. Bay trees shade the stream and Humboldt Lilies are plentiful and bloom in June. This is indeed a beautiful place.

Leave the area by going back downstream until reaching the center fork — about 10 minutes of walking — then turn right and go upstream. Fifteen minutes after starting up the Center Fork a stream enters from the left and ahead. Don't take the West Fork, but angle right and continue along the Center Fork for another eight minutes at which time you look very diligently for an almost invisible trail — the Bee Tree Trail — on your right. There is an old Oak on each side of the stream just below the trail (the Oak on our right has recently fallen across the streambed requiring us to stoop as we go under. The beehive is still in the tree so don't thump the log); then a curving Sycamore, broken off at about 20 feet, that is on your left; and just upstream is a dead Oak snag — how long this will stand is unknown. don't expect to see any cairn of rocks or other sign. Now that you have found the way, let the next hiker have the same sense of accomplishment .

The upward trail is steep enough, and gains 650' elevation in less than one half mile. There are some truly enchanting stretches of the path where high chaparral completely covers overhead and you get the feeling of being in an airy tunnel. Most of the trail is through open chaparral however, and good views of the canyon below are available. About two thirds of the way up, the trail levels off on a ridge for a short distance; at this point a faint trail on the right goes south on the ridge. Don't take it, but continue north, downhill briefly before making a turn to the right and head for the firebreak. The trail crests out on the firebreak that comes south from Gizmo Peak.

Follow the firebreak north over four small bumps, and just before the firebreak goes steeply up to Gizmo Peak look right for a segment of the Bent Arrow Trail. Take it, and upon reaching the top continue east to Mulholland Drive where you left the car.

Big-Leaf Maple

Blue Gorge

235

HIKE 60

SULLIVAN CANYON
and West Ridge from
Mulholland Drive (loop)

Maps:	Canoga Park, topo
	Topanga, topo
Distance:	9 miles
Elevation:	1300' gain and loss
Terrain:	Fireroad, streambed and
	some trail
Time:	4 hours
Trailhead:	Mulholland Drive

The trailhead is on Mulholland Drive at Fireroad 26 — 3.6 miles west of the San Diego Freeway.

This hike offers several options: (1) Sullivan Canyon and return; (2) Sullivan Canyon then up to Sullivan Ridge; and (3) Sullivan Ridge West then down the trail to the Canyon and return by way of the canyon. I will describe the canyon route and give clues on modifying the hike to take in the other options.

Walk around the fireroad gate and south on an almost level road. One-half mile from the trailhead a side road on the left leads down into upper Sullivan Canyon. Take this road past a gate and a couple of switchbacks, quickly losing 300 feet, then another 300 feet more gradually. The vegetation in this part of Sullivan Canyon and the ridges is chaparral, but upon reaching the bed of the stream you enter a riparian woodland that continues all the way to the effective end of the canyon in Brentwood.

You will pass a Eucalyptus tree on the right, and a number of smaller seedlings nearby. This is a good landmark, as it indicates almost two miles from the trailhead, and is a convenient turnaround point for a short hike. The floods of early 1980 wiped-out most of the road downstream and soon you will be walking on the gravel streambed. Sullivan Creek is an intermittent stream cycling from a torrent that sweeps the entire floor of the canyon, to a trickle that surfaces   only on occasion. Each year the trail pattern changes, depending on the effects of the floods.

About 2½ miles downstream from the eucalyptus tree, look for a trail that goes up the slope to the west of the stream. Because a lot of hikers like to keep the mountains in an untouched state, you may not find a sign or pile of rocks to show where the trail is. I recognize the area by looking for a number of natural markers. Out in the gravel bed of the stream are two trunks of Oaks leaning northwest. One trunk has a scar around it as though many years ago some barbed wire was wrapped around and never removed. There is a small arroyo across the stream on the east, and some Sycamores nearby with broken tops; two are upstream on the same side as the trail. There is also an island Oak nearby; that is, an Oak out in the streambed with a lot of gravel piled up around it. Look for the beginning of the trail on the west side, at a point where you can see all these natural features. If you don't find the trail, continue downstream a short distance to Queensferry Rd, then return the way you came.

If you do find the trail and would like to make a loop out of the hike and return by way of Sullivan Ridge West, go up the trail to the ridge, a 200 ft. gain in ten to fifteen minutes. Upon reaching the road (paved at this point) turn right and go north, passing by the entrance to Camp Josepho on the left. By staying on the ridge road, you will return to your car.

Option #3 is to do the reverse and go down the ridge first then up the canyon. Finding the short trail to the canyon may be a small challenge. Go 1/3 mile south beyond the Camp Josepho Road along the ridge road. You will pass under some telephone wires and go around a bend in the road to the right. One of the poles on the left is numbered 43975. Continue a few hundred feet farther and look for the start of the trail on the left. This trail takes you to the stream, then go upstream to the trailhead. This option allows another variant. Upstream from the Eucalyptus tree, 15 or 20 minutes, the road makes a "U" turn left. At this point a branch road on the right leads to a steep trail to Mulholland Drive — 250 yards east of where you left your car.

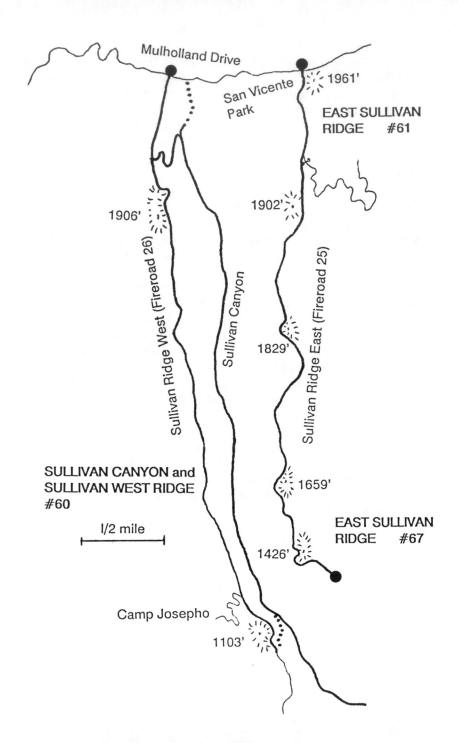

Mulholland Drive

San Vicente Park

1961'

EAST SULLIVAN
RIDGE   #61

1906'

1902'

Sullivan Ridge West (Fireroad 26)

Sullivan Canyon

Sullivan Ridge East (Fireroad 25)

1829'

**SULLIVAN CANYON and
SULLIVAN WEST RIDGE
#60**

1659'

1/2 mile

**EAST SULLIVAN
RIDGE   #67**

1426'

Camp Josepho

1103'

HIKE 61

EAST SULLIVAN RIDGE ROAD
(Fireroad 25)
from Mulholland Drive

Maps:	Topanga, topo
	Canoga Park, topo
Distance:	6½ miles
Elevation:	1050' loss and gain
Terrain:	Fireroad
Time:	2½ hours
Trailhead:	Mulholland Drive

San Vicente Mountain Park is the site of a former Nike missile base and is now a Los Angeles city park. Great views of the Los Angeles Basin and the San Fernando Valley are available from several knolls.

This hike is over the same terrain as we cover on hike 67. The difference is that we begin at the north end of Fireroad 25 rather than the south end. Another difference is, we will come uphill at the end of this hike.

Reach the trailhead by driving 7½ miles east of Topanga Canyon Blvd (State Hwy 27) on Mulholland Drive, or 2-3/4 miles west of the Mulholland overpass at the San Diego Freeway. Fireroad 25 begins on the south side of Mulholland.

Walk around the gate and head south along the road. On the left, one-half mile from the start, a Department of Water and Power service road drops down to Mandeville Canyon. (On the right, a bushwhack route enters the upper part of Sullivan Canyon and makes it possible to intersect the trail so as to get to Fireroad 26, making about a 3½ mile loop trip. I would do this only after hiking the rest of the available trails.) Continue south on the road, actually gaining some altitude for awhile. We will have walked 2½ miles before the road makes a serious move to lose altitude, and we might elect to shorten the hike at this point if the temperature is high. The turnaround point is at the gate near paved roads.

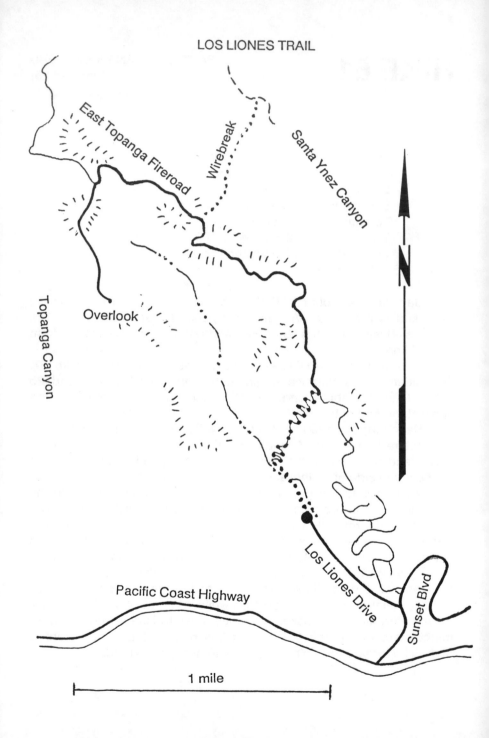

LOS LIONES TRAIL

HIKE 62

Map:	Topanga, topo
Distance:	6 miles roundtrip
Elevation:	1500' gain and loss
Terrain:	Trail and fireroad
Time:	3 hours
Trailhead:	Los Liones Drive

Los Liones Canyon is a rugged, steep sloped, secluded area near civilization yet apart from the urban scene. A hiking trail in this part of Topanga State Park is welcome.

Drive east .3 mile on Sunset Blvd. from the Pacific Coast Highway to Los Liones Drive and turn left. Park at the end of the street in a small parking area, avoiding the Church parking lot. Go around the fence to the left by the Lemonade Berry bush and follow the trail north along the intermittent stream. About 300 yards from the trailhead we make an abrupt turn right and go up steeply. The trail makes many switchbacks through chaparral and temporarily levels out on a mesa after gaining 300 feet. After this brief respite we go into a Bigpod Ceanothus forest and gain another 400 feet as the trail makes countless switchbacks up the steep hillside. Abruptly, the East Topanga Fireroad nears and we turn left and follow it uphill. The road continues uphill until easing up in about two-thirds of a mile and a 500 foot gain. About 20 minutes later we look for a trail that follows the top of a ridge heading south. One half mile along the ridge brings us to the "Overlook," an area with a great view of the ocean and the seacoast. Palos Verdes Penninsula and Catalina Island are visible on clear days.

The 1973 Trippet fire burned the slope south of the Overlook and for a few years a passable route went down the south ridge, but the chaparral has recovered so that the route is not in use.

Return the way we came but take the time to look west into Topanga Canyon and the 1300 foot drop to the stream. One-half mile along East Topanga Fireroad we can look left down the "Wirebreak" and see Santa Ynez Canyon.

This hike has some steep sections of trail that give most of us a good workout — but I have seen people run it.

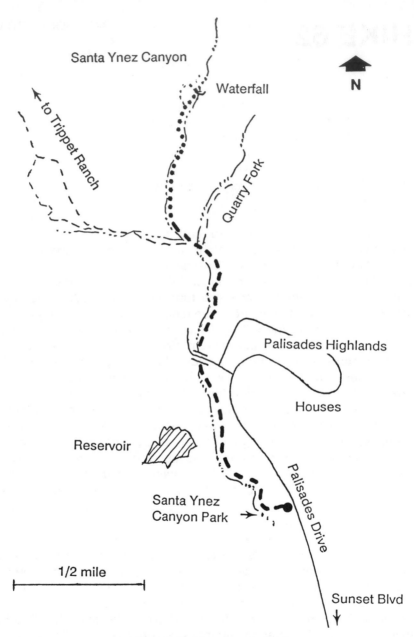

Santa Ynez Canyon

Waterfall

N

to Trippet Ranch

Quarry Fork

Palisades Highlands

Houses

Reservoir

Palisades Drive

Santa Ynez
Canyon Park

1/2 mile

Sunset Blvd

SANTA YNEZ WATERFALLS
from Santa Ynez Canyon Park

HIKE 63

SANTA YNEZ WATERFALLS
from Santa Ynez Canyon Park

Maps:	Topanga, topo
	Topanga State Park Map
Distance:	4 miles roundtrip
Elevation:	300' gain and loss
Terrain:	Trail and Boulder
	hopping
Time:	2½ hours
Trailhead:	Palisades Drive

This is not a strenuous trip at all unless you elect to climb up the waterfalls in the canyon. The footing can be difficult because the winter rains wipe out trails and bring down small trees and brush.

The trailhead is reached from Sunset Blvd. Turn north on Palisades Drive (.3 mile from Pacific Coast Highway), and in 1-3/4 miles a sign on the left indicates entry to Santa Ynez State Park. Park outside and walk in, reaching the stream in a minute or two.

Walk upstream, initially staying on a trail that follows along the east bank. Later on, the trail crosses and recrosses the stream many times, and even loses its identity as a trail on occasion. When in doubt, use the stream as a guide. 1/2 mile from the trailhead you walk through a cement culvert, then past a cement apron water drainage on the right and continue the gentle upstream walk.

The canyon narrows, and some cliff forming sandstone rock becomes prominent on both sides of the stream. Caves, or rockshelters, can be seen near stream level as well as higher on the cliffs. An intermittent stream comes down steeply from the right. At that point, and for 100 feet, there is a limestone outcropping along the trail and showing in the stream.

Continue upstream and you soon come to a gate. Immediately beyond the gate is a fork in the stream and the trail. Take the left fork as the right fork goes to Quarry Canyon. Before crossing the stream notice a large sandstone rock that has a mortar hole on the top side. The size and shape indicate that this was used by the

Indians for grinding acorns. Cross the stream and continue 100 yards, reaching another fork in the trail. This time, turn right, cross the stream, and follow the north fork upstream. An old Cabin Site is on the point of land between the streams above their junction. Two stone chimneys about 30 feet apart are all that remain of the buildings. Trees have grown up into what was once the building and have all but completely hidden the chimneys. The vegetation is so thick that there is some difficulty getting to the area. Part of the vegetation is Poison Oak; and to further dissuade careless exploration, there is a resident rattler (as of May 1980) on the indistinct trail leading to the site.

Twenty minutes on the north fork of boulder hopping and some trail, takes you through a lot of Poison Oak, Ferns, Humboldt Lilies and water-loving plants. Look for Pacific tree-frogs on overcast, cool days, or in sheltered places; tadpoles can be found in April and May. When hearing the "kreck-eck" of the Pacific tree-frog you

Rock Shelter in Lower Santa Ynez Canyon

might expect to see a large animal, if measured by the sound volume; but look for a 1½ inch long frog that blends with the surroundings and is not likely to be close to a tree. Also notice the characteristic black stripe that runs from the nostril to behind the eye.

The canyon walls become steep and rugged, the stream narrows, and you feel that the waterfalls are close. Several small falls come first, and you are challenged in climbing up some rock; then around to the right of a turn in the canyon is a beautiful, twelve foot waterfall. Occasionally climbers with ropes will continue farther and even go to the source of the stream at Eagle Spring; but this is the turnaround point of this hike because of the difficult rock climbing.

Return the way you came, and remind yourself to come back again at the tail end of a good rainstorm for a real spectacle.

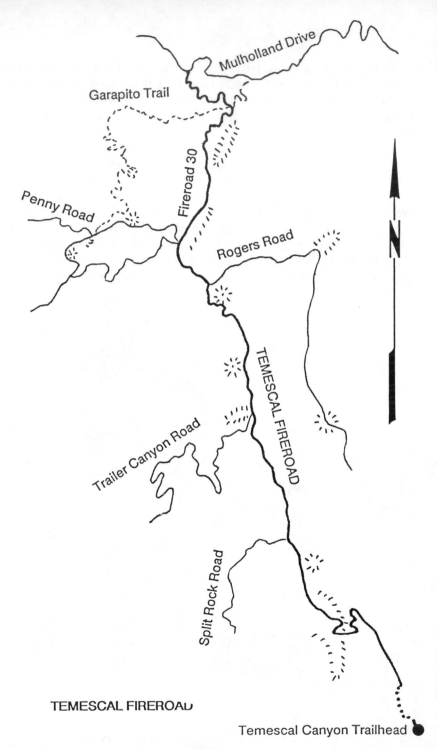

Mulholland Drive

Garapito Trail

Penny Road

Fireroad 30

Rogers Road

N

TEMESCAL FIREROAD

Trailer Canyon Road

Split Rock Road

TEMESCAL FIREROAD

Temescal Canyon Trailhead

HIKE 64

Maps:	Topanga, topo
	Canoga Park, topo
Distance:	17.5 mi. roundtrip
Elevation:	3300 ft. gain and loss
Terrain:	Fireroad
Time:	8 hours including lunch
Trailhead:	Temescal Canyon

This hike starts at the Presbyterian Conference Center on Temescal Road in Pacific Palisades, goes to Mulholland Drive, and back by way of Fireroad 30. The Conference Center and some of the ridge are private property, so the use of this trail is subject to conditions determined by the owners. As of this writing, conditions that are suitable in the Park are acceptable in the private area. Watch for any posted notices and comply with them. Because you go and return by the same route, you have the option of turning around short of the destination or of arranging a car shuttle at the north end. The hike crosses Topanga State Park in a south to north direction by use of a dominant ridge. Excellent views are presented of Santa Ynez, Temescal, Rustic, and Garapito Canyons. The San Fernando Valley can be seen from the north end of the hike and the Los Angeles Basin from the south. This route clearly shows the expanse of wildland that exists within the city.

Sign in on the roster at the entrance to the Center, and walk along the road about 100 feet beyond the gate, and take a trail on the left to go uphill. The route parallels the stream far enough away so as to avoid the housing area. Once beyond the last house the trail drops down to follow the creekbed upstream along a washed-out road then climbs through the narrow gorge of the canyon. The gorge offers some interesting features: a thin waterfall called "The Drip," on the east side of the trail could become serious after a rainstorm; cliff forming conglomerate rock adds a rugged accent to the steep canyon walls; and Temescal Creek cascades down a narrow gorge.

The trail crosses the stream where a wooden bridge once spanned the 15 to 20 foot distance from bank to bank. The Mandeville fire of 1978 came through Temescal Canyon and burned the bridge, so now you must use your own resources to get to the other side. The trail crosses the stream, makes a switchback to the left as it goes steeply up the wall of the canyon, then tops out on a ridge going northwest. The fireroad stays near the crest of the ridge, gaining altitude moderately. Upper Temescal Canyon to the east is totally undeveloped, whereas both Pulga Canyon and Santa Ynez Canyon to the west show building activity. This part of the hike was in the path of the 1978 Mandeville fire and was completely blackened. The recovery by resprouting chaparral and flowering plants is striking, and few signs of the fire are evident.

Split Rock Road comes in on the left, and about 1 mile farther north, Trailer Canyon Road comes up from Santa Ynez Canyon. A microwave facility, locally called "Radio Peak," is about half way between the two points. The route continues north on a reasonably level grade, intersecting with Rogers Road about 1½ miles beyond the Trailer Canyon intersection. The highest point in Topanga State Park, Temescal Peak (2126)', is near the intersection and may be climbed by a short but steep firebreak for a good view of the head of Temescal Canyon and of Rustic and Santa Ynez Canyons.

Continue north on the fireroad, which is a segment of the Backbone Trail at this point, passing Cathedral Rock in 1/2 mile, then on to Hub Junction — a four-way intersection. The left road goes to Trippet Ranch by way of Eagle Spring; the next left road goes to Trippet Ranch by way of Eagle Rock, and the road straight ahead is a continuation of Fireroad 30, the route of this hike. One-and-a-half miles from the Hub, the Bent Arrow Trail has its beginning by clinging to the wall of Upper Rustic Canyon and working its way east, eventually to parallel Mulholland Drive. On the west, opposite the Bent Arrow Trail, look for the beginning of Garapito Trail.

You have:
-- just walked through a wilderness area — all within the city limits — and probably have met other hikers and some animals but not many distractions.
-- earned the beauties of the recesses of the Park by hard physical work; and must feel a sense of accomplishment that few others do.
-- should be tired. Unless a car shuttle has been set up, turn around and walk the 8-3/4 miles back.

HIKE 65

Maps: Canoga Park, topo
Topanga, topo
Distance: 9½ miles roundtrip
Elevation: 1250' gain and loss
Terrain: Road and gravel streambed
Time: 4 hours 15 minutes
Trailhead: Queensferry Road

In Brentwood go 2.3 miles west of the San Diego Freeway on Sunset Blvd. Turn north onto Mandeville Canyon Road for 0.3 mile to Westridge Road, turn left and follow the twists and turns for 1.1 miles turning left at Bayliss Road, then 0.3 mile to Queensferry Road, turn left and park. The trail is on a private road and presently posted "No trespassing."

This hike is along the floor of a narrow steep-walled canyon. During the heavy flood stage, water covers the entire floor and distributes a large amount of 150 million year old gravel (called Santa Monica Slate) rather indiscriminately along the entire area. The floods of early 1980 eliminated most of the road and trails in the canyon, restoring it to a near pristine state.

Pick your way along the bottom of the canyon as it very gently ascends to the north. You will cross the stream many times — this will be of concern only early in the year when the water is high. As soon as summer arrives, the surface water disappears but the stream continues to flow down in the gravel several feet below.

The floor of the canyon is shaded with Sycamore trees, Coast Live Oaks, Walnuts, and other moisture-loving trees. A wide variety of native wild flowers, some grasses, and small shrubs including Poison Oak are found here. Both sides, up from the canyon floor, are covered with chaparral. A fire early in 1978 burned the slopes and ridges except at the head of the canyon, but the chaparral recovered immediately by rootsprouting and new lush plant growth.

Two pipelines run down the valley floor, usually covered from view but sometimes exposed by flood waters. Remnants of a dirt service road exist for a short distance on the east slope a hundred

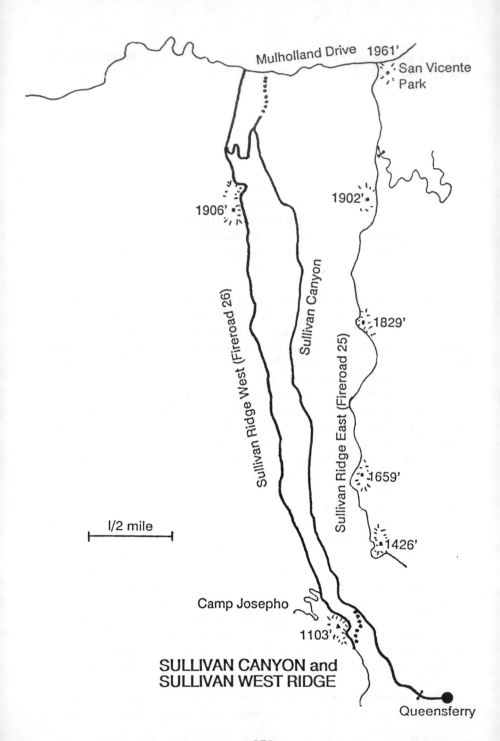

Mulholland Drive 1961'

San Vicente
Park

1906'

1902'

Sullivan Canyon

Sullivan Ridge West (Fireroad 26)

Sullivan Ridge East (Fireroad 25)

1829'

1659'

1426'

1/2 mile

Camp Josepho

1103'

**SULLIVAN CANYON and
SULLIVAN WEST RIDGE**

Queensferry

feet or so up. Trails go to both ridges but are presently overgrown and difficult to locate from below. Only one is in good condition, going to the west ridge.

The canyon floor continuously presents shady rest spots without many significant landmarks. About 1½ miles from the trailhead there is a 6' waterfall on the east side. This dries up early, but is clear cool water in the spring. Occasional outcroppings of the Santa Monica Slate bedrock can be seen on both sides of the canyon. The blue-gray color is sometimes covered by a layer of limonite that was deposited by percolating waters along joints and bedding planes. This brown color is deceptive because it makes the slate difficult to recognize. Farther up the canyon a tall Eucalyptus tree on the left makes a good landmark. It has reseeded and now some smaller ones are growing. This point is about 3 miles from the trailhead and is often used as a turnaround point for a shorter hike, as the trail becomes steeper from here on.

Continuing up the stream, you will be on an old road that is high enough above the stream to avoid being washed out. In about a half mile, a road forks to the right and dead-ends into a steep trail going up through the chaparral to Mulholland Drive. I prefer the left fork, staying on the road until reaching the fireroad on the ridge. Turn right and follow this to Mulholland.

The return trip presents two options: you may go back the same way you came or go back by way of the Sullivan Ridge Road West (Fireroad 26). The fireroad stays high on the ridge and goes south without many turns. It's best to pick a cool day for this trip as little shade exists except for a small clump of Oaks about half way.

A little over 3 miles from Mulholland a road goes downhill on the right to Camp Josepho. Stay on the ridge and one third mile farther a trail on the left leads down to the floor of Sullivan Canyon. Watch closely for the start of this trail as it is not marked. While still on the road, you pass under some telephone wires and go around a bend to the right; look to your left. A pole with the number 43975 is a good indicator. Go a few hundred feet farther to find the trail, overgrown and steep. In 15 minutes you reach the streambed and turn right. It is one-half mile to the end of the hike.

HIKE 66

Maps:	Topanga, topo
	Will Rogers State Park
Distance:	5½ miles
Elevation:	1300'gain and loss
Terrain:	Trail, very steep with poor
	footing at times
Time:	2½ hours
Trailhead:	Will Rogers S.H.P.

This hike combines exercise with a bit of nostalgia. Will Rogers bought the ranch in 1922 and it became a state park in 1944. The house and grounds are preserved as they were. Although Will was astride a horse when he travelled these trails I believe no one had a closer feel for this land.

Reach the trailhead by driving north on Will Rogers State Park Road from Sunset Blvd 4.6 miles from the Pacific Coast Hwy in Pacific Palisades. A fee is charged for parking. If you come by RTD bus, get off at the Evans Rd stop on Sunset Blvd. A trail leads into the Park.

Hike north along the trail near the tennis courts west of Park Headquarters. The trail goes uphill onto the ridge overlooking Rivas Canyon and passes close to Inspiration Point, then forks left beginning a steady uphill climb.

The trail is steep in places, and rocky. Shade is rare so wind and sun play an important part in your comfort. The ridge you are on separates Rustic Canyon on the east from Rivas Canyon on the west; as you go higher, the canyon views and the ocean scene are spectacular. The trail levels out comfortably on top with some slight up and down as you go from one little peak to another. A trail breaks right and goes to the floor of Rustic Canyon. Farther on, as you start up a slight rise, a trail angles off to the left into Rivas Canyon. Take this trail and follow along the east slope of the canyon. Staying on this road takes you to the head of Rivas Canyon and the saddle overlooking Rustic Canyon. This is the turnaround point of the hike. A 4-trunked Oak tree provides a sheltered spot to rest and relax. Rogers Road leaves this point going north toward Trippet Ranch and deeper into Topanga State Park.

Return to Will Rogers State Park by picking up the ridge trail east of the point where you came up the road. There will be a few short uphill stretches, but it is mostly downhill to the parking lot.

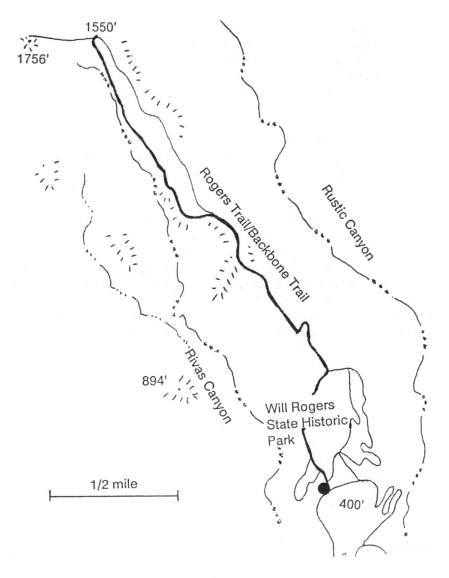

1550'

1756'

Rogers Trail/Backbone Trail

Rustic Canyon

Rivas Canyon

894'

Will Rogers State Historic Park

1/2 mile

400'

HIKE 67

Maps:	Topanga, topo
	Canoga Park, topo
Distance:	6½ miles roundtrip
Elevation:	1050' gain and loss
Terrain:	Fireroad
Time:	2½ hours
Trailhead:	Westridge Road

In Brentwood from the corner of Sunset Blvd. and Mandeville Canyon Road go north on Mandeville 3/10 mile to Westridge Road. Turn left and follow Westridge to the end of the road at the locked gate. This is a residential area and the only parking available is on the street.

Walk around the gate onto the dirt road that heads north along the ridge. This is Fireroad 25 and stays close to the ridge between Mandeville Canyon on the east and Sullivan Canyon on the west.

The altitude gain is moderate and the footing good. The view to the west into Sullivan Canyon is rugged and impressive. The floor of the canyon is 750' below the trail, making the trail down in the canyon look narrow. Sullivan Ridge is a favorite evening hike. Some spectacular sunsets are seen over the ridge to the west. In the summer, late afternoon is a lot cooler on this shadeless ridge.

Farther along the ridge the road follows the eastern edge of the crest giving a good view of Mandeville Canyon on the east. The floor of the canyon here is also 700-800 feet below the trail. A number of homes have been built in this narrow canyon.

The fireroad comes to an inactive military installation near San Vicente Mountain, now a city park. By taking the road turning left at the gate and climbing a short distance to the top of the knoll, a magnificent view of the San Fernando Valley and the Los Angeles Basin spreads before you.

Return the same way you came.

(This hike is the same as Hike #61 — in reverse.)

HIKE 68

Maps:	Canoga Park, topo
	Topanga, topo
Distance:	10½ miles roundtrip
Elevation:	2100' gain and loss
Terrain:	Gravel streambed, road, trail, chaparral, bush-whack, and class 2 rock climbing
Time:	8 hours incl. lunch and side trips
Trailhead:	Queensferry Road

This trip is difficult, requiring hiking experience and some climbing ability. The route finding is involved — it is best done in a group led by someone that knows the terrain. The route crosses Boy Scout property at Camp Josepho. Prior permission is required.

Arrive at the start of the hike by driving 0.7 mile west of the San Diego Freeway on Sunset Blvd. Turn north onto Mandeville Canyon Road for 0.3 mile to Westridge Road, turn left and follow the twists and turns for 1.1 miles turning left at Bayliss Road, then 0.3 mile to Queensferry Road, turn left and park.

Walk north along the floor of Sullivan Canyon for about 3 miles, passing a Eucalyptus tree. Depending on storm damage, there should be a road at this point that goes north, becoming steeper as the head of the canyon is reached. The road makes a climbing U-turn to the left then swings right and intersects the Sullivan Ridge Road west (Fireroad 26). Turn right and continue to Mulholland Drive. If on schedule you are now 2¼ hours out from the trailhead.

Turn left on Mulholland and walk 1/4 mile, coming to Fireroad 27A, on the left. Go around the gate and follow the fireroad 1/3 mile west along the Gizmo Peak ridge until coming to the Bent Arrow Trail on the left. The trail makes a couple of switchbacks coming out on the firebreak south of the peak. Travel the firebreak about 1/2 mile until coming to a trail on the right. This trail is difficult to spot. Look for a cleared area that extends west of the firebreak. This precedes the low place before the last knob on the ridge. Go to the edge of the clearing and drop straight down a trail to the west. After losing 250 feet of altitude we make a turn left and head south. Stay with the trail until it turns right and drops down to the center fork. Get off the trail and continue following the ridge. At least two rattlers reside in the area and might be obscured by the heavy low buckwheat brush, so exercise more than usual care.

Drop down the south point of the ridge through light chaparral, losing 500 feet. You will reach the stream in an Oak shaded lunch spot about 3½ hours after leaving the trailhead.

After lunch there is an optional side trip. The ridge that you came down separates the main fork of Rustic Creek and the east fork. Take a 35 minute roundtrip up the east fork to "Blue Gorge." This broad canyon soon begins to narrow and after ten minutes of walking you will enter the gorge.

Water, running through the east fork for centuries, has carved a narrow canyon through the blue-black rock. Blue Gorge is a rare little world set aside to be witnessed by only the hardy and daring. You sense the adventure that lies ahead while walking upstream. Suddenly a massive smooth rock grotto 30 feet high confronts you. A five foot waterfall spills into a pool at your feet. Upon closer approach you see that the appearance of a cave is deceptive because the narrow passage turns as it comes through the rock. Climb to the top of the waterfall and you are in a cool microscene of smooth rocks, waterfalls, Humboldt Lilies, Moss, Ferns, Bay and Maple Trees overhead. It is difficult to believe that 100 feet up the mountain is a stand of tough chaparral.

Upon leaving the lunch area, head downstream. Ideally the route follows the stream to Camp Josepho, then up the road to Sullivan Ridge; but unless permission has been obtained to cross the Boy Scout property, an alternate route must be used. (a) The point of a ridge comes down to the stream below the east fork entry. This slope is steep at the bottom but becomes gentler after about 200' gain. It is the best route to Sullivan Ridge Road. (b) A more difficult route goes up the steep baranca just 200 yards south of the ridge. The baranca received the name "Falls Gorge" because of the many 8 to 12 foot waterfalls we climbed up. This route takes close to an hour and a half to gain 600 feet to Sullivan Ridge Road. From that point go south on the road, coming to a small clump of Oak trees with a board wedged in for a seat. Continue south on the ridge to the side road that drops down to Camp Josepho on the west.

My recommendation is to follow the streambed to Camp Josepho rather than fight chaparral climbing uphill. Upon reaching Camp Josepho walk up the road to Sullivan Ridge on the east. Turn right and walk one-third mile and look for the trail down to Sullivan Canyon. While still on the road you will cross under some telephone wires and go around a bend in the road to the right. A few hundred feet beyond a pole with the number 43975 you will find the trail on the left. The trail is overgrown and steep, but is solid footing compared with some of the day's travel. Upon reaching the streambed turn right for the easy one-half-mile-walk to the trailhead and your car.

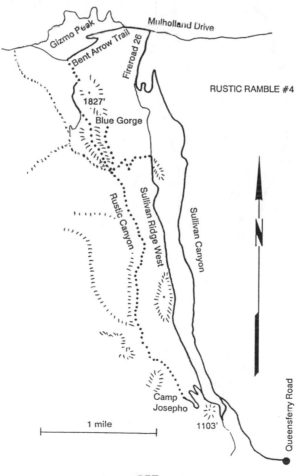

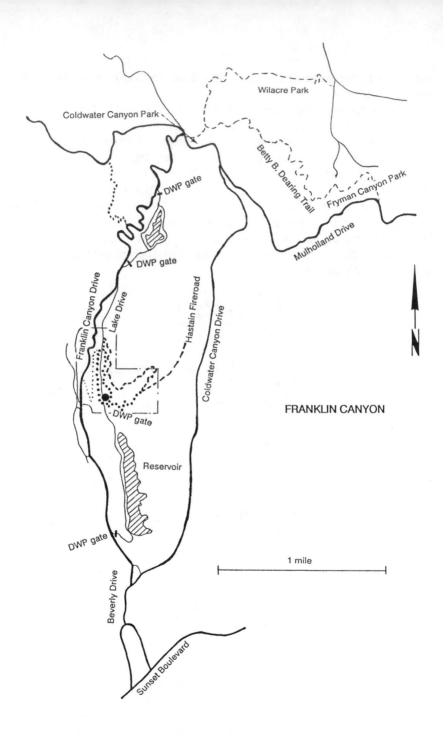

Coldwater Canyon Park

Wilacre Park

DWP gate

Betty B. Dearing Trail

Fryman Canyon Park

Mulholland Drive

DWP gate

Franklin Canyon Drive

Lake Drive

Hastain Fireroad

Coldwater Canyon Drive

FRANKLIN CANYON

DWP gate

Reservoir

DWP gate

1 mile

Beverly Drive

Sunset Boulevard

N

HIKE 69

Maps:	Beverly Hills, topo; Thomas Brothers Maps	
	#1	#2
Distance:	2 miles	.2 mile
Elevation:	400 ft	none
Terrain:	Steep trail	Trail
	Fireroad	
Time:	45 min.	30 min.
Trailhead:	Franklin Cyn	Franklin Cyn
	Ranch	Ranch

Franklin Canyon Ranch is part of the multi-agency and multi-organizational recreational complex of the Cross Mountain Park. National Park Service rangers and docents from William O. Douglas Outdoor Classroom (WODOC) provide outdoor educational programs on a reservation basis and the general public can use the area without charge. Facilities include a parking lot, restrooms, drinking water, pay telephone, picnic area, trails, National Park Service Ranger Station Nature Center.

Both above and below the ranch, the L.A. City Department of Water and Power maintains reservoirs. These are part of the scenery for the hikes, but are closed to the general public. WODOC provides environmental educational programs on a reservation basis at the upper reservoir. The special facilities include trails for senior citizens, a handicapped and Braille trail, and a series of student educational trails. Open seven days a week throughout the year, WODOC provides an exceptional schedule of opportunities for many who would not have a chance for outdoor experiences.

Reach Franklin Canyon from Beverly Hills by driving north on Beverly Drive from Sunset Blvd. 1.2 miles from the Coldwater Canyon Drive intersection, turn onto Franklin Canyon Drive; then after 1.7 miles more, turn right onto Lake Drive. Go to the parking lot.

From the San Fernando Valley drive south on Coldwater Canyon Avenue until reaching Mulholland Drive. Cross Mulholland onto Franklin Canyon Drive and go 1.7 miles to Lake Drive, turn left and go to the parking lot. Part of Franklin Canyon Drive is not paved and should not be used in wet weather.

I will describe two hikes in the Franklin Canyon Ranch area: (1) Hastain Trail, and (2) Discovery Trail. Dr.

To hike the Hastain Trail counterclockwise we leave the parking lot and walk south across the lawn toward a lath house. A steep trail leads us up the east flank of the ridge. Immediately we are surrounded by a mixed plant community of Coastal Sage Scrub and Chaparral. In bloom seasonally are Popcorn Flower, Bush Sunflower, Everlasting, Peony, Golden Yarrow and many others. The trail switches back as it climbs, and the narrow trail is steep. In 15 minutes we will intersect a fireroad and are entitled to a rest to view the canyon and reservoir below. We have climbed 400 feet. A right turn onto the fireroad will take us higher on the ridge and give views of the canyons below, Los Angeles, and on a clear day, the ocean. A left turn at the fireroad will take us downhill at a comfortable slope for about 1 mile before intersecting Lake Drive. Turn left and return to the parking lot.

Discovery Trail is an almost level self-guided walk over a trail on one side of Lake Drive and back down on the other side. Begin at the southeast corner of the parking lot and walk north on the trail. On occasion we use the road because of the steep hillside. "Discovery" is a good title because this trail allows us to notice the plants and animals about us. We will see Walnut Trees, Elderberry Bushes, Poison Oak, and many different flowers. A colony of Poison Hemlock (an introduced plant that gained fame in 399 B.C. when Socrates died in Athens) grows along the road. Don't even touch it. Cross the road and come back along the trail.

The Canyon Trail, and others are available for exploration.

HIKE 70

Fryman Canyon Park, Wilacre Park and Coldwater Canyon Park, in conjunction with Franklin Canyon Ranch and two Franklin Canyon reservoir areas, are referred to as the Cross Mountain Park.

WILACRE PARK

Wilacre Park is 129 acres of rugged ridges and canyons in Studio City. Surrounded by residential areas, this park is a greenbelt of wild land set aside for recreational use. Access is gained by three trailheads: one from Coldwater Canyon Park on Mulholland Drive, one from Laurel Canyon Boulevard, and the other from the upper end of Iredell Street. I'll describe a hike from Laurel Canyon on the Betty B. Dearing Trail.

Reach the trailhead by driving 1.6 miles south of the Ventura Freeway on Laurel Canyon Boulevard to Fryman Canyon, and park. Limited curb-side space is available; there is no parking lot.

We walk west on a paved road that is restricted to non-motorized vehicles and those on foot. Dogs are allowed on leash. We immediately begin an uphill climb that will total a 500 foot elevation gain when we reach Coldwater Canyon Park. Plan for a 30 minute brisk walk through the shade of Walnut trees, some introduced pines, but mostly chaparral. We will notice several levelled places that may in time become overnight campgrounds. Upon reaching Coldwater Canyon Park, a right fork at station #14 will put us on the "Magic Forest" nature trail and we can make a loop into the Park.

A left turn at station #14 takes us on a near level trail heading south. In ten minutes we become hemmed-in on the left by a cyclone fence and almost immediately find ourselves on Iredell Street. We are now out of the Park but continuing ahead, another trail starts up from the right. You may elect to turn around at this time or proceed southeast on the trail as it contours around to Fryman Canyon, and then up to Fryman Canyon Overlook. Part of this trail is on private property over which the owners have granted trail access.

FRYMAN CANYON PARK

Fryman Canyon is a steep chaparral-covered 59 acres of north facing hillside near Mulholland Drive. The Trailhead for the Betty B. Dearing Trail is on Mulholland Drive 2 miles east of Coldwater Canyon Park and .8 of a mile west of Laurel Canyon Boulevard. Ample parking for cars and a few buses is provided at a scenic overlook.

The trail goes downhill, initially, and later contours west through a chaparral forest. We cross an intermittent stream in the shade of riparian woodlands and, incidentally, walk by an automobile graveyard — I counted 10. The trail intersects an old road and continues west. We return the way we came, or continue on to Coldwater Canyon Park or to Wilacre Park. A car shuttle could be set up if we don't want to climb back up the hill.

COLDWATER CANYON PARK

Coldwater Canyon Park is a 12 acre Los Angeles City, Department of Recreation and Parks property managed under lease by the Tree People. The focus of activities is on a variety of educational and community services, using a number of buildings left when fire station 108 vacated the premises in 1977. A forestry nursery, landscaping display, and nature trail are some of the features. Trails connect with the Wilacre Park trail system.

Coldwater Canyon Park is located on the north side of Mulholland Drive, east of Coldwater Canyon Avenue. A parking lot, drinking water, restrooms, and an information center are available.

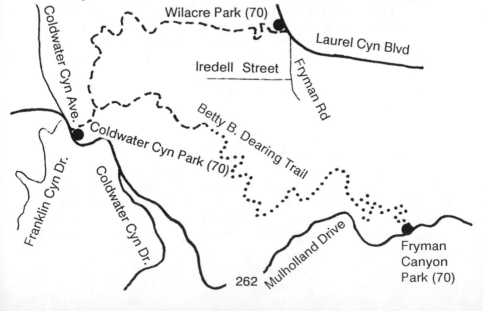

262

HIKE 71

Maps:	Hollywood Street Map
Distance:	1/2 mile roundtrip (at most)
Terrain:	path
Time:	15 minutes
Trailhead:	Fern Dell Drive

This isn't a hiking trail in the same sense as most of the trips to be found in this book; it is a secluded spot within a city where one may escape the busy streets, relax for awhile, or take a romantic stroll.

In Hollywood near the intersection of Los Feliz Blvd. and Western Avenue go north on Fern Dell Drive to Red Oak Drive. The entry gate is on the east side of Fern Dell.

Moco-Cahuenga Canyon is a verdant haven in a populated area. A stream courses through the canyon, dappling over waterfalls into pools surrounded by ferns and moss covered rocks. Overhead a dense canopy of large Sycamore trees shades this narrow strip of a Park.

Moco-Cahuenga is an Indian Language name with "Moco" meaning the post and council grounds and "Cahuenga" identifying the chief of that tribe.

Surprise yourself some day when in Hollywood — take a few minutes and relax in this truly delightful spot.

HIKE 72

FERNDELL PICNIC AREA
from Griffith Observatory
(loop)

Maps:	Hollywood, topo
	Griffith Park map
Distance:	2 miles roundtrip
Elevation:	500' gain and loss
Terrain:	Trail and bridle path
Time:	1 hour
Trailhead:	Griffith Observatory

In Hollywood, drive north on Vermont Avenue past Los Feliz Blvd. where the name changes to Vermont Canyon road. The road passes several picnic grounds, a golf course, the Greek Theatre, and a bird sanctuary. After climbing a short distance, the road ends at the Griffith Observatory parking lot.

Walk toward the Observatory and before reaching the building go to your left toward the shrubs and trees. The trail starts down the hill, gently at first but with some loose rocks and a perceptibly steeper grade farther on. As you leave the activity at the observatory the remoteness of the area is apparent. Vegetation, mostly chaparral, lines the trail but is not so dense that good views of the valley and city below are blocked out. After about 350 yards down the trail there is a choice of several routes; take the second trail on the right and continue downhill.

In a few hundred yards more there is another fork in the trail. This time take either one — they both lead to the picnic grounds. I like the left trail because the source of the Ferndell stream starts near the trail. The stream stays within sight and sound all the way to the picnic grounds, which are complete with restrooms, tables, charcoal grills, trees, a running stream, and grass.

The Moco-Cahuenga Canyon is just downstream of the picnic grounds. This little park is a delightful retreat of waterfalls, moss and ferns. Moco-Cahuenga is a mini-hike of its own, but if you have extra time on this hike, it is certainly worth a few minutes' visit.

Return to the Observatory by going upstream through the picnic grounds. Stay on the west side of the stream until picking up the bridle path that starts at the bend of Western Canyon Road as it makes a big left turn upon leaving the picnic area. Stay on the path as it climbs through the broad canyon. Do not be concerned that the Observatory is not visible; a ridge separates this path from the one on which you descended and obscures the view. The path stays on the left of the streambed and is a gradual climb making a big wide sweep to the right. Western Canyon Road parallels the path and is uphill on the left. As the path nears the ridge, it crosses Western Canyon Road, at which time you turn right and follow the paved road to the parking lot. You can avoid walking along the road by crossing it and continuing up the path until it reaches the ridge and intersects the trail between Mt. Hollywood and the Observatory. Turn right and follow the trail to the parking lot.

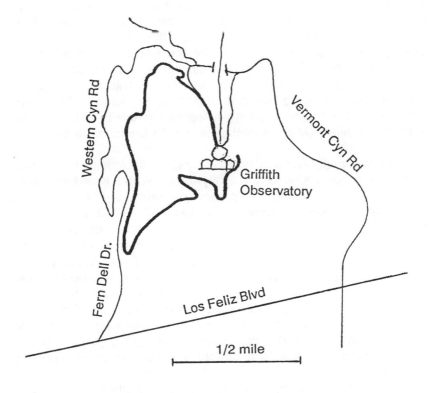

HIKE 73

Maps:	Burbank, topo
	Hollywood, topo
Distance:	2½ miles roundtrip
Elevation:	500' gain and loss
Terrain:	Bridle path and
	foot trail
Time:	1 hour 15 minutes
Trailhead:	Griffith Observatory

The path leaves the north end of the Griffith Observatory parking lot climbing gently along a tree-lined ridge. In about 350 yards the path crosses along a ridge that is above the Mt. Hollywood Drive Tunnel. At this point the bridle path coming up from the Ferndell picnic area joins from the left. Continuing uphill you will notice a steep side trail on the right. This also leads up to Mt. Hollywood, but is steeper and rougher going. The path climbs gently, but steadily, making a big switchback to the west. In less than 1/3 mile after the switchback a path branches in from the left.

Take this path, heading north at first as it circles around the west then the north side of Mt. Hollywood. A grove of trees and benches and cool drinking water shortly appears to the left of the path. This is known as Captain's Roost and is a fine place for lunch or a rest. Continue up the trail as it circles the peak and you notice several bridle paths coming up from the left. One of these leads to a water tank, another comes up from Mt. Hollywood Drive, another from Vista Del Valle. Mt. Hollywood can be climbed from a number of different points so it is worth noting that there are a lot of trails leading back down the mountain, most of which don't lead to the parking lot, so it pays to be observant. Continue on the path, and at the first opportunity turn right to go to the top of Mt. Hollywood. There is a bench, a sign, and an exceptional view of the city.

For variety, return by a slightly different route. Leaving the peak, retrace your steps for about 250 yards to the road, turn right, then at the next junction turn right again — the plan being to circle the peak meeting up with the path that brought you up. Notice Dante's View, a cool grove of trees with benches and water — another beautiful lunch stop. Continue along the path to the junction then head downhill back to the parking lot.

Several well defined trails lead down the ridge to the observatory. If you become adventurous and explore, keep an eye out for a steep trail leading down the east slope. This goes to the bird sanctuary rather than the parking lot, but is not a serious problem; a 1/2 mile walk up Vermont Canyon Road would put you back in the parking lot.

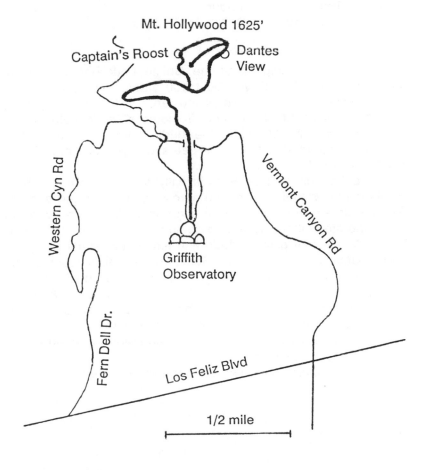

HIKE 74

Maps:	Burbank, topo
	Griffith Park Map
Distance:	2 miles roundtrip
Elevation:	250' gain and loss
Terrain:	Bridle path and
	foot trail
Time:	1 hour
Trailhead:	Griffith Park Hdqtrs

From the parking lot at the Griffith Park Ranger Station go west on Griffith Park Drive about 100 yards, crossing the road at the intersection. At the end of the fence a trail goes up the hill; take this trail about 100 ft. until it meets a bridle path, then turn left. After about 300 yards the bridle path forks; take the left fork. Almost immediately you will see a sign pointing out "Bee Rock Trail" to the right.

The trail up to Bee Rock initially follows a stream that has debris control dams constructed across it. Most of the season will find the stream dry, but a heavy rain brings down sand and gravel. Along the streambed, Sycamore, Walnut, and Oak are the dominant trees. As the trail gains altitude and leaves the stream, Toyon and Laurel Sumac become plentiful. Some Poison Oak is near the trail.

Thirty minutes after leaving the parking lot should find you at a ridge. Turn left and walk out onto Bee Rock. A fenced-in corridor has been placed to prevent falling. A good view of the eastern end of the Park is possible from the top of the rock. The Park Ranger Headquarters, Park Center and merry-go-round area can be seen through the trees.

This is a short, easy hike; return the way you came.

HIKE 75

Maps:	Hollywood, topo
	Griffith Park Map
Distance:	1/2 mile roundtrip
Elevation:	100' gain and loss
Terrain:	Trail
Time:	1/2 hour
Trailhead:	Griffith Park

This trail begins southwest of the Griffith Park merry-go-round on the other side of the road.

Built near an intermittent stream in chaparral, this self-guided nature trail identifies a number of plants. The plant selection includes chaparral, as well as streamside vegetation. Markers are set up along the trail and a guide pamphlet may be available. I have made comments for each station, but keep in mind that plants grow up and die, markers get changed, and other factors enter into the chance that this trail could change.

1. This tall tree is a Deodar Cedar and is not native to this area. It has been planted extensively in southern California and lines both sides of Los Feliz Blvd.
2. The berries of the Sugar Bush have a tart waxy covering. Soaking them in water makes a drink used by Indians.
3. Coffee Berry, also called Pigeon Berry and Yerba del oso, is not eaten; but when roasted and ground, the seeds make a palatable coffee substitute. Coffee Berry bark is known to be a laxative.
4. The Blue Elderberry Bush produces an edible berry late in the summer. It is edible only when fully ripe. The leaves and stems of the plant are mildly poisonous, but are used as a diuretic and purgative.

5. Oak tree

6. The light gray-green tree near the stream is a white alder. This tree is native to the area and may grow to 100 feet in height.

7. The mottled light green and gray barked tree across the stream is a California Sycamore. This tree will grow only near a perpetual or intermittent stream or in moist gulches. It prefers poor, rocky soil.

8. Poison Oak. As a skin irritant the juice of the plant is very poisonous. Direct contact anytime of the year will cause a severe skin rash. If you view this in the fall or winter the red leaves may have fallen to the ground. They are still poisonous.

9. The tree on the opposite side of the dam is an Arroyo Willow, or Creek Willow. This is an important flood and erosion control plant, the sturdy but flexible branches can catch debris and slow running water.

   (Don't bump your head on that California Walnut.)

10. The Holly-leaf Cherry across the stream is an evergreen bush that produces a tasty cherry that is mostly seed. Islay is its common name. It is an important plant of the chaparral.

11. This Southern California black walnut is usually found on margins of streams in gravelly or sandy soils but sometimes on dry hillsides. The nuts are edible — small and hard to crack, but of excellent Flavor.

12. This tall bush is Toyon, or "California Holly." It thrives in the deep soil of canyon bottoms,or competes well in the chaparral. The berry is edible.

13. The Lemonade-berry Bush is similar to the Sugar Bush (Station 2). The berry can be soaked in water to make an acid drink. The Wild Blackberries, also seen here, grow near streams.

   Cross the stream on a footbridge then turn right. From this point on, most of the numbered posts are missing. Recross the stream and go up the trail to the ridge. Cross the ridge and follow down the stream on the other side.

14. Laurel Sumac is related to Lemonade-berry and Sugar Bush. This aromatic bush grows well throughout the Santa Monicas.

15. This is a Coast Live Oak. The leaf curls some — to the degree that if it were to fall in the water upside down it would float like a boat. The bark of the tree is rough and corky looking.

16. This fern-like plant is Poison Hemlock, and although not native to this hemisphere it is widely distributed in the moist areas of the Santa Monicas. The plant dries up in the summer holding some of the seeds on the tall stalks. In early October the new plants start growing at the base of the old plant. All parts of this plant are poisonous.

17. This is another toyon. To the left is a Fuchsia Flowering Gooseberry. The plant dries up in late summer and drops its leaves, thereby reducing its need for water.

18. This is another gooseberry. You may notice the three very stout spines at the branch nodes. In general, gooseberries have spines; currants do not.
    The small single needle pine (Pinus edulis) is not a native of the Santa Monicas.

19. Burned over area across the arroyo. There are some everlasting plants on the uphill side of the trail. These flowers have an odor resembling brown sugar — even when dry.

20. Lemonade-berry, Gooseberry, and Walnut. A Scrub Oak is on the other side of the trail.

21. This is a clump of Giant Rye Grass. A native in the Santa Monicas and used by the Indians, it dries up in the fall.

22. The yucca plants on the hillside across the arroyo are commonly called Our Lord's Candle. In the spring when in bloom, the plant has a tall spike covered with cream colored blossoms. By late summer a dry spike remains. The Indians used the fibers from the leaves to make baskets and as thread. The seeds were ground and made into mush.

23. Notice the small oak seedling near the base of the larger oak. Also, the seasonal California wall fern or licorice fern grows here. Don't expect to see it after a long dry spell.

24. This hillside has a number of Black Sage plants growing three or more feet high. The leaf and flower whorls on the stems give rise to other names of Ball Sage and Button Sage.

BACKBONE TRAIL

The Backbone Trail is a 64.1 mile (more or less) equestrian and hiking trail that runs west and east through the Santa Monica Mountains. The western terminus is at the Pacific Ocean at Point Mugu State Park, the eastern terminus, at Will Rogers State Historic Park. Parts of the trail have been in existence many years, other segments are still on the drawing board. Land for the eastern half has been procured; we have major gaps in land acquisition of the western half.

The concept of a Backbone Trail has been talked about for many years, not always by the name "Backbone," but the idea of an east-west ridge trail is certainly not recent. Work to procure land, design the trail, and build it has been going on for several years. Cooperative effort of the California State Park system, the Santa Monica National Recreation Area, the Santa Monica Mountains Conservancy, the Sierra Club, elected representatives, and a great number of volunteers has had a direct positive effect on keeping the project moving.

The following maps and brief descriptions are meant to give an overview of the trail, rather than a detailed description. Those segments of the trail that have been completed should not present a route finding problem but for the segments not yet built, the information here should be augmented with topo maps and personal contact with someone who has walked the route, before attempting it on your own.

The names of the trail segments listed here are temporary until either common usage dictates or someone with authority to name trails does so. A problem with naming a trail segment that hasn't been built is that the builders of the trail are the ones that will, for one reason or another, come up with an appropriate name. As an example, "The Dead Horse Trail" had no name during construction — but a lot of suggestions were being made — until one day as the trail neared completion, the crew arrived at the trailhead to find that overnight someone had buried a horse (pony) in the trail. "Dead Horse Trail" has been the accepted name since. So until such time as designated names are established, I would like to consider these as "working" names to be temporary for this edition of the book, and will plan to update later.

The "Miles" column is the accumulated mileage for the entire trail, starting at the west end and ending at the east end. My bicycle odometer reads in tenths of a mile so where measured and known, distances are rounded off to the nearest tenth. Where not measured and particularly when the trail has not been built, I've made a studied determination (wild guess) of the mileage.

Locations listed are identifiable places on the maps, usually a trail junction, or road or stream crossing. Information as to the location of water or restrooms is included. In general, the nicetles and conveniences of a well-established trail are missing. We don't expect trail signs or mileages to be posted in the immediate future and those of us who choose to walk this trail in the next few years should do so with an explorer's attitude. A group of us have been walking the trail as an annual pilgrimage, starting in 1983, and have a realistic feeling for the magnitude of work that has been accomplished as well as the task ahead. We should be prepared for difficulty where the trail has not been built, and appreciate a trail after its construction.

I will briefly describe the trail from west to east

KEY;

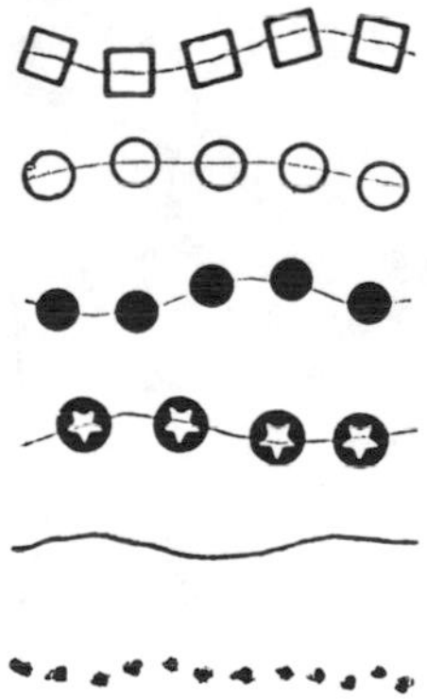

Proposed alignment

Temporary trail route

Existing trail

Flagged trail

Other trails

Trails not maintained,
or very steep

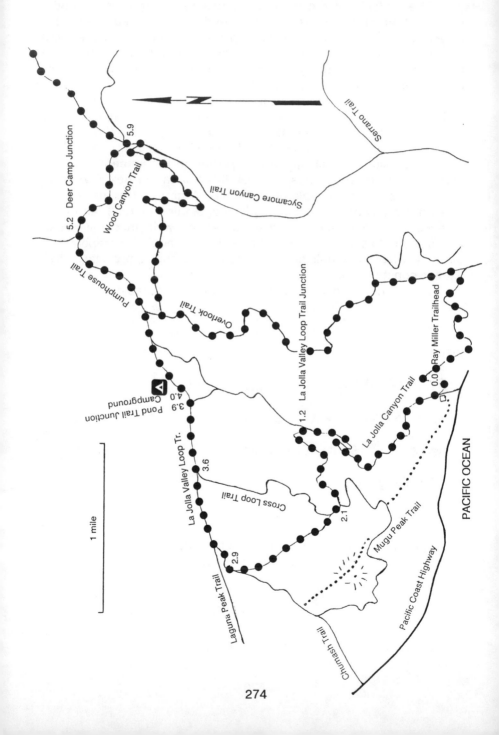

SEGMENT OF TRAIL	MILES	LOCATION
La Jolla Canyon Trail	0.0	Ray Miller Trailhead, La Jolla Cyn
	1.2	La Jolla Valley Loop Trail Junction
La Jolla Valley Loop Tr.	1.2	La Jolla Canyon Trail Junction
	2.1	Mugu Peak Trail Junction
	2.2	Cross Loop Trail Junction
	2.4	Oak Grove
	2.9	Mugu Peak Trail Junction
	3.0	Laguna Peak Trail Junction
	3.6	Cross Loop Trail Junction
	3.9	Pond Trail Junction
	4.0	Campground
	4.3	Trail Junction
	4.5	Overlook Trail Junction
Pumphouse Trail	4.5	Overlook Trail Junction
	5.2	Deer Camp Junction
Wood Canyon Trail	5.2	Deer Camp Junction
	5.9	Sycamore Canyon Trail Junction

The Ray Miller trailhead is an excellent staging area for the beginning or the end of your hike along the Backbone Trail. A large parking lot, locked at night, gives us a good assembly spot. Restroom facilities and drinking water are available. Overnight camping is available at nearby La Jolla Beach and at Sycamore Campground. A walk-in campground is located at mile 4 of the trail (two miles from the trailhead by short-cutting). Restrooms, drinking water, and picnic tables are available at the walk-in camp. Restrooms and picnic tables are also available at Deer Camp Junction. Total elevation gain for this segment is about 1000'.

The lower part of the trail comes through narrow, rocky La Jolla Canyon, closed to all but foot traffic. Because the Backbone Trail is an equestrian-hiker trail, alternate routes have long been considered as suitable for horses. The Chumash Trail could not be changed because to do so would constitute a gross irreverence to its heritage of being one of the oldest trails known in continuous use (possibly for the last 7000 years). The Ray Miller Trail, constructed in 1989, heads east and connects to the Scenic and Overlook Trails. Horses can use this trail.

275

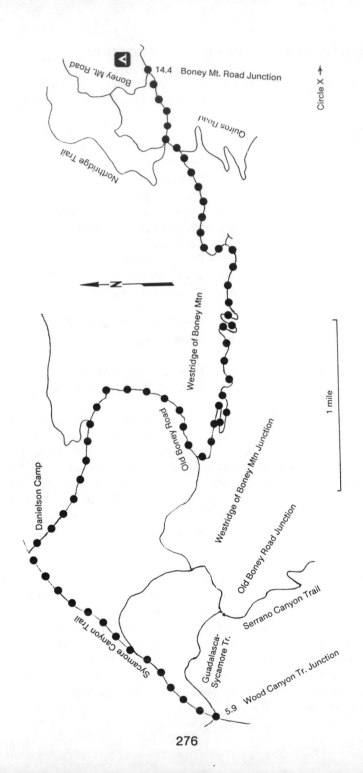

Circle X →

14.4   Boney Mt. Road Junction

Boney Mt. Road

Quiros Road

Northridge Trail

← N

Westridge of Boney Mtn

Old Boney Road

Danielson Camp

Westridge of Boney Mtn Junction

Old Boney Road Junction

Serrano Canyon Trail

Sycamore Canyon Trail

Guadalasca-
Sycamore Tr.

5.9   Wood Canyon Tr. Junction

1 mile

SEGMENT OF TRAIL	MILES	LOCATION
Sycamore Canyon Trail	5.9	Wood Canyon – Sycamore Junction
	7.2	Road to Ranch Center
	7.5	Danielson Camp
Blue Canyon Trail	7.5	Danielson Camp
	9.5	Blue Meadow Junction
Westridge of Boney Mtn Trail	9.5	Blue Meadow Junction
	14.4	Camp Allen

The original plan for the Backbone Trail route was to use the segment of the Guadalasca Trail that goes uphill east of Sycamore Canyon. This trail is more than 20° steep in many places and would require complete rebuilding. A decision has been made to reroute the Backbone Trail along Sycamore Canyon as far as Danielson Camp. This change allows a moderate grade and the benefit of passing a campground with many facilities.

The Westridge Trail segment was built primarily by California Conservation Corps crews during 1990. A reliable source of water does not exist between Danielson Camp and the Ranger Station at Circle X Ranch. The Altitude change, the distance, and the remoteness of this section mandate careful planning for anyone attempting this hike.

Three other trails connect Sycamore Canyon with the Westridge Trail. Each one is unique and worth hiking. The Serrano Canyon Trail is not suitable for horses.

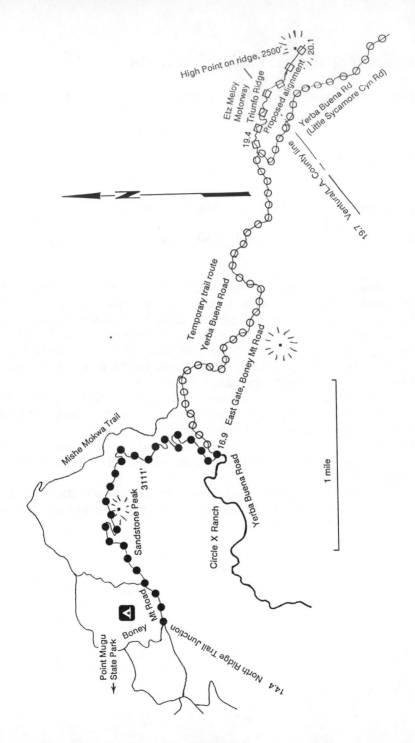

High Point on ridge, 2500'

Etz Meloy Motorway

Triunfo Ridge

Proposed alignment

/, 20.1

19.4

Yerba Buena Rd (Little Sycamore Cyn Rd)

19.7 Ventura/L.A. County line

Temporary trail route

Yerba Buena Road

East Gate, Boney Mt Road

16.9

Circle X Ranch

Yerba Buena Road

Mishe Mokwa Trail

Sandstone Peak

3111'

Point Mugu State Park

Boney Mt Road

14.4 North Ridge Trail Junction

1 mile

N

SEGMENT OF TRAIL	MILES	LOCATION
Boney Mt Road	14.4	North Ridge Trail Junction
		Camp W. Herbert Allen
	15.7	Trail to Sandstone Peak
	16.9	Yerba Buena Road Junction
Yerba Buena Road	16.9	East Gate, Boney Mt Road
Triunfo Pass segment	19.4	Triunfo Ridge
(Property has not been		
procured and trail		
does not exist)		
Triunfo Ridge	19.4	Yerba Buena Road Junction
(Property has not been	19.7	Ventura/L.A. County line
procured and trail	20.1	High Point on ridge, 2500'
does not exist)		

Access is available by trail from (1) Yerba Buena Road and (2) Point Mugu State Park.

This section of the Backbone Trail has not been constructed, with the exception of existing routes in Circle X Ranch. The status of land procurement is not known.

Boney Mountain Road climbs to 3000' but to gain the top of Sandstone Peak we must leave the highest point on the road and climb a steep trail to the top. At 3111' Sandstone Peak is the highest point in the Santa Monica Mountains. I can give no reliable explanation why this massive volcanic mountain is called "sandstone." Because of his many years of devoted work to develop Circle X Ranch as a Boy Scout camp, W. Herbert Allen was honored by having the peak named after him. The new name was not officially accepted so it remains "Sandstone Peak."

Upon reaching Yerba Buena Road, the trail no longer exists until arriving at Clarke Ranch Road. Until such time as a corridor is procured we can walk on Yerba Buena Road and then Mulholland Highway to the beginning of Clarke Ranch Road, a total of 5.2 miles. Pavement on a decent grade might even be welcome after the rock on Boney Mountain. The proposed route is on Triunfo Ridge along Etz Meloy Motorway.

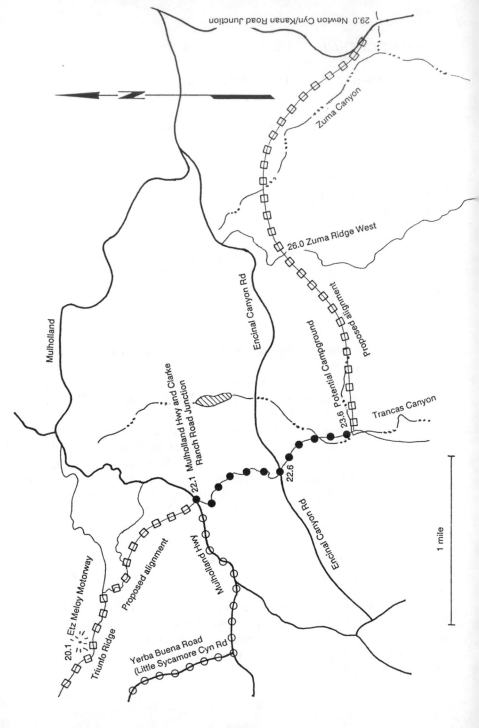

SEGMENT OF TRAIL	MILES	LOCATION
Triunfo Ridge	20.1	High Point on ridge, 2500'
(Property has not been	22.1	Mulholland Hwy and Clarke
procured and trail		Ranch Road Junction
does not exist)		
Clarke Ranch Road	22.1	Mulholland Hwy Junction
(not procured)	22.6	Encinal Canyon Rd Junction
Trancas Canyon	22.6	Encinal Canyon Rd Junction
(Portion of trail	23.6	Potential Campground
corridor owned by	26.0*	Zuma Ridge West
N.P.S. Trail not		
constructed)		
Zuma Canyon	26.0	Zuma Ridge West
(Portion of trail	27.5*	Zuma Canyon
corridor owned by	29.0	Newton Cyn/Kanan Road Junction
N.P.S. Trail not		
constructed)		

* The Actual proposed route is unknown. The distance is based upon the terrain and elevation change.

  Access is available from (1) Little Sycamore Canyon Road, (2) Mulholland Highway, (3) Encinal Canyon Road, and (4) Kanan Road.

  This section of the Backbone Trail promises to be of exceptional interest. Areas for potential campgrounds are found in both Trancas and Zuma Canyons. Trancas Canyon is a steep walled winding slit through massive rock and offers great chances for exploration. Zuma Canyon is known for spectacular waterfalls, rock pools and fern covered grottos. Lower Newton canyon between Zuma Canyon and Kanan Road supports three waterfalls, two of which are dramatic.

  A large parking area along Kanan Road, at the north end of the tunnel nearest the ocean, can be used for a staging area for this trail section. Room for horse trailers will be no problem.

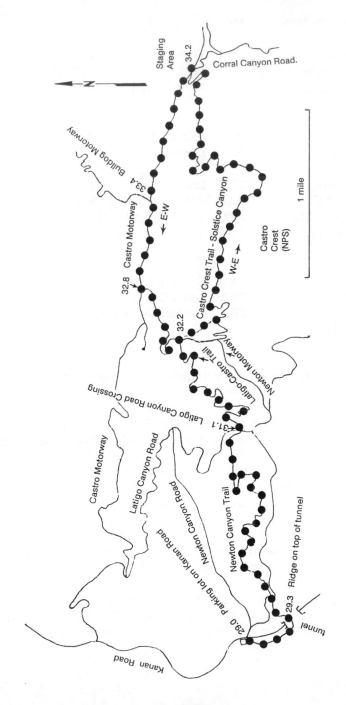

Staging Area
34.2
Corral Canyon Road.

←—N—

1 mile

Bulldog Motorway

33.4
Castro Motorway
E-W

Castro Crest Trail - Solstice Canyon

W-E

Castro Crest (NPS)

32.8

32.2

Newton Motorway

Latigo-Castro Trail

Latigo Canyon Road Crossing

31.1

Castro Motorway

Latigo Canyon Road

Newton Canyon Road

Parking lot on Kanan Road

Newton Canyon Trail

Ridge on top of tunnel

29.3

tunnel

29.0

Kanan Road

282

SEGMENT OF TRAIL	MILES	LOCATION
Newton Canyon Trail	29.0	Parking lot on Kanan Road
	29.3	Ridge on top of tunnel
	31.1	Latigo Canyon Road Crossing
Latigo-Castro Trail	31.1	Latigo Canyon Road Crossing
	32.2	Newton Motorway Junction
Newton Motorway	32.2	Latigo-Castro Trail Junction
	32.8	Castro Motorway Junction
Castro Motorway	32.8	Newton Motorway Junction
	33.4	Bulldog Motorway Junction
	34.2	Corral Cyn Rd Parking lot and Corral Crest Trail Junction

Access is available from (1) Kanan Road (Southern-most Tunnel), (2) Latigo Canyon Road, and (3) Corral Canyon Road.

The trail follows the old road south to the ridge on top of the tunnel, then turns east. The property owner has granted a trail easement to the National Park Service from the tunnel to a driveway. Please respect the rights of the property owner and stay on the trail.

The trail from Latigo Canyon Road to Newton Motorway is complete and in use. Newton Motorway is a steep climb, 300' gain, to Castro Motorway. Six-tenths of a mile after getting on Castro Motorway, Bulldog Motorway comes up from the left. An alternate — and maybe favored — route starts on Bulldog, drops down to Malibu Creek, and follows it into the floor of the valley.

Otherwise, stay on Castro Motorway until you reach Corral Canyon Road staging area. There are no facilities.

Another alternate route takes us to Corral Canyon Road staging area via Solstice Canyon. This is preferred as a west-to-east route because it eliminates the steep climb up Newton Motorway to Castro Motorway. This may be 1/2 mile longer than the fireroad but on a beautiful trail.

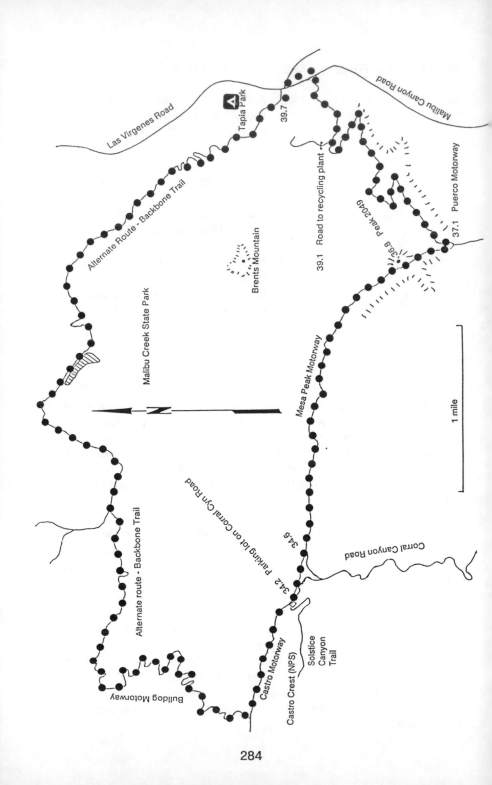

SEGMENT OF TRAIL	MILES	LOCATION
Mesa Trail	34.2	Parking lot on Corral Cyn Road
	34.6	Mesa Peak Motorway Junction
Mesa Peak Motorway *	34.6	Mesa Trail Junction
	36.8	Peak 2049
	37.1	Puerco Motorway Junction
	39.1	Road to recycling plant
	39.6	Malibu Creek Road Junction
Malibu Canyon Road	39.5	Mesa Peak Motorway Junction
	39.7	Parking lot at Tapia Park

* The 1/2 mile between Malibu Canyon Rd and the road to the recycling plant is "technically" not Mesa Peak Motorway.

This section of the Backbone Trail is on existing Fireroads.

Access is available from (1) Corral Canyon Road and (2) Malibu Canyon Road.

A ridge trail all the way has good views of Malibu Creek State Park on the left and Corral Canyon on the right. After passing Peak 2049 and starting down to the east we are treated to grand panoramas of Malibu Creek.

At Malibu Canyon Road we cross the road and turn left. Cross the bridge on the walkway, then recross Malibu Canyon Road and walk to Tapia parking lot.

Camping, restrooms, drinking water, and picnic tables are available.

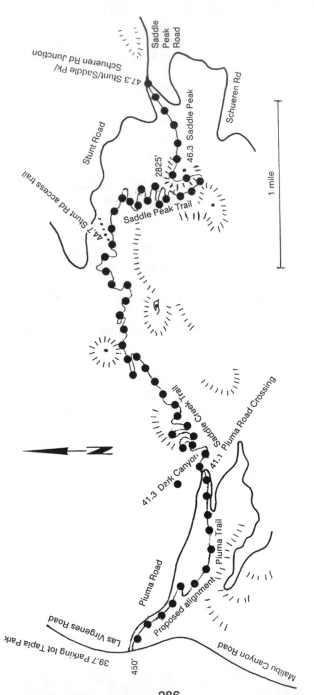

Saddle Peak Road

Saddle Peak Road

47.3 Stunt/Saddle Pk/ Schueren Rd Junction

Schueren Rd

46.3 Saddle Peak

Stunt Road

2825'

44.7 Stunt Rd access trail

Saddle Peak Trail

1 mile

Saddle Creek Trail

Piuma Road Crossing

N

41.3 Dark Canyon

41.1 Piuma Road Crossing

Piuma Trail

Piuma Road

Proposed alignment

Las Virgenes Road

39.7 Parking lot Tapia Park

450'

Malibu Canyon Road

SEGMENT OF TRAIL	MILES	LOCATION
Piuma Trail	39.7	Parking lot: Tapia Park
(Property has been	41.1	Piuma Road Crossing
procured; trail has		
not been constructed)		
Saddle Creek Trail	41.1	Piuma Road Crossing
	41.3*	Dark Canyon
	44.7	Stunt Road access trail
Saddle Peak Trail	44.7	Stunt Road access trail
	46.3	Saddle Peak
	47.3**	Stunt/Saddle Pk/Schueren Rd Junction

*   This section of the Backbone Trail is being built at the present time (1987).

**   The eastern .3 mile of this trail comes very close to some houses, so please respect the rights of property owners and stay on the trail.   Although it is over existing public easement (the Brown-Latigo Motorway/Saddle Peak Road), it is overgrown and not maintained. Efforts are being made to relocate the trail.   In the next few years that will elapse before that segment is constructed, we can anticipate a timely resolution of the actual route of the trail segment.

Access is available from (1) Malibu Canyon Road, (2) Piuma Road, (3) Stunt Road, and (4) Stunt Road/Saddle Peak Road Junction.

It is characterized by elevation changes from 450' at Malibu Creek to 2825' on Saddle Peak. Most of the trail is in chaparral.

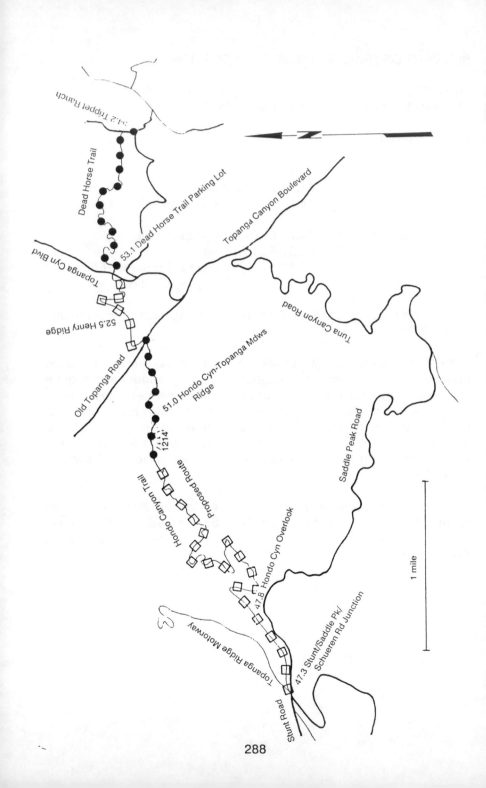

54.2 Trippet Ranch

Dead Horse Trail

Topanga Cyn Blvd

53.1 Dead Horse Trail Parking Lot

Topanga Canyon Boulevard

52.5 Henry Ridge

Old Topanga Road

Tuna Canyon Road

51.0 Hondo Cyn-Topanga Mdws Ridge

1214'

Hondo Canyon Trail

Proposed Route

Saddle Peak Road

47.8 Hondo Cyn Overlook

Topanga Ridge Motorway

47.3 Stunt/Saddle Pk/ Schueren Rd Junction

Stunt Road

N

1 mile

288

SEGMENT OF TRAIL	MILES	LOCATION
Hondo Canyon Trail	47.3	Stunt/Saddle Peak Rd Junction
	47.8	Hondo Cyn Overlook
	51.0	Hondo Cyn-Topanga Mdws Ridge (1214')
	52.0	Old Topanga Road Crossing
	52.5	Henry Ridge
	53.0	Topanga Cyn Blvd Crossing
	53.1	Dead Horse Trail Parking lot
Dead Horse Trail	53.1	Dead Horse Trail Parking lot
	54.2	Trippet Ranch

The section of the Backbone Trail between the Stunt/Saddle Peak Road Junction to the Dead Horse Trail Parking lot has not been constructed. The land has been procured. Because of the elevation change and terrain I have estimated actual trail distance at 5.8 miles. Point to point distance is 2.7 miles.

Access is available from (1) Stunt/Saddle Peak/Schueren Road Junction, (2) Old Topanga Road, and (3) Dead Horse Trail Parking lot.

The western half mile of this section will follow an obscured trail parallel to Saddle Peak Road. Upon dropping down into Hondo Canyon the new trail (not yet built) will enter an area that has been isolated from use by steep slopes and dense brush. Rock formations and precipitous views dominate the high part of the area. The Grasslands and Oak Woodlands of Topanga Meadows make a radical change in scenery as the trail crosses the ridge south of Hondo Canyon. From the east side of Old Topanga Road the trail will cross Henry Ridge north of Topanga school. Even though the trail hasn't been flagged, the route is not difficult and drops down a ridge to Greenleaf Road and Topanga Canyon Boulevard crossing. The Dead Horse Trail segment is complete and in use.

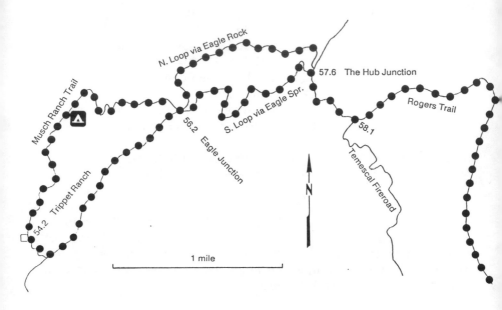

The section of the Backbone Trail between Trippet Ranch and Will Rogers State Historic Park has been in existence for a number of years.

Access is available from (1) Trippet Ranch and (2) Will Rogers State Historic Park.

Trippet Ranch is headquarters of Topanga State Park and offers a Ranger Station, pay telephone, picnic tables, restrooms, drinking water, and a bulletin board. Will Rogers State Historic Park, at the other end of this section of trail, offers all this plus tours of the home, a bookstore, and a museum. In between are 10 miles of good walking on fireroads and trails.

Immediately, at Trippet Ranch, two routes are offered: (1) the fireroad to Eagle Junction; and (2) Musch Ranch Trail (goes past an overnight camping area). Both trail segments are about 2 miles long and meet at Eagle Junction. At Eagle Junction two more options are available: (1) North Loop past Eagle Rock and, (2) South Loop past Eagle Spring. Both Segments are about 1.4 miles long and meet at the Hub. From the Hub the route is south on ridges, losing altitude as we approach Will Rogers State Historic Park.

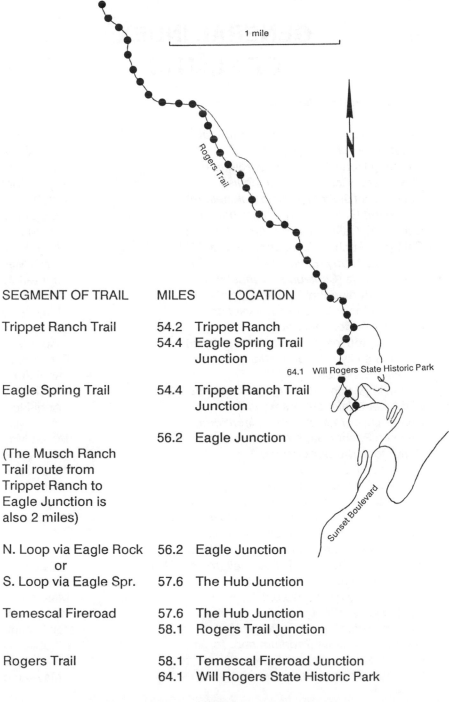

1 mile

N

Rogers Trail

SEGMENT OF TRAIL	MILES	LOCATION
Trippet Ranch Trail	54.2	Trippet Ranch
	54.4	Eagle Spring Trail Junction
Eagle Spring Trail	54.4	Trippet Ranch Trail Junction
	56.2	Eagle Junction
(The Musch Ranch Trail route from Trippet Ranch to Eagle Junction is also 2 miles)		
N. Loop via Eagle Rock or S. Loop via Eagle Spr.	56.2	Eagle Junction
	57.6	The Hub Junction
Temescal Fireroad	57.6	The Hub Junction
	58.1	Rogers Trail Junction
Rogers Trail	58.1	Temescal Fireroad Junction
	64.1	Will Rogers State Historic Park

64.1 Will Rogers State Historic Park

Sunset Boulevard

GENERAL INDEX
OF PLANTS

Flowering and Herbaceous

Baby Blue-eyes *(Nemophila menziesii)*	March-April
Bedstraw *(Galium spp. [3])*	March-June
Bleeding Heart *(Dicentra ochroleuca)*	May-June
Blow-wives *(Achyrachaena mollis)*	April
Blue Dicks *(Dicholostemma pulchellum)*	March-April
Blue-eyed Grass *(Sisyrinchium bellum)*	March-April
Buttercup, Calif. *(Ranunculus californicus)*	Feb.-March
California Fuchsia *(Zauschneria spp. [2])*	Aug.-Nov.
California Poppy *(Eschscholzia spp. [2])*	March-May
Canchalagua *(Centaurium venustum)*	June-July
Catchfly [Indian Pink] *(Silene laciniata)*	April-June
Checkerbloom *(Sidalcea malvaeflora)*	May-June
Chia *(Salvia columbariae)*	March-April
Chinese Houses *(Collinsia heterophylla)*	April-May
Chocolate Lily *(Fritillaria biflora)*	Feb.-March
Clarkia *(Clarkia spp. [5])*	April-June
Clematis [Virgin's Bower] *(Clematis spp. [2])*	March-May
Cliff Aster *(Malacothrix saxatilis)*	April-Nov.
Cream-cups *(Platystemon californicus)*	April-May
Crimson Pitcher Sage *(Salvia spathacea)*	March-May
Curly Dock *(Rumex crispus)* *	March-June
Dodder *(Cuscuta spp. [4])*	March-June
Dudleya [Live-forever] *(Dudleya spp. [3])*	April-June
Dudleya, Chalk-leaved *(Dudleya pulverulenta)*	August
Eucrypta *(Eucrypta chrysanthemifolia)*	March-April
Evening Primrose *(Camissonia spp. [5])*	April-May
Evening Primrose, Hooker's *(Oenothera hookeri)*	May-June
Everlasting [Cudweed] *(Gnaphalium spp. [7])*	Jan.-Oct.
Fennel *(Foeniculum vulgare)* *	May-July
Fiddleneck *(Amsinckia spp. [2])*	March-May
Fiesta Flower *(Pholistoma auritum)*	March-April
Figwort *(Scrophularia californica)*	March-June
Filaree [Storksbill] *(Erodium spp. [4])* *	Feb.-May
Fire Poppy *(Papaver californicum)*	April
Fleabane *(Erigeron foliosus)*	May-June

Four O'clock *(Mirabilis laevis)* — March-June
Gilia *(Gilia spp. [2])* — April-May
Globe Lily *(Calochortus albus)* — April-May
Goldenrod *(Solidago californica)* — Aug.-Nov.
Golden Yarrow *(Eriophyllum confertiflorum)* — April-May
Golden Stars *(Bloomeria crocea)* — April-May
Goldflelds *(Lasthenia spp. [2])* — April-May
Gourd *(Cucurbita foetidissima)* — June-July
Ground Pink *(Linanthus dianthiflorus)* — April
Groundsel, Bush *(Senecio douglasii)* — April-May
Groundsel, Common *(Senecio vulgaris)* * — Jan.-May
Gumweed *(Grindelia robusta)* — April-June
Hedge Nettle *(Stachys bullata)* — March-May
Hedge Nettle, White *(Stachys albens)* — June-Aug.
Heliotrope *(Heliotropium curassavicum)* — June-Aug.
Hemlock, Poison *(Conium maculatum)* * — May-July
Horehound *(Marrubium vulgare)* * — March-May
Humboldt Lily *(Lilium Humboldtii)* — June-July
Indian Paintbrush *(Castilleja spp. [4])* — March-May
Indian Warrior *(Pedicularis densiflora)* — Feb.-April
Jewel-flower *(Streptanthus heterophyllus)* — March-April
Jimson-weed *(Datura wrightii)* — May-July
Lacepod [Fringepod] *(Thysanocarpus curvipes)* — March-May
Larkspur, Blue *(Delphinium spp. [2])* — March-May
Larkspur, Scarlet *(Delphinium cardinale)* — June-July
Leather Root *(Psoralea macrostachya)* — June-Aug.
Lomatium *(Lomatium spp. [4])* — Jan.-May
Lotus *(Lotus spp. [7])* — March-Aug.
Lupine *(Lupinus spp. [8]* — March-May
Man-root [Wild Cucumber] *(Marah macrocarpus)* — Jan.-April
Mariposa Lily, Catalina *(Calochortus catalinae)* — March-April
Mariposa Lily, Plummers *(Calochortus plummerae)* — June-July
Mariposa Lily, Yellow *(Calochortus clavatus)* — May
Matilija Poppy *(Romneya coulteri)* * — April-May
Milkmaids *(Cardamine californica)* — Feb.-April
Milkweed, Calif. *(Asclepias californica)* — March-June
Milkweed, Narrowleaf *(Asclepias fascicularis)* — May-Sept.
Miners' Lettuce *(Claytonia perfoliata)* — March-April
Monkeyflower, Bush *(Diplacus longiflorus)* — April-June
Monkeyflower, Common *(Mimulus guttatus)* — March-May
Monkeyflower, Scarlet *(Mimulus cardinalis)* — June-Aug.
Monkeyflower, Yellow *(Mimulus brevipes)* — March-May

Morning Glory *(Calystegia macrostegia)*	Feb.-June
Mountain Dandelion *(Agoseris grandiflora)*	May-June
Mustard, Common *(Brassica campestris)* *	All year
Mustard, Black *(Brassica nigra)* *	March-July
Onion, Wild *(Allium spp. [2])*	March-May
Owl's Clover *(Orthocarpus purpurascens)*	March-May
Pansy [Johnny-Jump-up] *(Viola pedunculata)*	April-May
Pea, Wild Sweet *(Lathyrus laetiflorus)*	Feb.-June
Pennyroyal *(Monardella hypoleuca)*	June-July
Penstemon, Climbing *(Keckiella cordifolia)*	May-July
Penstemon, Foothill *(Penstemon heterophyllus)*	April-June
Penstemon, Showy *(Penstemon spectabilis)*	April-May
Peony *(Paeonia californica)*	Jan.-March
Perezia *(Perezia microcephala)*	June-July
Phacelia, Caterpillar *(Phacelia cicutaria)*	March-June
Phacelia, Large-flowered *(Phacelia grandiflora)*	April-June
Phacelia, Sticky *(Phacelia viscida)*	April-June
Pimpernel *(Anagallis arvensis)* *	March-June
Pincushion, Pink *(Chaenactis artemisiaefolia)*	May-June
Pincushion, Golden *(Chaenactis glabriuscula)*	March-April
Pineapple Weed *(Matricaria matricarioides)*	Feb.-May
Popcorn Flower *(Cryptantha spp. [4])*	March-May
Popcorn Flower *(Plagiobothrys spp. [3])*	March-May
Radish, Wild *(Raphanus sativus)* *	All year
Redmaids *(Calandrinia)*	April-May
Rock-rose *(Helianthemum scoparium)*	Feb.-May
Sanicle *(Sanicula spp. [4])*	March-May
Saxifrage, Calif. *(Saxifraga californica)*	March-May
Scarlet Bugler *(Penstemon centranthifolius)*	April-May
Shooting Stars *(Dodecatheon clevelandii)*	Jan.-March
Skullcap *(Scutellaria tuberosa)*	March-April
Snapdragon, Rose *(Antirrhinum multiflorum)*	May-June
Snapdragon, Twining *(Antirrhinum kelloggii)*	March-April
Snapdragon, Violet *(Antirrhinum nuttallianum)*	April-May
Snapdragon, White *(Antirrhinum coulterianum)*	April-May
Soap Plant *(Chlorogalum pomeridianum)*	May-June
Sow Thistle *(Sonchus spp.)* *	All year
Stream Orchid *(Epipactis gigantea)*	May-June
Sunflower, Canyon *(Venegasia carpesioides)*	March-May
Sunflower, Bush [Shrub] *(Encelia californica)*	March-June
Sunflower, Prairie *(Helianthus annuus)* *	April-Sept.
Sunflower, Slender *(Helianthus gracilentus)*	April-Sept.

Sweet Clover *(Melilotus spp. [2])*	March-June
Tarweed *(Hemizonia spp. [2])*	April-June
Tarweed *(Madia spp. [3])*	April-June
Telegraph Weed *(Heterotheca grandiflora)*	June-Aug.
Thistle, Calif. *(Cirsium californicum)*	April-June
Thistle, Bull *(Cirsium vulgare)* *	June-Oct.
Thistle, Milk *(Silybum marianum)* *	May-July
Thistle, Star *Centaurea melitensis)* *	May-July
Thistle, Western *(Cirsium coulteri)*	March-June
Tidy Tips *(Layia platyglossa)*	March-May
Turkish Rugging*(Chorizanthe staticoides)*	April-June
Verbena *(Verbena lasiostachys)*	April-Sept.
Verbena, Beach *(Abronia spp. [2])*	April-June
Vetch *(Vicia spp. [3])*	March-May
Vinegar Weed *(Trichostema lanceolatum)*	May-June
Wallflower *(Erysimum spp. [2])*	March-May
Whispering Bells *(Emmenanthe penduliflora)*	March-May
Woodland Star *(Lithophragma affine)*	April-May
Woolly Aster *(Corethrogyne filaginifolia)*	June-Sept.
Yarrow [White] *(Achillea borealis)*	May-June
Zygadene [Star Lily] *(Zygadenus fremontii)*	March-April

* alien (non-native) plants

This list of annuals and perennial flowering plants is not meant to be complete. Their abundance or rarity each year is related not only to habitat and seasonal weather variations, but also to the periodic occurrence of fire. Almost all of the listed plants produce an abundance of bloom the first season after fire that is way beyond the normal; some of them only bloom after a fire.

Trees

Alder, White *(Alnus rhombifolia)*
Laurel [Bay] *(Umbellularia californica)*
Maple, Bigleaf *(Acer macrophylla)*
Oak, Coast Live *(Quercus agrifolia)*
Oak, Valley *(Quercus lobata)*
Sycamore *(Platanus racemosa)*
Walnut, Calif. *(Juglans californica)*

Shrubs
RIDGES AND HIGHER SLOPES

Bricklebush *(Brickellia spp. [2])*	Sept.-Nov.
Buckwheat, Calif. *(Eriogonum fasciculatum)*	April-July
Buckwheat, Coastal *(Eriogonum cinereum)*	June-Sept.
Buckwheat, Conejo *(Eriogonum crocatum)*	May-June
Buckwheat, Longstem *(Eriogonum elongatum)*	Aug.-Oct.
Bush Sunflower *(Encelia californica)*	March-June
Chaparral Pea *(Pickeringia montana)*	April-May
Ceanothus, Bigpod *(Ceanothus megacarpus)*	Feb.-April
Ceanothus, Buckbrush *(Ceanothus cuneatus)*	Feb.-April
Ceanothus, Greenbark *(Ceanothus spinosus)*	March-May
Ceanothus, Hairyleaf *(Ceanothus oliganthus)*	March-April
Ceanothus, Hoaryleaf *(Ceanothus crassifolius)*	March-April
Chamise *(Adenostoma fasciculatum)*	May-June
Cherry, Hollyleaf *(Prunus ilicifolia)*	April-May
Coyote Brush *(Baccharis pilularia)*	Aug.-Nov.
Deerweed *(Lotus scoparius)*	March-June
Goldenbush *(Haplopappus spp. [4])*	Sept.-Oct.
Laurel Sumac *(Rhus Laurina)*	May-June
Mallow, Bush *(Malacothamnus fasciculatus)*	May-Oct.
Manzanita, Bigberry *(Arctostaphylos glauca)*	Jan.-March
Manzanita, Eastwood *(Arctostaphylos glandulosa)*	Jan.-March
Mountain Mahogany *(Cercocarpus betuloides)*	March-May
Poppy, Bush or Tree *(Dendromecon rigida)*	Feb.-May
Prickly Phlox *(Leptodactylon californicum)*	Jan.-April
Rattleweed [Locoweed] *(Astragalus spp. [5])*	March-June
Redberry, Hollyleaf *(Rhamnus ilicifolia)*	Feb.-April
Redshanks *(Adenostoma sparsifolium)*	August
Sage, Black *(Salvia mellifera)*	April-June
Sage, Purple *(Salvia leucophylla)*	May-July
Sage, White *(Salvia apiana)*	April-June
Sagebrush, Coastal *(Artemesia californica)*	Aug.-Oct.
Scrub Oak *(Quercus dumosa)*	March-April
Silk Tassel *(Garrya veatchii)*	Jan.-March
Squaw Bush *(Rhus trilobata)*	March-April
Sugar Bush *(Rhus ovata)*	March-May
Toyon *(Heteromeles arbutifolia)*	May-June
Woolly Blue-curls *(Trichostema lanatum)*	April-June
Yerba Santa *(Eriodictyon crassifolium)*	April-May
Yucca *(Yucca whipplei)*	May-June

Shrubs

STREAMSIDE

Blackberry *(Rubus ursinus)*	March-April
Cat-tail *(Typha latifolia)*	Aug.-Oct.
Mugwort *(Artemesia douglasiana)*	July-Nov.
Mulefat *(Baccharis viminea)*	Jan.-May
Willow *(Salix spp. [3])*	Jan.-March

OCEAN FACING

Coreopsis *(Coreopsis gigantea)*	March-May
Lemonadeberry *(Rhus integrifolia)*	Feb.-April
Prickly Pear *(Opuntia littoralis)*	May-June
Saltbush *(Atriplex lentiformis)*	July-Oct.

CANYONS AND LOWER SLOPES

Castor-bean *(Ricinus communis)* *	All year
Cinquefoil *(Potentilla glandulosa)*	April-June
Coffeeberry, Calif. *(Rhamnus californica)*	May-June
Currant, Chaparral *(Ribes malvaceum)*	Dec.-Feb.
Currant, Golden *(Ribes aureum)*	March-April
Elderberry *(Sambucus mexicana)*	April-Aug.
Gooseberry, Fuchsia-flowered *(Ribes speciosum)*	Jan.-March
Honeysuckle *(Lonicera subspicata)*	May-July
Lupine, Pauma *(Lupinus longiflorus)*	April-June
Nightshade, Black *(Solanum douglasii)*	All year
Nightshade, Purple *(Solanum xantii)*	Jan.-Aug.
Ocean Spray [Creambush]*(Holodiscus discolor)*	April-May
Poison Oak *(Toxicodendron diversilobum)*	Feb.-March
(old name: *Rhus diversiloba)*	
Rose, Calif. Wild *(Rosa californica)*	April-May
Snowberry *(Symphoricarpos mollis)*	April-May
Spanish Broom *(Spartium junceum)* *	April-June
Tobacco, Tree or Bush *(Nicotiana glauca)* *	All year

* Denotes alien (non-native) plant

NON-FLOWERING PLANTS AND GRASSES

Birdsfoot Fern *(Pellaea mucronata)*
Bracken Fern, Western *(Pteridium aquilinum)*
Chain Fern, Giant *(Woodwardia fimbriata)*
Coffee Fern *(Pellaea andromedifolia)*
Giant Rye *(Elymus spp.)*
Goldback Fern *(Pityrogramma triangularis)*
Horsetail *(Equisetum spp.)*
Maidenhair Fern *(Adiantum spp.)*
Woodfern, Coastal *(Dryopteris arguta)*

The list of shrubs and trees for the Santa Monica Mountains is not complete. There are some rarely found plants that are not included because of space limitations. The division of shrubs according to habitat is not meant to be taken literally; there is much overlapping of species in the areas listed. Blooming months are also meant only as a guideline; there can be variations related to both the particular year's weather and the individual habitat.

The information in this appendix has been compiled by Jim Kenney.

GENERAL INDEX OF ANIMALS

AMPHIBIANS
Arboreal Salamander *(Aneides lugubris)*
Arroyo Toad *(Bufo microscaphus)*
Bullfrog *(Rana catesbeiana)*..an introduced frog
California Newt *(Taricha torosa torosa)*
California Slender Salamander *(Batrachoseps attenuatus)*
California Treefrog *(Hyla cadaverina)*
Ensatina or Eschscholtz's Salamander *(Ensatina eschscholtzi)*
Garden Slender Salamander *(Batrachoseps major)*
Pacific Treefrog *(Hyla regilla)*
Western Spadefoot *(Scaphiopus hammondi)*
Western Toad *(Bufo boreas)*

BIRDS
Acorn Woodpecker *(Melanerpes formicivorus)*
Allen's Hummingbird *(Selasphorus sasin)*
Anna's Hummingbird *(Calypte anna)*
Barn Owl *(Tyto alba)*
Barn Swallow *(Hirundo rustica)*
Bewick's Wren *(Thryomanes bewickii)*
Black-chinned Hummingbird *(Archilochus alexandri)*
Black-crowned Night Heron *(Nycticorax nycticorax)*
Black-headed Grosbeak *(Pheucticus melanocephalus)*
Black-throated grey warbler *(Dendroica nigrescens)*
Bluebird *(Sialia mexicana)*
Brown Towhee *(Pipilo fuscus)*
Bushtit *(Psaltriparus minimus)*
California Quail *(Lophortyx californicus)*
California Thrasher *(Toxostoma redivivum)*
Coot *(Fulica americana)*
Dark-eyed "Oregon" Junco *(Junco hyemalis)*
Ducks - various migratory:
    Pintail *(Anas jamaicensis)*
    Ruddyduck *(Oxyura jamaicensis)*
    Shoveler *(Anas clypeata)*
    Green-winged teal *(Anas crecca)* winter
    Cinnamon teal *(Anas cyanoptera)* summer
Golden Eagle *(Aquila chrysaetos)*

Goldfinch, Lawrencis *(Carduelis lawrencei)*
Great Blue Heron *(Ardea herodias)*
Great Horned Owl *(Bubo virginianus)*
House Finch *(Carpodacus mexicanus)*
Kingfisher *(Megaceryle alcyon)*
Lark Sparrow *(Chondestes grammacus)*
Lesser Goldfinch *(Carduelis psaltria)*
Loggerhead Shrike *(Lanius ludevicianus)*
Mallard Duck *(Anas platyrhynchos)*
Mourning Dove *(Zenaida macroura)*
Nuttail's Woodpecker *(Picoides nuttallii)*
Phainopepla *(Phainopepla nitens)*
*Plain Titmouse (Parus in*ornatus)
Raven *(Corvus corax)*
Red-shouldered Hawk *(Buteo lineatus)*
Redtail Hawk *(Buteo jamaicensis)*
Redwing Blackbird *(Agelaius phoeniceus)*
Rough-winged Swallow *(Stelgidopteryx ruficollis)*
Rufus-sided Towhee *(Pipilo erythropthalmus)*
Scrub Jay *(Aphelocoma coerulescens)*
Song Sparrow *(Melospiza melodia)*
Turkey Vulture *(Cathartes aura)* Buzzard
Western Tanager *(Piranga ludoviciana)*
White-breasted Nuthatch *(Sitta carolinensis)*
White-crowned Sparrow *(Zenotrichia leucophrys)*
Wood Peewee *(Contopus sordidulus)*
Wrentit *(Chamaea fasciata)*

Technical names of birds correspond with those found in the Audubon Society Field Guide to North American Birds - Western Region.

MAMMALS

Bat *(various species)*
Bush Rabbit *(Sylvilagus bachmanii)*
Black-tailed Jackrabbit (Lepus Californicum)
California Mule Deer *(Odocoileus hemionus)*
Cottontail Rabbit *(Sylvilagus audubonii)*
Coyote *(Canis latrans)*
Deer Mouse *(Peromyscus maniculatus)* White-footed
Feral Domestic Cat *(Felis domesticus)*
Gray Fox *(Urocyon cinoreoargenteus)*

Gray Whale *(Cochruchtius robustus)*
Ground Squirrel *(Otospermophilus beacheyii)*
Kangaroo Rat *(Dipodomys Sp.)*
Long-tailed Weasel *(Mustela frenata)*
Meadow Mouse *(Microtus californicus)*
Mole
Mountain Lion *(Felis concolor)*
Pocket Gopher *(Thommys bottae)*
Raccoon *(Procyon lotor)*
Ring-tailed Cat *(Bassariscus natantus)* ?
Shrew
Striped Skunk *(Mephitis mephitis)*
Western Gray Squirrel *(Scinrus griseus)* ?
Wild Cat
Woodrat *(Neotoma sp.)*

REPTILES

California Legless Lizard *(Anniella pulchra)*
California Mountain Kingsnake *(L. Zonata)*
California Striped Whipsnake *(Masticophis lateralis)*
Coachwhip [Red Racer] *(Masticophis flagellum)*
Coast Horned Lizard *(Phrynosoma coronatum)*
Common Kingsnake *(Lampropeltis getulus)*
Gilberts Skink *(Eumeces gilberti)*
Gopher Snake *(Pituophis melanoleucus)*
Night Snake *(Hypsiglena torquata)*
Racer *(Coluber constrictor)*
Ringneck Snake *(Diadophis punctatus)*
Side-blotched Lizard *(Uta stansburiana)*
Southern Alligator Lizard *(Gerrhonotus multicarinatus)*
Southern Pacific Rattlesnake *(Crotalus viridis)*
Striped Racer *(Masticophis lateralis)*
Western Aquatic Garter Snake or Two Striped Garter
    Snake *(Thamnophis couchi hammondi)*
Western Fence Lizard *(Sceloporus occidentalis)*
Western Pond Turtle *(Clemmys marmorata)*
Western Skink *(Eumeces skiltonianus)*
Western Whiptail *(Cnemidophorus tigris)*

Red-tailed Hawk

Bobcat

Coyote

Cottontail

Mule Deer

Mountain Lion

Gray Fox

Calif Ground Squirrel

GLOSSARY OF TERMS

alluvium | unconsolidated gravel, sand, and fine rock debris deposited principally by running water.

anticline | a fold of stratified rock, convex upward.

arroyo | stream

barranca | a vertical walled gully cut by an intermittent stream

basalt | a fine grained rock

boca | entrance

brea | tar

breccia | a rock containing abundant angular fragments. They can be sedimentary, volcanic, tectonic, landslide or other

bushwhack | travel through dense vegetation, usually chaparral

caballero | a Spanish gentleman (horseman)

cajon | box

cienega | swamp

conejo | rabbit

conglomerate | a sedimentary rock consisting of larger rounded rock imbedded in a finer, usually sandy matrix, and all cemented together

diatomite | a sedimentary rock consisting of the silaceous skeletons of single celled algae

encinal | grove of live oak

erosion	removal of rock material by any natural process
fault	a fracture in the earth's crust
formation	a rock unit of distinctive characteristics which formed over a limited span of time and under some uniformity of conditions
granite	a coarse-grained intrusive rock rich in silica, potassium, sodium
habra	dale
igneous rock	a class of rocks formed by the crystallization of a molten state
intrusive rock	rock that has injected into other rock, usually in a molten state
loma	top of a hill
milling stone	a shallow stone which was used by the Indians for grinding seeds
mortar	a deep bowled grinding stone used for acorns
muller	a flat sandstone used by the Indians for grinding small hard seeds
mya	one million years ago..
nogales	walnut trees
pestle	a slender pounding stone used for acorn grinding
pismo	tar
playa	beach
potrero	pasture for horses
puente	bridge

ridge	long narrow crest of a mountain
roble	deciduous oak
saddle	a low place on a ridge
sandstone	a sedimentary rock formed by cementation of sand
savannah	a grassland containing scattered trees
seco	dry, barren
sedimentary rock	a class of rocks of secondary origin made up of transported and deposited rock and mineral particles
serrano	mountaineer, highlander
shale	a sedimentary rock made of very fine particles
siltstone	a sedimentary rock made of silt — finer than sand, coarser than clay
slate	weakly metamorphosed shale
strata	sheetlike masses of sedimentary rock of one kind, usually in layers between beds of other kinds
syncline	a downfold in layered rocks
temescal	sweat house
trancas	a barrier
vallecitos	small valley
yucaipa	wet marshy land

PLACE-NAME INDEX

BIBLIOGRAPHY

BIBLIOGRAPHY

ANDERSON, E.N.
    1968   The Chumash Indians of S. California
           Malki Museum Press, Banning, California

BECK, Warren A. and Haase, Ynez D.
    1974   Historical Atlas of California
           Univ. of Okla. Press, Norman Oklahoma

BOLTON, Herbert E. (Editor)
    1916   Spanish Expl. in the S.W. 1542-1706
           Charles Scribner's Sons, N.Y.

    1927   Fray Juan Crespi, Missionary Explorer on the Pacific
           Coast, 1769-1774. U. of C. Press, Berkeley, California

BOOTH, E. S.
    1968   Mammals of Southern California
           U. of C. Press, Berkeley, California

CAUGHEY, John W.
    1953   California
           Prentice Hall, N.J.

CAUGHEY, John and LaRee
    1962   California Heritage
           Ward Ritchie Press, Los Angeles

COLLINS, Barbara J.
           Key to Coastal and Chaparral Flowering Plants of
           Southern California
           California State University, Northridge

CRITTENDEN, Mabel and Telfer, Dorothy
    1973   Wildflowers of the West
           Celestial Arts, Millbrae, California

FULTZ, Francis M.
    1927   The Elfin-Forest of California
           The Times-Mirror Press, Los Angeles

GRANT, Campbell
    1966   The Rock Paintings of the Chumash
           U. of C. Press, Berkeley, California

HEAD, W. S.
    1972   The Calif. Chaparral, an Elfin Forest
           Naturegraph publishers, Healdsburg

HEIZER, R. F.
    1966   Languages, Territories and Names of California
           Indian Tribes
           U. of C. Press, Berkeley, California

    1968   The Indians of Los Angeles County
           S.W. Museum, Highland Park, California

    1978   Handbook of North American Indians Vol 8,
           California
           Smithsonian Institution

HEMERT, E.; Adolph, V.; Taggart, F.J. (Editors)
           The Narrative of the Portola Expedition
           of 1769-1770 by Miguel Costanso, Publ. of the
           Academy of Pacific Coast History, Vol. 1, No. 4,
           91-159. U. of C. Press, Berkeley, California.

HOGUE, C. L.
    1974   The Insects of the Los Angeles Basin
           Natural History Museum, Los Angeles

JEPSON, Willis L.
    1951   A Manual of the Flowering Plants of California
           U. of C. Press, Berkeley, California

KROEBER, A. L.
    1925   Handbook of the Indians of California
           Bulletin 78; Bureau Amer. Ethnology. Wash.

LANDBERG, Leif C. W.
    1965   The Chumash Indians of S. California
              Southwest Museum Papers, Los Angeles

McAULEY, Milt
    1982   Hiking Trails of Point Mugu State Park
    1983   Hiking Trails of Malibu Creek State Park
    1984   Hiking in Topanga State Park, 2d edition
    1985   Wildflowers of the Santa Monica Mountains
              Canyon Publishing Company, Canoga Park, California

MONROE, Keith
              Near and Different

MUNZ, Philip A. & Keck, David D.
    1959   A California Flora
              U. of C. Press, Berkeley, California

MUNZ, Philip A.
    1961   California Spring Wildflowers
              U. of C. Press, Berkeley, California

    1974   A Flora of Southern California
              U. of C. Press, Berkeley, California

OAKESHOTT, G. B.
    1971   California Changing Landscape
              McGraw-Hill

RAVEN, Peter H.; Thompson, Henry J.; & Prigge, Barry A.
    1966   Flora of the Santa Monica Mtns, 2d edition
              UCLA, Los Angeles

ROBINSON, W. W.
    1958   The Malibu
              The Ward Ritchie Press, Los Angeles

SANTA MONICA MOUNTAINS COMPREHENSIVE PLANNING COMM.
    1978   Santa Monica Mtns Comprehensive Plan
              (Preliminary Report)

SAUNDERS, C. F.
    1923   The Southern Sierras of California
            Houghton Mifflin Co., Cambridge

SHARP, Robert P.
    1978   Coastal Southern California
            (a Geology Field guide)
            Kendall/Hunt Publ. Co., Dubuque, Iowa

SPELLENBERG, R.
    1979   The Audubon Society Field Guide to North American
            Wildflowers, Western Region
            Alfred A. Knopf, Inc.

STEBBINS, R. C.
    1934   Amphibians & Reptiles of Western North America
            McGraw-Hill Book Co., N.Y.

SUDWORTH, George B.
    1908   Forest Trees of the Pacific Slope
            USDA, Washington

UVARDY, M.
    1977   The Audubon Society Field Guide to North American
            Birds - Western Region
            Alfred A. Knopf, Inc.

UNIVERSITY OF CALIFORNIA AT LOS ANGELES
            Archaeological Survey, Annual Reports

WALLACE, W. J.
    1956   The Little Sycamore Shellmound
            Archaeological Research Association,
            Los Angeles

YERKES, R. F. and Campbell, R. H.
    1979   Stratigraphic Nomenclature of the Central Santa Monica
            Mountains, Los Angeles County, California. Geological
            Survey Bulletin 1457-E
            U.S. Government Printing Office, Washington, D.C.

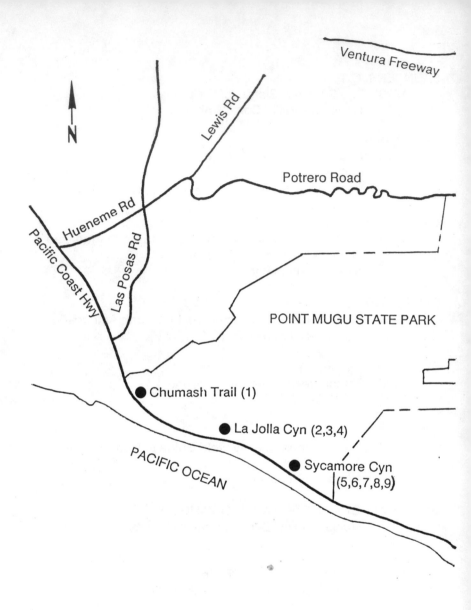

N

Ventura Freeway

Lewis Rd

Potrero Road

Hueneme Rd

Pacific Coast Hwy

Las Posas Rd

POINT MUGU STATE PARK

● Chumash Trail (1)

● La Jolla Cyn (2,3,4)

PACIFIC OCEAN

● Sycamore Cyn
(5,6,7,8,9)

TRAILHEAD MAP

These six map pages cover the
Santa Monica Mountains from
West to East.

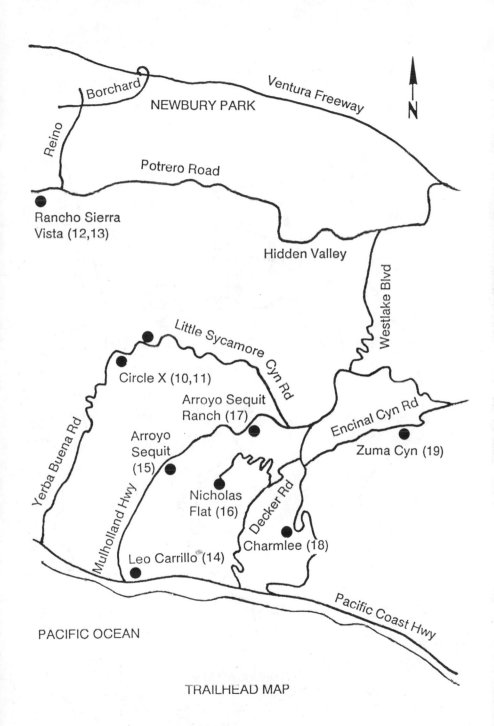

TRAILHEAD MAP

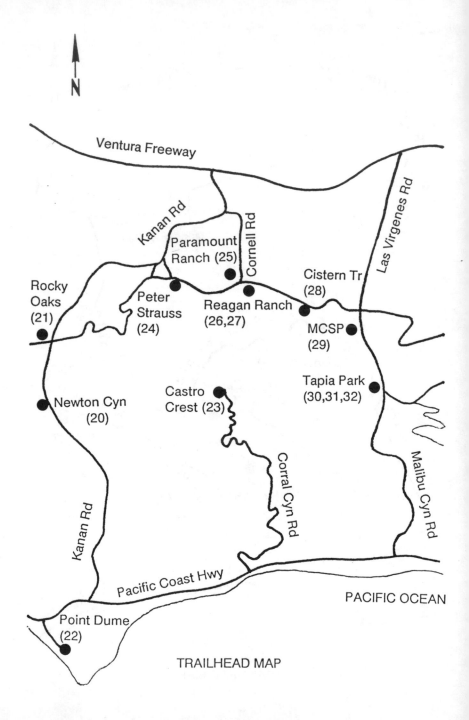

N

Ventura Freeway

Kanan Rd

Cornell Rd

Las Virgenes Rd

Paramount
Ranch (25)

Rocky
Oaks
(21)

Peter
Strauss
(24)

Reagan Ranch
(26,27)

Cistern Tr
(28)

MCSP
(29)

Newton Cyn
(20)

Castro
Crest (23)

Corral Cyn Rd

Tapia Park
(30,31,32)

Kanan Rd

Malibu Cyn Rd

Pacific Coast Hwy

PACIFIC OCEAN

Point Dume
(22)

TRAILHEAD MAP

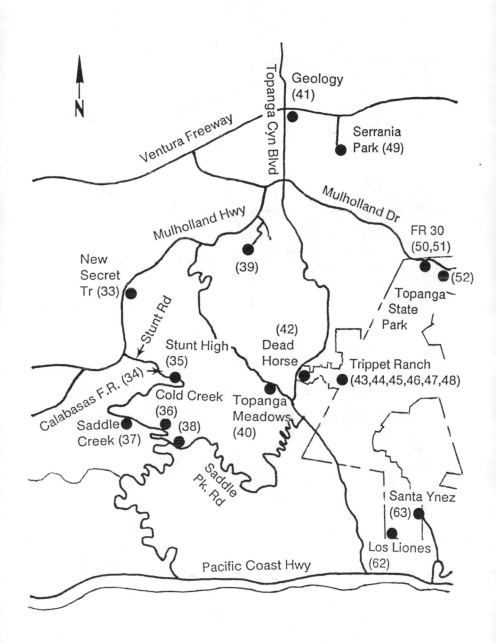

TRAILHEAD MAP

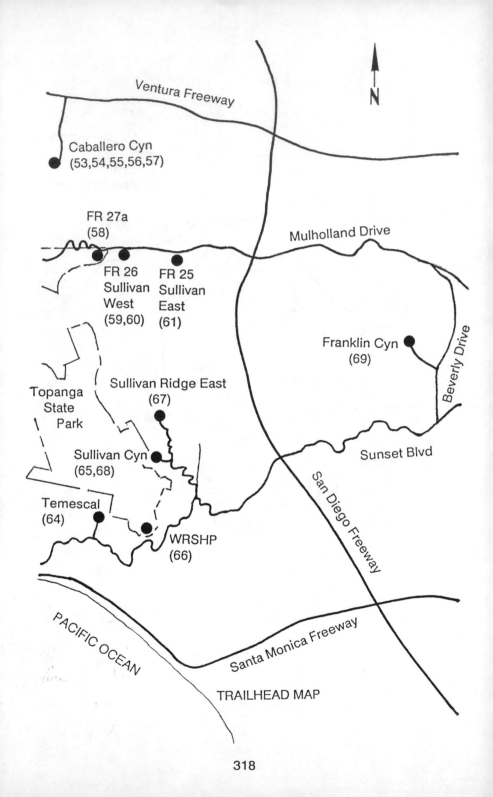

Ventura Freeway

N

Caballero Cyn
(53,54,55,56,57)

FR 27a
(58)

Mulholland Drive

FR 26
Sullivan
West
(59,60)

FR 25
Sullivan
East
(61)

Franklin Cyn
(69)

Beverly Drive

Sullivan Ridge East
(67)

Topanga
State
Park

Sullivan Cyn
(65,68)

Sunset Blvd

Temescal
(64)

WRSHP
(66)

San Diego Freeway

PACIFIC OCEAN

Santa Monica Freeway

TRAILHEAD MAP

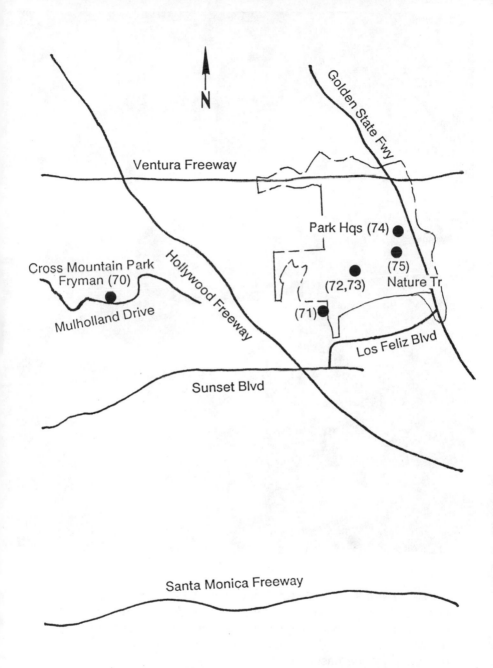

TRAILHEAD MAP

HIKING TRAILS OF THE SANTA MONICA MOUNTAINS by Milt McAuley, is a complete guide to finding the known and not so well-known places in this mountain recreational area. This book is destined to be the main reference for the casual as well as the serious hiker. The easy to read descriptions and the clear maps will take you from the beginning to the end of each hike in complete confidence.